THE PEOPLE'S VICTORY

'Lucy Noakes's fascinating chronicle of VE Day, 8 May 1945, draws on the hundreds of contemporary accounts in the Mass Observation Archive to create a vivid picture of the hopes, fears, and excitement of ordinary people across Britain at the moment the war in Europe ended.' Professor Alan Allport, award-winning author of *Britain at Bay*

'*The People's Victory* is an intimate, and profoundly moving, encounter with ordinary lives in a moment of extraordinary change. Drawing on the unparalleled riches of the UK's Mass Observation Archive, it shows us that wartime people were complex, surprising and thoughtful – in fact people quite like us. The book is authoritative, enlightening, and narratively gripping, as it takes us on a journey through the last days of war in the company of those who lived through it.' Professor Claire Langhamer, Director of the Institute of Historical Research

'Drawing on the fabulous Mass Observation Archive, Noakes has written an entirely new social history of the Second World War. *The People's Victory* is a moving and engaging account of ordinary people's everyday experiences, and responses to, one of the most significant moments in twentieth-century British history. It is a compelling read.' Professor Emerita Penny Summerfield

'Ambitious in its span and nuanced in its analysis, *The People's Victory* offers a compelling portrait of a nation at war. Lucy Noakes has rescued from relative obscurity a rich and complex archive, one that lends insight into the hopes, dreams and fears of an embattled generation. This book is a tour de force and a major contribution to the way we remember war.' Professor Bruce Scates, Australian National University

Lucy Noakes is the Rab Butler Professor of Modern History at the University of Essex, a Trustee of the Mass Observation Archive and the current President of the Royal Historical Society. A historian of twentieth-century Britain and an expert on the social and cultural history of the Second World War, her publications include three single-authored books – *War and the British: National Identity and the Second World War* (1998, with a revised edition released in 2023), *Women and the British Army 1907–1948* (2007) and *Dying for the Nation: Death, Grief and Bereavement in Second World War Britain* (2020) – and three edited collections.

THE PEOPLE'S VICTORY

VE DAY THROUGH THE EYES OF THOSE WHO WERE THERE

Lucy Noakes

Atlantic Books
London

First published in hardback in Great Britain in 2025 by Atlantic Books, an imprint of Atlantic Books Ltd.

Copyright © Lucy Noakes, 2025

The moral right of Lucy Noakes to be identified as the author of this work has been asserted by her in accordance with the Copyright, Designs and Patents Act of 1988.

All rights reserved. No part of this publication may be reproduced, stored in a retrieval system, or transmitted in any form or by any means, electronic, mechanical, photocopying, recording, or otherwise, without the prior permission of both the copyright owner and the above publisher of this book.

No part of this book may be used in any manner in the learning, training or development of generative artificial intelligence technologies (including but not limited to machine learning models and large language models (LLMs)), whether by data scraping, data mining or use in any way to create or form a part of data sets or in any other way.

Every effort has been made to trace or contact all copyright holders. The publishers will be pleased to make good any omissions or rectify any mistakes brought to their attention at the earliest opportunity.

Credit for the image on p. 26 to © National Portrait Gallery; the image on p. 29 reproduced courtesy of © Plymouth City Council (Arts and Heritage); credit for the image on p. 218 to © Imprint / Alamy Stock Photo

10 9 8 7 6 5 4 3 2 1

A CIP catalogue record for this book is available from the British Library.

Hardback ISBN: 978 1 83895 512 0
E-book ISBN: 978 1 83895 514 4

Printed in Great Britain by CPI Group (UK) Ltd, Croydon CR0 4YY

Atlantic Books
An imprint of Atlantic Books Ltd
Ormond House
26–27 Boswell Street
London
WC1N 3JZ

www.atlantic-books.co.uk

Product safety EU representative: Authorised Rep Compliance Ltd., Ground Floor, 71 Lower Baggot Street, Dublin, D02 P593, Ireland. www.arccompliance.com

For all Mass Observers, past, present and future.

And for my parents, with love.

Contents

Map	Geographical Distribution of Wartime Mass Observation Diarists	ix
	A note on sources and terminology	xi
Prologue:	'An Anthropology of Our Own People'	1
Chapter One:	The Second World War in British Myth and Memory – 'I Had a Pretty Quiet War Really'	7
Chapter Two:	Mass Observation and the Second World War – 'They Speak for Themselves'	27
Chapter Three:	Mass Observers at War – 'War Begins at Home'	59
Chapter Four:	1–6 May 1945 – 'A Week of Confusion and Fluctuating Emotions'	93
Prologue:	7 May 1945: The Funeral of Germany	125
Chapter Five:	Daytime, Monday 7 May – 'The Most Unsettling Day of All'	135
Chapter Six:	Evening, Monday 7 May – 'I Still Rejoiced with All My Heart'	163

Prologue:	8 May 1945 – An End and a Beginning	197
Chapter Seven:	Daytime, Tuesday 8 May – 'So, This Is V Day'	213
Chapter Eight:	Evening, Tuesday 8 May – 'This Is Your Victory'	243
Afterword:	'It Is All Very Difficult to Imagine We Have Peace'	277
	Acknowledgements	301
	Notes	303
	Index	323

MAP

Geographical Distribution of Wartime Mass Observation Diarists

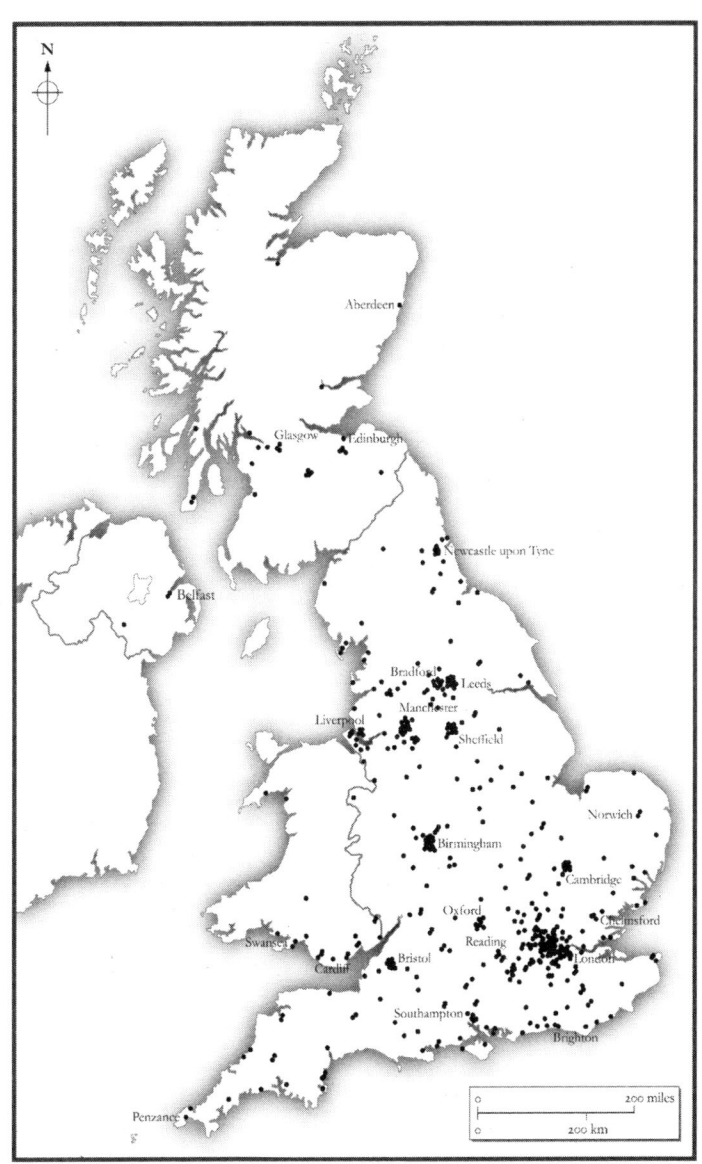

A note on sources and terminology

This book tells the story of how Britain marked the end of the war in Europe in May 1945, through the words of a group of people whom we know as 'Mass Observers'. These volunteer authors were writing for the eccentric and pioneering social-survey organisation Mass Observation, which started to collect material on the lives of British people in 1937. By 1945 many hundreds of individuals were writing for it, some keeping and donating wartime diaries and others forming a 'National Panel' that responded to Mass Observation's regular and eclectic open-ended questionnaires, known as Directives. Some did both.

The material collected by Mass Observation gives us a unique perspective on the lives of people living in the United Kingdom during the Second World War. It enables us to see how hundreds of individuals experienced, described and felt about wartime, from the declaration of war in 1939 to its end in 1945. These Mass Observers were volunteers, self-selecting individuals who were attracted by the idea of recording their experiences, thoughts and feelings for posterity, and who could find the time and the commitment to write for the organisation. Compiled at the time, and thus not shaped by memory or changing social attitudes, the observations used language that may now appear outdated. They were not a 'representative sample' of the British population, carefully selected for the way they gave voice to people of different regions, political and religious beliefs, ages, genders and social classes. Indeed, Mass Observation's volunteer writers often (but not always) came from large cities, most notably London and the Home Counties, were more likely to be English than Scottish, Welsh or Irish and were often (but again not always) left-leaning in their politics.

Mass Observation also employed a small pool of 'professional' observers, referred to as Investigators, often themselves volunteers, who were sent out into wartime Britain to question the people they met and to record what they saw. Material from some of these reports is included here. In these, Mass Observation attempted to classify people by gender, age and social class, using a similar model for social class to that used today by the British census. Thus some of the descriptions in this book might categorise people as 'F45D', which translates as 'Female, aged 45, Social Class D' (manual labour) or M25B: 'Male, 25, Social Class B' (intermediate managerial, administrative, professional), and so on. Usually these judgements were made quickly, perhaps solely on the basis of an overheard conversation, and so they might tell us more about the preoccupations and prejudices of the time than about the people who were being categorised.

Most of the material used in this book was donated to Mass Observation either in the form of diaries or as responses to the Directive questionnaires. Each of these was given a code number by Mass Observation to ensure the privacy of the writer, and these have been used again here, with the exception of two of its best-known authors – Nella Last and Naomi Mitchison – both of whom have subsequently had their Mass Observation diaries published. Endnotes give the authors' Mass Observation number and either list them as a Diarist or as a Respondent to a Directive, with the date of the Directive included (usually May 1945, which was when Mass Observation asked its panel of writers to record their activities on VE Day). The careful reader, who is keen on source notes, will also notice some references to Topic Collections, which was Mass Observation's catch-all phrase for material that did not fit elsewhere, including drafts of publications, newspaper cuttings and ephemera; to File Reports, which were Mass Observation's summaries of their findings; and to Day Diaries, which were the organisation's first attempt at surveying the life of the nation in the late 1930s.

Mass Observation continues today, having been revived in 1981. The papers of both the original archive and of the new project are held at The Keep Archive Centre, Brighton and are a part of the University of Sussex's Special Collections. Currently about 500 people write for the project, and every 12 May Mass Observation asks the public to keep a 'Day Diary' and to send it into the Archive as a 'snapshot' of life in Britain. You can see more details of Mass Observation today here: massobs.org.uk/about-mass-observation/

PROLOGUE

'An Anthropology of Our Own People'

During the cold winter of January 1937 a young worker in the cotton mills of Bolton, Lancashire found himself intrigued by a letter in the *New Statesman*, inviting volunteers to take part in an 'anthropology of our own people'.[1] The mill worker was the anthropologist and polymath Tom Harrisson, recently returned from studying the people of the New Hebrides and now living and working in Bolton in order to research everyday life in an industrial working-class town, and the author of the letter was Charles Madge, a journalist and poet living in Blackheath, south London. Inspired by coverage of the abdication crisis of 1936, when newspapers claimed to speak 'for the people' without necessarily asking their opinions, Madge believed that an organisation that could represent and understand 'ordinary people' was vital to a democracy like Britain. What, he wondered, would the people say, if they were asked?

Mass Observation, the organisation that they founded, went on to observe and record the lives of British people in the middle years of the twentieth century. Among the tumultuous events of that period detailed by Mass Observation are the 1937 coronation of King George VI, the Munich Crisis of 1938 and the foundation of the National Health Service in 1948. But at the heart of its millions of pages of diaries, questionnaires and observations, which are described in more detail in Chapter Two, is the material that it collected on life in Britain during the Second World War.

Mass Observation's work enabled the people who lived through the war in Britain to describe their experiences, feelings, hopes and fears in their own words. Men and women from across the country, and from almost every walk of life, responded to the call for wartime diaries and volunteers to reply to Mass Observation's frequent open-ended questionnaires, known as Directives. Alongside this, the organisation's small number of paid employees and larger number of volunteer observers travelled around the country, watching people, listening to conversations, recording and reflecting on the impact of war and the public mood.

It is Mass Observation that tells us how the people – not the press or politicians – felt about the fall of France in 1940, and about the invasion of Britain that was expected to come any day. Researching morale for the Ministry of Information, Mass Observers sent back detailed daily reports from across the country. As the last troops were being evacuated from Dunkirk on 8 June, people in Birmingham were worried about a Fifth Column, with 'spies seen all over the place'. Meanwhile in Tunbridge Wells the 'general feeling is that news is not too bad', perhaps because 'many think Hitler will invade first Eire [Ireland] and then Cornwall'.[2]

While the Blitz 'proper' (the heavy bombing at night of London and other major cities and towns in 1940 and 1941) started at tea-time on Saturday 7 September 1940 and continued for the next fifty-seven nights without a break, it is Mass Observation that reminds us that there had been other, more scattered air raids in the weeks and months beforehand. A twenty-four-year-old woman living in Grays, Essex, described an air raid on her town four days before the first heavy raid on London:

> During the night bombs fell nearby damaging some of the windows of my home. By now I'm quite used to the nightly barrage of gunfire, but the noise of one's 'first' bombs, whose distance cannot be gauged from previous knowledge is a terrifying experience. The bombs fell ⅓ of a mile away from us at least, but as they whistled down I thought they were over my head. I am not afraid of death, but all my resolutions to keep calm, and almost all my faith in God, seemed to depart at that moment, and my whole body and mind registered only one emotion – fear! But still I am alive to carry on my job, and next time I shall not be afraid.

Nevertheless, she was shocked by the severity of the raid on 7 September, writing on 10 September that:

> I just can't find words to describe my feelings about the bombing of London. There is so much of London that is part of us all, so much that is sacred to British people everywhere, that it *must not* be demolished by German bombs... I see no reason why London shouldn't be completely flat with the ground by the end of this year.[3]

London, of course, survived the war, but alongside other major cities, such as Berlin, Tokyo, Shanghai and Antwerp, it took many years to recover from the fierce, destructive nature of war from the air.

It's also Mass Observation that reminds us that London was not the only British city to be subjected to heavy air raids. Its researchers travelled to other towns and cities as they came beneath the bombs, faithfully recording the impact of air raids on local life. Hull in East Yorkshire was one of the most heavily bombed cities in the country, and when Mass Observers visited in the spring of 1941 they discovered that morale was poor, particularly in the 'poverty stricken' district of St Paul's – a legacy, they argued, of 'enervating pre-war social conditions that prevailed in this area'. Far from the image of a stoical and humorous 'Blitz Spirit', they observed a feeling of 'complete helplessness and resignation' in the poor and much-bombed district.[4] In Bristol, heavily bombed during the Blitz of 1940–41, they found ' a shortage of cigarettes, chocolate, fancy cakes and other semi-luxuries'. More worryingly, they also found a sense of resentment and a belief that the city's suffering was not well known:

> We've been told it's worse down here than it was in Coventry or Birmingham, but we haven't had as much said about us. Anybody'd think Coventry people were the only ones who could take it.[5]

Being bombed might have been a widely shared event for those living in Britain's cities, but Mass Observation showed that this was not necessarily a unifying experience.

It also captured the less dramatic elements of wartime life. Rationing ('the only grumble is the shortage of fish'), queuing ('this is as unpopular as ever') and the blackout ('I enjoy driving in it as it is something of an adventure') all received Mass Observation's attention, revealing a nation of mildly fed-up people who nevertheless generally accepted the need for unpopular wartime measures.[6] Above all, Mass Observation reminds us that wartime Britain was made up of millions of individuals, largely united in the war effort, but with their own distinct considerations, irritations and preoccupations.

Mass Observation is unique in recording the feelings and experiences of so many 'ordinary' people in wartime. The war was, of course, a *world* war, experienced by many millions of people across more than fifty countries. This book includes short prologues to the chapters on VE Day that provide snapshots of life around the world on the same day. Some of these draw on press reports or the observations of diplomats and official recorders. Others come from the private diaries and papers of individuals. But these were rarely collected systematically, and their existence today is often a matter of luck, dependent on decisions made by individuals, families, archivists, historians and publishers, as well as the wartime conditions that enabled, or prevented, writing. Occupation by an enemy power, population movement, imprisonment, conscription and forced labour, and the dangers of recording individual thoughts and beliefs when living under an authoritarian regime were all potent blocks to diary-writing.

By contrast, in Britain we are lucky to have the material gathered so diligently by Mass Observation, which was later almost forgotten in a damp basement in the organisation's old headquarters in London until it was rescued in the 1960s by Tom Harrisson and the historian and founder of the University of Sussex, Asa Briggs. It provides a counterweight to better-known stories, often those of political and military leaders, and reminds us of the voices and views that can be difficult to discern in our dominant memories of the war years. This book tells the *people*'s story of VE Day through their own words, views and experiences.

CHAPTER ONE

The Second World War in British Myth and Memory

'I Had a Pretty Quiet War Really'

One unseasonably cool and damp spring evening in May 1961, Alan Bennett walked onto the stage at Brighton's Theatre Royal. His particular stiff-legged gait would have been familiar to anyone in the audience who had seen Kenneth More in the popular film *Reach for the Sky*, released five years previously in 1956. This was a biopic of the RAF pilot Group Captain Douglas Bader, who had lost both legs in a flying accident in 1931, yet had gone on to fly in the Battle of Britain, being credited with at least twenty-two victories before being shot down over France and imprisoned in various prisoner-of-war (POW) camps, from which he went on to make numerous escape attempts. Bennett's character, like Bader, had been one of 'the few', the RAF pilots who defended Britain from the Luftwaffe's attacks in the aftermath of the 1940 fall of France. By 1960, and with the aid of More's sympathetic portrayal, Bader had come to exemplify the best of Britain's Second World War, almost single-handedly symbolising British stoicism, determination and quiet heroism. Bennett's character reminisced:

> I had a pretty quiet war really. I was one of 'the few'. We were stationed down at Biggin Hill. One Sunday, we got word Jerry

was coming in, over Hastings I think. I got up first because I could, and everything was very calm and peaceful. England lay like a green carpet below. The war seemed worlds away. I could see Tunbridge Wells, the sun glinting on the river. I remembered that last weekend I spent there with Celia, that summer of '39. Suddenly, Jerry was coming at me out of a bank of cloud, I let him have it and I, well, I think I must have got him in the wing, because he spiralled past me out of control. As he did so, I always remember this, I caught a glimpse of his face, and do you know, he smiled. Funny thing, war.[1]

It's fair to say that Bennett's gentle and affectionate observations of a particular kind of British war hero did not go down well that evening. Audience members booed and jeered, affronted by this perceived insult to a British war hero by a man far too young to have fought in the war himself.[*] In a foreshadowing of the as-yet-unseen social changes waiting just over the horizon of the 1960s, a generation gap between those who had experienced the war as adults, and had learned to pleasurably relive aspects of it through the many war films of the 1950s, and those who had been children during the war years or had been born in its aftermath was very apparent that evening.

Bennett's monologue was part of a much longer sketch called 'The Aftermyth of War', written and performed as part of the satirical revue show *Beyond the Fringe*, which had received rave reviews in the 1960 Edinburgh Festival and was now touring the provinces in preparation for a transfer to London's West End later that month. *Beyond the Fringe* was a new kind of comedy revue, which delighted in surreal sketches that satirised British

---

[*] Bennett had been born in 1934 and was employed as a junior lecturer in medieval history at Magdalen College, Oxford.

society, identifying and poking fun at the British establishment, authority figures and social structures. Peter Cook, the revue's driving force and key writer, told journalists that the show would be 'anti-establishment, anti-capital punishment, anti-colour bar and anti-1960. But it will all be very serious stuff. Sharp, bitter and to the point.'[2] With Peter Cook, Jonathan Miller and Dudley Moore, Bennett dissected the collective memory of the war years as a story of 'plucky Brits' banding together, against the odds, to beat the Germans. Best known for the sketch in which Cook's upper-class RAF officer tells Miller's junior (but still upper-class) pilot, 'Perkins, I want you to lay down your life. We need a futile gesture at this stage, it will raise the whole tone of the war', 'The Aftermyth of War' skewered the idea of the Second World War as 'Britain's finest hour' in which plucky cockneys and stoical officers muddled through and overcame divisions of social class and status to unite and defeat Nazi Germany. *Beyond the Fringe*, with its willingness to poke fun at national myths and much-admired public figures (famously including the prime minister Harold Macmillan), is often credited with heralding the end of 'the age of deference' and the beginning of the 1960s. The theatre critic of the *Daily Mail*, never the most liberal or adventurous of newspapers, heralded the show's 1961 London opening with glee:

> The targets aimed at are hit dead centre every time and left sprawling. Everything that could make the middle classes uneasy… is aired with gusts of freshness. Mr Macmillan's empty telly-chats, rock 'n' roll, religion, the cosy tolerance of apartheid, those nostalgic myths prettifying the last war, the absurdities of Civil Defence by Brown Paper, inept Church of England sermons, the depth (in all of us) of class and race prejudice.[3]

The targets may have been hit dead centre, but even the skill and wit of Alan Bennett and his fellow satirists could do little to dent the mythology of Britain's Second World War.

There had, of course, been successful comedies about, or referencing, the war years before *Beyond the Fringe*. The popular comedy films *Passport to Pimlico* and *Whisky Galore!*, both released by Ealing Film Studios in 1949, played with the idea of a wartime nation in which everyone was united and willing to put the collective war effort uncomplainingly above and beyond their own freedoms, liberties and desires. *Passport to Pimlico* was set just after the war and told the tale of the working-class London suburb of Pimlico, fed up with post-war bureaucracy, red tape and rationing, discovering that it was a part of the ancient French kingdom of Burgundy and briefly declaring and enjoying independence, before reluctantly but inevitably returning to the fold of the greater British nation. Likewise, *Whisky Galore!* – set on Todday, a fictional Scottish island where the locals overcome rationing and outwit the bureaucracy of Customs and Excise when they salvage and distribute some of the 50,000 cases of whisky that wash ashore after a shipwreck – celebrated the power of a small, united community to overcome a more powerful opponent. Both films were nostalgic and sympathetic representations of the war years, with the small communities of Pimlico and Todday standing in for wartime Britain, portraying them as a period of social unity and cohesion, and emphasising the idea of the British people as individualistic, inventive and pragmatic, drawn together by a shared sense of fair play and common purpose. Like *Beyond the Fringe*, they were very funny. Unlike *Beyond the Fringe*, they were created by teams that had themselves recently experienced the war and embraced, rather than subverted, the mythology of wartime Britain that had grown up during those years. It seemed that you could laugh at the 'nostalgic myths prettifying the war', but only if you had been a part of it yourself.

But only eight years after that Brighton audience had recoiled from Bennett's gentle parody it seems they were ready once again to laugh at the war and, by implication, themselves. On 31 July 1968 the BBC aired the very first episode of what was to become one of its best-loved sitcoms, *Dad's Army*. Like 'The Aftermyth of War' sketch, which in its entirety was well over ten minutes long, the characters and stories that it played with would have been immediately recognisable to much of the audience. A character-led comedy, *Dad's Army* had at its heart the unspoken class conflict between the pompous and insecure middle-class bank manager and local Home Guard commander Captain Mainwaring (Arthur Lowe) and his urbane upper-middle-class deputy in both the bank and the Home Guard, Sergeant Wilson (John Le Mesurier). Other key characters included a spiv from London, a Scottish undertaker prone to gloom-laden pronouncements and an elderly but enthusiastic veteran of the 1898 Battle of Omdurman. The masculine identity of Home Guard members was also central to the comedy, with the contrast between the undoubted bravery and willingness of the platoon to defend their country, and their actual ability to do so, driving many of the plotlines. Like *Passport to Pimlico* and *Whisky Galore!*, many of the pleasures of *Dad's Army* lay in its ability to both show the social divisions and contradictions of Britain and yet at the same time emphasise the achievement of wartime unity. The first episode, 'The Man and the Hour', opened in the present day, with Mainwaring addressing his old platoon on the then-current 'I'm Backing Britain' campaign, a briefly popular but ultimately doomed attempt to lift the British economy by reviving the wartime spirit and encouraging workers to volunteer for unpaid overtime in order to boost productivity. Told in flashback, the first episode set the tone of affectionate nostalgia for the unity and togetherness of the war years that was to dominate the series. Peter Black, the *Daily Mail*'s television reviewer, noted perceptively that the programme 'makes sub-Ealing film whimsy out of the old Home Guard days'. He continued:

> This is summer, 1940, when the heart of England beat with a single pulse, and we are entitled to laugh at the Home Guard if we want to… It is, of course, traditionally English. Here's Arthur Lowe, recruiting the men with John Le Mesurier. 'A dispatch rider, he's got a packet.' 'Poor devil. What was it, a sniper?'[4]

Still deservedly popular today, *Dad's Army* shows us an attractive and idealised picture of the wartime nation: brave, humorous and self-deprecating, able to overcome internal disputes and divisions in pursuit of a shared public good and honourable shared aims. *Dad's Army* may be a (very funny) comedy that relentlessly poked fun at its characters, but it is also a picture of the war years as Britain's 'finest hour'.

The war was not just familiar to audiences through comedy series, films and sketches. It was also present in the overgrown bombsites in many cities or in the stubs of ration coupons in the bottom of kitchen drawers. It was a staple of boys' comics and of British cinema, with more than 110 war films retelling the war years to an appreciative audience between 1945 and 1970, the majority of them in the 1950s. In the later 1950s dramatic British war films retelling the war from a military perspective, such as *The Dam Busters* (1955), *Reach for the Sky* (1956) and *The Battle of the River Plate* (1956), did especially good business at the box office, matched in popularity only by the *Doctor in the House* comedy series starring Dirk Bogarde and Donald Sinden, who were themselves familiar to audiences from their contemporaneous roles in war films. The war was, and remains, one of the most recognisable events in modern British history.

It is a period that resonates through widely recognised images and sounds as well as films, television and novels. 'St Paul's Survives' is the photographer Herbert Mason's famous image of St Paul's Cathedral surrounded by the destruction visited on the City on the night of 29 December 1940 by the Luftwaffe, standing as a symbol of resilience and survival under fire. Photos of small children, name-tags hanging around their necks as they walk to city train stations at the start of their evacuation journey, remind us of the pity of war, but also of national togetherness, as the towns and villages of rural Britain provided sanctuary for urban children fleeing the conflict. Tired soldiers returning from Dunkirk in 1940, or leaving for the beaches of Normandy in 1944, and dogfights in the sky above southern England in the summer of 1940, represent the military fight, while the sounds of an air-raid siren evoke images of people sheltering on Tube-station platforms or huddled with their families in damp Anderson shelters at the end of their gardens.

Popular culture continues, in the early years of the twenty-first century, to be determined to revisit the war years as often as possible. The war even has its own festival: the *We Have Ways Fest*, a three-day event first held in 2021 and which advertises itself as 'a festival like no other', bringing together real ale, military historians, entertainers, weaponry and hardware to an appreciative (and largely male) audience. Perhaps appealing to a wider audience, *Foyle's War*, a popular drama running on ITV for eight series between 2002 and 2015, centred on Michael Kitchen's Chief Superintendent Christopher Foyle as he served with, first, the wartime police force on England's south coast, and subsequently with MI5 during and immediately after the war. Quiet, honourable, self-effacing and honest, Foyle embodied for many the best of the wartime spirit, upholding the importance of fairness and the impartiality of the law in the face of not only black marketeers and fifth columnists, but also an entitled elite, represented as being out of step with the values of the 'people's war'. Foyle's sidekick was his irrepressible driver, Samantha 'Sam' Stewart (played by Honeysuckle Weeks), a member of the Auxiliary Territorial Service (ATS, the women's section of the army) seconded to Sussex police force. Women in wartime also had stories to tell. *Home Fires* was a less successful but still popular television series, running for two years on ITV between 2015 and 2016 and following members of the Women's Institute in Cheshire as they dealt with the changes, difficulties and opportunities provided by the war, while *Land Girls* ran for three series on the BBC between 2009 and 2011, allowing daytime viewers to follow the imagined lives of women working on the land during the war years.

But it was perhaps in the cinema that the war found its most successful twenty-first-century storytellers. Christopher Nolan's epic *Dunkirk*, depicting the story of the evacuation from those beaches in 1940, with the different timelines and narrative complexities familiar to audiences from his other films, was the second-highest grossing film at the UK box office in 2017, beaten only by Disney's live-action *Beauty and the Beast*. Joe Wright's *Darkest Hour*, released the following year and starring a prosthetically enhanced and Oscar-winning Gary Oldman as Winston Churchill, also played to packed cinemas. Both films retold key moments in the war that were presumably familiar to audiences with a sense of the traditional wartime narrative. In Nolan's *Dunkirk*, Mark Rylance stoically skippers his small boat to Dunkirk, avoiding Nazi attacks to rescue troops waiting on the beaches, all the while quietly mourning the death of his son in the RAF. Soldiers returning from Dunkirk, expecting disdain and despair from the British public, are astounded to discover that they are welcomed back as heroes. Its final scene showed Spitfire pilot Tom Hardy calmly destroying his plane on the beaches of Dunkirk while awaiting captivity – an image not of defeat, but of defiance, and of a promised return. Meanwhile Wright's *Darkest Hour* imagined Oldman's Churchill, just after his appointment as prime minister, taking the London Underground to the Houses of Parliament for the debate on Dunkirk on 4 June 1940, in which he gave his famous 'We shall fight on the beaches' speech. In Wright's film, however, Churchill is undecided: should he follow his instincts and declare defiance or succumb to those in his party who saw no chance of victory and urged a negotiated peace with Nazi Germany? It is the bravery, determination and good humour of the ordinary Londoners that he meets on the Underground, who declare themselves ready to 'fight them in Piccadilly' and 'never surrender', that finally set Churchill on his path of continued armed resistance to Nazi military might.

Stoical, defiant, brave: both films represented a wartime Britain in which its civilians, its military and its political leaders were united in their willingness to endure hardship rather than surrender, and to place collective national interests above those of the individual. This was a comforting story that British audiences felt familiar with, skilfully handled by two experienced film-makers. Crucially, it was a story that could make Britain feel better about itself in a time of ongoing national turmoil, argument and division following the 2008 financial crash, the years of austerity and the divisive Brexit referendum of 2016. Perhaps a Britain 'alone', isolated from the rest of Europe, could once again find itself and come together in the face of adversity, to triumph against the odds?

Of course much is missing from this memory of the war. Most of those rescued from the beaches of Dunkirk returned to Britain on the ships of the Royal Navy, not fishing boats and pleasure craft. While the recovery of more than 338,000 troops was undoubtedly cheering, the defeat of the British Expeditionary Force and the vast loss of military materiel were nonetheless – in Churchill's own words – 'a colossal military disaster'.[5] Britain never fought alone, but at the head of a large, multinational and multicultural military made up of volunteers from the British Empire and refugees from occupied Europe; 574 pilots volunteered from across the Empire, from occupied Europe and from Ireland to fly missions during the Battle of Britain, and later in the war Bomber Command crews were made up of airmen from sixty different countries. Many of these men paid the ultimate price for their service and are listed on the Runnymede Air Forces Memorial and on the Battle of Britain Roll of Honour in Westminster Abbey. Mohinder Singh Pujji, one of the twenty-four Indian men who were selected for pilot training when they volunteered to fly with the RAF in 1940, was awarded the Distinguished Flying Cross at the end of the war. Of these twenty-four volunteers, Pujji was one of only two survivors.

The first men to go ashore in the D-Day landings of June 1944 were not the first Allied troops to set foot on continental soil since 1940, or the first to be part of a successful invasion force: they had been preceded not only by Commando raids on the French coast but, crucially, by the invasion of Sicily and the Italian mainland one year earlier. The invasion forces included troops from across the Empire, and from occupied European nations, alongside those of the United States and Britain. While most people opposed Nazi Germany and imperial Japan, many hundreds of fascist sympathisers were interned in 1940 alongside the British Union of Fascists leader Oswald Mosley and his wife Diana Mitford, being suspected of plotting to undermine the war effort. 1942 saw MI5 working undercover to identify and undermine the attempts of remaining Nazi sympathisers to send important information to Berlin.

St Paul's may have survived the Blitz, but Mason's photo also captures the utter destruction of the historic buildings that surrounded it. Many of the evacuees who left the cities in August and September 1939 had returned home in time for the air raids that began in earnest in September 1940, and in which more than 60,000 were to die during the course of the war.[6] The government initially closed Tube stations to the crowds seeking shelter there, fearing both the loss of life if one should suffer a direct hit, and that the largely working-class shelterers – who often lacked the gardens necessary for the Anderson shelters that had been distributed as war loomed in the late 1930s – might simply refuse to return to the surface and go back to work in the vital war industries. After the first few weeks of the Blitz many Londoners simply stayed in their own beds, so tired of night by night air raids that they were willing to take the risk of being bombed in return for a night's sleep. More civilians died in the Allied bombing of France than during the Blitz, and German victims of Allied air raids numbered at least 380,000, according to recent estimates, and possibly as many as 635,000, with some 34,000 people perishing over one week in 'Operation Gomorrah', the raid on Hamburg in July 1943. Unsurprisingly, the history of a lengthy world war, even if focused on just one small country, is far more complex than memory and mythology can allow.

Uniting these dominant images and memories is the widely held belief that the Second World War was Britain's 'finest hour'. In contrast to the First World War, the military conflict is not central to the British collective memory of the Second World War. 'The few' of the RAF, and the troops of Dunkirk and D-Day, are present and correct, but they share their place with the people of the home front – not only Londoners sheltering from bombs, but the middle-class ladies of the Women's Voluntary Service, reliably dishing out tea and sympathy during air raids, members of the Women's Institute allocating evacuees to households, gardeners good-naturedly digging up beloved flower beds to grow vegetables, and housewives learning to 'make do and mend' as rationing bit deeper. Each of these has a place in the mythology of Britain's 'finest hour'. The war is remembered today as a time when everyone 'pulled together' to 'stand alone' in Europe, leading to a victory against the odds over a powerful enemy. The British people, united by good humour, stoicism and determination, appear in this memory as the polar opposite of the humourless, cruel and mechanistic Nazis, and it was these national characteristics that guaranteed the nation's eventual victory. Above all, the Second World War was a 'people's war' – fought and won by 'the people'. This mythology became central to the country's understanding of itself in the post-war decades; the war increasingly remembered as the nation's finest hour as its global power diminished.

And it has been an enormously useful and pliable mythology. Politicians and commentators across the political spectrum have drawn on the same images, and the same stories, in support of very different aims and views. The image of Britain fighting for democracy, and defending the rights of small nations to self-determination when threatened by their larger neighbours, was invoked in both the Falklands conflict of 1982 and the first Gulf War of 1991. In both conflicts the enemy leader – General Galtieri of Argentina and Saddam Hussein of Iraq respectively – was represented as the inheritor of Hitler, and those who opposed an armed response were reminded of the perils of appeasement. The Conservative MP Julian Critchley, writing in the *Daily Telegraph* after Britain's victory in the Falklands, saw the struggle as simply part of a longer pattern of British history:

> Compare the shared emotion at home and the superb morale of our fighting men in the freezing Falklands with what we know of the spirit of Agincourt, of the Elizabethans' response to the Spanish Armada, of Trafalgar or Waterloo, of the flood of volunteers at the start of the First World War or the Battle of Britain in the Second. It is the same inherited, untaught devotion to one's homeland which has survived all the changes and chances of our national life, untouched by all the plans of the twentieth century to ensure peace and the proliferation of international organisations.[7]

Less floridly, the editorial in the tabloid *Daily Star* paraphrased Churchill in its support for intervention in Iraq after that country annexed Kuwait in 1990:

> Fifty years ago we tried to appease Hitler. It failed. We must not let history repeat itself. It is time for the jaw jaw to stop. And the war war to start.[8]

The Second World War, so different in almost every way from both the Falklands conflict and the first Iraq War, nonetheless provided a recognisable, familiar template for explaining, and justifying, these battles of the late twentieth century.

More divisively, the idea of an island nation, standing alone in Europe, proved to be an enormously popular and powerful image for campaigners wanting to leave the European Union in 2016, and in the debates that followed. Nigel Farage, the populist anti-European Union politician and campaigner, was pictured in front of a poster for Christopher Nolan's *Dunkirk*, tweeting, 'I urge every youngster to go out and watch #Dunkirk.' Meanwhile the 'Vote Leave'-supporting Conservative MP Mark Francois explained that his childhood fascination with the Second World War helped to shape his belief that Britain's future lay outside Europe. Drivers negotiating the traditional bank-holiday traffic on Whitsun weekend 2016 may have been surprised, and possibly alarmed, by posters at the side of the busy M40 motorway urging them to 'Halt Ze German Advance', while three years later Nigel Farage and Arron Banks's Leave.EU organisation had to withdraw, and apologise for, a tweet showing the twenty-first-century German chancellor Angela Merkel with the words 'We didn't win two world wars to be pushed around by a Kraut.'

But it wasn't only campaigners to *leave* the EU who drew on the memory of the Second World War. When Britain did finally leave the European Union in January 2020, the event was marked by Led By Donkeys, a group originally formed to campaign against Brexit. They projected a video onto the White Cliffs of Dover, presented as their farewell to the rest of Europe. The campaigners chose Sid, a ninety-five-year-old veteran of the Second World War, to share a message of unity. He said:

> What I would like to say to you all in Holland and in Germany and in France, Belgium, everybody, this is a message from the White Cliffs of Dover, from Britain. I feel very, very sad about it all because we don't know which way things are going. First of all I'm Welsh and I'm British and I'm European, and I'm a human being. So let's all think of these lovely cliffs. Look from your side to this side, see these white cliffs, and we're looking across at you and feeling we want to be together. And we will be together before long, I'm sure.

For Sid, and for many others, the meaning of the war was clear: greater international unity, not less, was the way forward.

As Covid-19 tightened its grip on the world in 2020, the prime minister, Boris Johnson initially reacted by asking people to voluntarily avoid public gathering places such as pubs, cinemas and theatres so as to avoid contracting or passing on the virus to others. This request led to a flurry of activity on social media, as well as confusion in actual society. Godfrey Bloom, a controversial former Member of the European Parliament for Nigel Farage's United Kingdom Independence Party (UKIP), seems to have been the first person to publicly choose a Blitz analogy to make his point. He tweeted that 'we didn't close our pubs in the Blitz. 60,000 people killed then. What's happened to our country?' More than 10,000 people replied to explain to Bloom that a contagious virus was quite different from a bomb. The lack of a clear government strategy to prevent Covid-19 spreading in the early weeks of the pandemic didn't stop the health minister Matt Hancock calling on Britons to emulate their grandparents' behaviour in the Blitz, reminding his audience that:

> Our generation has never been tested like this. Our grandparents were, during the Second World War, when our cities were bombed during the Blitz. During the pounding every night, the rationing, the loss of life, they pulled together in one gigantic national effort. Today our generation is facing its own test, fighting a very real and new disease.[9]

The fundraising efforts for the NHS of ninety-nine-year-old Captain Tom Moore, for which he raised more than £30 million by walking 100 lengths of his garden, were aided by his status as both a centenarian and a Second World War veteran. Although the major public events planned to mark the seventy-fifth anniversary of VE Day in May 2020 were cancelled, individuals and communities continued to celebrate, with socially-distanced street parties, bunting, flags, wartime images and – in the case of at least one village – VE Day scarecrows. When HM the Queen addressed the nation in the early weeks of the pandemic, she began by recalling her first public broadcasts as a young princess during the war, and ended by echoing the popular wartime singer Vera Lynn:

While we may have more still to endure, better days will return; we will be with our friends again, we will be with our families again. We will meet again.[10]

In her evocation of the separations, sacrifices and spirit of the Second World War, the Queen's speech wove together the national mythology of wartime with the isolation, trials and tribulations of Covid-19, and the unity needed to overcome this new crisis. The experience of wartime, she reassured her audience, showed both that Britain and its people would rise to this new challenge and that normal life would one day resume.

It is not the intention of this book to try and demolish this myth, not least because there is some truth to it. Wartime Britain was largely (but never entirely) united, and although it was at the head of the world's biggest and most powerful empire and, after 1941, fought alongside the major powers of both the United States and the Soviet Union, it sometimes *felt* alone, especially after the fall of France and the evacuation from Dunkirk in 1940. This 'Spitfire Summer' – bookended by the retreat and evacuation of the remains of the British Expeditionary Force from Dunkirk in late May and early June, and the beginning of the Blitz in September, with the Battle of Britain sitting in between – lies at the heart of Britain's wartime mythology. This is the period recalled as Britain's 'finest hour', when the British people (military and civilian alike) faced down the overwhelming might of Hitler's Germany to emerge eventually victorious, largely united in both their defiance of the Nazi state and in their determination to build a better world once the war ended.

This image of the war has run through modern British society like the wording in a stick of rock. When the England football team played Germany at Wembley in the semi-final of the 1996 European Championships, the *Daily Mirror* paraphrased Chamberlain's declaration of war in September 1939:

> I am writing to you from the Editor's office at Canary Wharf, London. Last night the *Daily Mirror*'s ambassador in Berlin handed the German government a final note stating that, unless we heard from them by 11 o'clock that they were prepared to withdraw their football team from Wembley, a state of soccer war would exist between us. I have to tell you now that no such undertaking has been received, and that consequently we are at soccer war with Germany.[11]

Tongue-in-cheek, yes. But instantly recognisable to its audience, almost sixty years after the event. Germany went on to win, on penalties. Perhaps supporters were able to draw on the 'Blitz spirit' in the game's aftermath, much as Londoners were urged to display this 'spirit' following the London Tube and bus bombings of 7 July 2005, or maybe they drowned their sorrows with a pint or two of Shepherd Neame's Spitfire Amber Ale, advertised as the 'Bottle of Britain'? Certainly their counterparts two decades later may have found themselves looking at a ubiquitous 'Keep Calm and Carry On' fridge magnet if they hoped to find consolation in a post-match snack, after England was knocked out of the same competition by Iceland in 2016. How much comfort was offered by either snack or slogan – itself taken from a wartime poster that was never used – is questionable.

This myth-making is not new. The war was mythologised as it happened, as commentators from across the political spectrum sought to shore up morale and reassure the British people that although this was a war that would be hard, it would inevitably end in victory. We are *au fait* with much of this material: Churchill's speeches; newsreel footage of volunteer firefighters struggling with the massive conflagrations of the Blitz; wartime films that have become staples of Sunday-afternoon television, such as Noël Coward and David Lean's *In Which We Serve* (1942), telling the story of the survivors of the sinking of HMS *Torrin*, bonded by experience, shared war aims and good humour, their life-raft a model of social cohesion and unity. These words and images are familiar to many of us, interesting and often pleasurable reminders of the (imagined) harmony and determination of the war years. But the people who formed the original audience for these were also writing their own war, their words captured by the social-survey organisation Mass Observation. The next chapter looks at this organisation and some of the people who wrote for it, whose words give us such a vivid picture of life in Britain during the turmoil of the Second World War.

Mass Observation founders Tom Harrisson (left) and Charles Madge (right) in 1938, the year after the organisations' founding.

CHAPTER TWO

Mass Observation and the Second World War

'They Speak for Themselves'

By the spring of 1945 the naval city of Plymouth in southwest England was looking far from its best. Like many of its inhabitants, it was tired and weary after years of war and hardship. With its extensive docks and large naval base, the city on the coast of Devon had been the target of repeated bombing raids by the Luftwaffe. Four years earlier Plymouth had endured its own intensive period of 'blitzing', when more than 1,000 civilians were killed and thousands more injured by 6,600 high-explosive bombs and 200,000 incendiary bombs, which were dropped on the city in March and April 1941. By the war's end Plymouth was one of the most devastated cities in England, with more than 4,000 houses destroyed and another 18,000 seriously damaged. Despite the creation of a 'bold and comprehensive' plan for reconstruction in 1941, rebuilding of the city centre wouldn't begin until 1947.[1] By 1945 residents had learned to pick their way around the rubble and bombsites as they journeyed across the city, and to live with (and often in) bomb-damaged houses. As it became clear that the war in Europe was drawing to a close, the people of Plymouth had good reason to celebrate.

When 'Victory in Europe Day' – usually known today as VE Day, and at the time often simply as 'V Day' – finally dawned on 8 May 1945, Plymouth celebrated the end of almost six long years of war in Europe. Like other cities, towns and villages across Great Britain and Northern Ireland, and in many other countries across Europe and around the world, solemn commemorative parades and church services were combined with street parties, dances and gatherings of all shapes and sizes. Lady Nancy Astor, Conservative MP for Plymouth Sutton, joined in the dancing on Plymouth Hoe, and a church service was held in the ruins of St Andrew's Church in the city centre. A nine-year-old boy watched the Lord Mayor lead a victory parade through the city, remembering in adulthood 'the tanks and armoured cars pass by… in an endless stream' through 'scenes of devastation'.[2] Bands played, crowds danced and impromptu tea parties were held in streets across the city, as neighbours dragged tables and chairs out into the street and shared the cakes and sandwiches they had made with the rationed sugar, flour and eggs that had been carefully saved for this day. Many a child fell asleep long before the celebrations ended that night.

Mass Observation, which had been watching and recording the activities, feelings and habits of the British people since 1937, was keen to discover both how people *planned* to celebrate victory in Europe and how they *actually* marked the end of the war. A young man from Plymouth, one of Mass Observation's panel of volunteer writers, decided to act as an observer himself, conducting a systematic survey of 190 of his fellow Plymouth citizens. He asked them the question that Mass Observation had asked of him: 'What do you propose to do the day peace is declared?' The answer from the 130 men that he asked was unanimous:

*Nancy Astor dancing with a Royal Navy
sailor on Plymouth Hoe, 1942.*

Twenty men from the dockyard, approximate age 28: said they would get drunk

Twenty men from the dockyard, approximate age 50: said they would get drunk

Twenty demolition (workers), approximate age 30: get drunk

Twenty railwaymen, approximate age 28: get drunk

Twenty transport men, approximate age 30: get drunk

Ten army get drunk, ten navy get drunk, ten air force get drunk.

The plans of the sixty women questioned were slightly more nuanced. They were expecting to hold parties, to visit the local pub and to go dancing, all activities in which alcohol could undoubtedly play a part, even if its consumption was not the main purpose. If anyone held hopes that the people of Plymouth would greet the defeat of Nazi Germany with the self-control and stoicism that had characterised the wartime 'Blitz spirit', they were about to be disappointed.[3] As the second 'total war' of the twentieth century drew to its close in Europe, the city's people were ready to celebrate.

The way that Britain 'remembers' VE Day eighty years on is almost entirely dominated by images like these: crowds celebrating in city centres; drinking and dancing in Trafalgar Square, Piccadilly and Westminster; gathering outside Buckingham Palace and in Whitehall to demand appearances by Winston Churchill and the Royal Family; and holding street parties in towns and villages across the land. For the first time since the outbreak of war, people could listen to the weather forecast on the BBC, predicting sporadic rain and thunderstorms for most of the country. Flags were bought or dug out of attics, pianos rolled into front gardens and bunting strung from lamp posts. In many places the figure of Hitler was quickly constructed, ready for burning on a communal bonfire. Food and drink, carefully saved to celebrate the victory, were shared with friends and neighbours. The blackout, which had seen the country plunged into darkness at sunset since 1939, had been largely lifted in April, and lanterns and street lights shone down on the parties as daytime stretched into evening and on into the night. Searchlights, no longer seeking out German bombers, lit up the night sky above London in a 'V for Victory' sign. Bonfires were set and fireworks exploded in a celebration of light and noise after years of blackout darkness. These are the images that dominate our collective memory of VE Day in twenty-first-century Britain.

Such images, however, are far from the whole story. As the reports, observations and diaries of VE Day began to roll into Mass Observation headquarters from around the country, it became clear that the end of the war in Europe was not a day of unalloyed joy for everyone. For those who had been bereaved by the war, and for those who still had loved ones reported as 'missing' (often many years after they had first disappeared), the day was bittersweet at best. For those who had family members, lovers and friends fighting in other 'theatres of combat' against the Japanese imperial army in Asia, the declaration of peace felt premature. Some of those who had fought in Europe or defended the home front found, to their surprise, that they were now part of Operation Downfall, the planned invasion of Japan that would have been led by the United States in the autumn of 1945, had Japan not surrendered in August of that year. Others were simply worn out by the long years of war or were pessimistic or anxious about the chances of a lasting peace. Individual feelings about VE Day in May 1945 – and what peace in Europe would bring – were as different and diverse as the people of wartime Britain.

The surrender of the Nazi regime that had torn Europe apart was undoubtedly a victory for Britain and the many other nations who had fought with the Allies, as well as for the millions who had endured and often tried to resist occupation across the continent. But the relief, and sometimes euphoria, that accompanied the end of the war in Europe was not universal. While the children's author Astrid Lindgren described Stockholm restaurants in neutral Sweden where 'all the diners sang and recited and did their party pieces', the anonymous author of *A Woman in Berlin* was reflecting on the experiences of women under Russian occupation in that city: the endless search for food and fuel, and the constant threat of rape from the soldiers who were flooding into the city, looking for alcohol, and women, with which to celebrate their victory.[4] Meanwhile in Czechoslovakia insurgents were battling the remnants of the Nazi occupiers of Prague, waiting in vain for the US Third Army to come to their aid; and further afield, French police tried to seize the pro-independence banners that were held by Muslim participants in a victory parade in Algeria, sparking a wave of attacks and reprisals that left 6,000–30,000 dead. Closer to home, the Channel Islands had to wait an extra day for liberation, when British forces arrived on 9 May.

This book traces *some* of what was happening in the world on those fateful days. While its focus is on the experiences, hopes and fears recorded by those on the British home front who wrote for the organisation Mass Observation, other voices are included alongside them, to remind ourselves that there were different experiences and different narratives of the time, and that these deserve a place in any history of a *world* war.

In Britain we are lucky to have the material that was collected by Mass Observation, the unconventional social-survey organisation founded in 1937. In December 1936 the country had plunged into a constitutional crisis when the new king, Edward VIII, abdicated after the Cabinet refused his request to marry Wallis Simpson, an American divorcee. The affair gripped the nation, dividing it between those who supported the errant king and those who implacably opposed the marriage. Soon after the affair became public, in her diary entry for 7 December 1936, the novelist Virginia Woolf tried to explain the sense of crisis that pervaded the nation, centred not just on the behaviour of the King, but on the uncertainties of public opinion:

> We can't have a woman Simpson for Queen, that was the sense of it. 'She's no more Royal than you or me' was what the grocer's young woman said. But today, before the PM makes his announcement to the House, we have developed a strong sense of human sympathy; we are saying hang it all, the age of Victoria is over. Let him marry whom he likes… They say Royalty is in Peril. The Empire is divided. In fact, never has there been such a crisis… Spain, Germany, Russia, all are elbowed out… [Oswald] Mosley is taking advantage of the crisis for his own ends. In fact we are all talking 19 to the dozen… things, empires, hierarchies – moralities – will never be the same again.[5]

Woolf captured the volatile nature of public opinion: did people support the King and his desire to marry Mrs Simpson, or the government and the Church of England, who argued that, as head of the Church, the King could not marry a divorcee? Politicians, bishops, newspaper editors and the King himself argued over who was in touch with public opinion, and what that public opinion meant for the future of the monarchy and, it seemed, the nation. What, in the end, did the people want? And what did the people *feel*?

Newspapers made claims and counter-claims about public feeling regarding the King and his desire to marry. While *The Times* and the *Daily Telegraph* largely sided with the Cabinet, the *Daily Express* reported that a crowd supportive of the King gathered outside Downing Street to sing the national anthem and booed ministers leaving a Cabinet meeting.[6] The *Daily Mirror* stated emphatically that:

> Every sensible man and woman in Britain today holds the view that anything that makes our monarch happy is good for the country.
> The King wishes to marry Mrs Simpson.
> And the people of Britain want his request to be granted.[7]

This was a situation for which there was no historical precedent, and the opportunity that it seemed to offer to study human behaviour 'in the raw' was to inspire a London-based poet and journalist, a documentary film-maker and an anthropologist then based in the industrial north-west to attempt just that.

The origins of Mass Observation can be found in the letters pages of the *New Statesman and Nation*, the progressive magazine edited by Kingsley Martin. The first letter was from an energetic schoolteacher, inventor and activist, Geoffrey Pyke, who wrote on 12 December 1936 to suggest that the abdication crisis could provide useful material for 'the anthropological study of our own civilization, of which we stand in such desperate need'. The journalist and poet Charles Madge replied on 2 January 1937 to claim that a project of 'mass observations' was already in existence, inviting volunteers to help as 'only mass observations can create mass science'. One of those to respond was the anthropologist Tom Harrisson, and on 30 January 1937 a letter signed by Madge, Harrisson and the documentary film-maker Humphrey Jennings appeared in the pages of the *New Statesman,* announcing the creation of Mass Observation and its ambition to develop 'an anthropology of our own people'. Ambitiously, if not a little pompously, the letter claimed that the new organisation:

> Develops out of anthropology, psychology, and the sciences which study man – but it plans to work with a mass of

observers… It does not set out in quest of truth or facts for their [own sake] or for the sake of an intellectual minority, but aims at exposing them in simple terms to all observers, so that their environment may be understood, and thus constantly transformed.[8]

Thus the people – 'the mass of observers' – would themselves become anthropologists, psychologists and social scientists and, through observing their lives, they would help to understand, and to change, wider society. The initial list of topics they proposed to explore was lengthy and eclectic. Everything, it seemed, was worth of study, including:

Behaviour at war memorials

Shouts and gestures of motorists

The aspidistra cult

Anthropology of football pools

Bathroom behaviour

Beards, armpits, eyebrows

Anti-Semitism

Distribution, diffusion and significance of the dirty joke

Funerals and undertakers

Female taboos about eating

The private lives of midwives.[9]

Anyone intrigued by this list was urged to write to Charles Madge at the home he shared with the poet Kathleen Raine in the comfortable suburb of Blackheath in south-east London.

The organisation was founded by three very different men.

Madge, the poet and journalist whose Blackheath home became the first headquarters of Mass Observation, was fascinated by psychoanalysis and surrealism, and was curious to see whether the study of responses to national crises, such as the abdication crisis, could reveal the unconscious thoughts and feelings of a nation to itself. He had been one of the journalists covering the crisis and he regarded the press's pronouncements on popular feeling as a 'massive piece of falsification'.[10] Madge was also all too aware of the dangerous fault lines and divides that were so present in 1930s Europe – economic, social and political. When 200 unemployed men had taken part in a 'hunger march' from the shipbuilding town of Jarrow in north-east England to deliver a petition to the government in distant London in 1936, Madge had spent time talking to some of the marchers when they stopped for the night in Cambridge. He was struck by the gulf that existed between the lives of the marchers and his own comfortable middle-class life in southern England. Some, of course, sought to benefit from such divisions. On continental Europe the Nazis had come to power in Germany on the back of economic crisis and resentment at the way the Versailles Treaty had punished Germany for its role in the First World War. The Spanish Civil War, with the involvement by proxy of the Communist Soviet Union, Fascist Italy and Nazi Germany, seemed to demonstrate the potential outcome of such division. At home, Mosley's British Union of Fascists fed on the divisions of the period to foment resentment and hatred of minorities and migrants. Understanding what people thought and felt, and sharing this understanding as widely as possible, appeared to be not only necessary, but also urgent.

Caught up in what his wife was to describe as a state of 'imaginative poetic exaltation', Madge saw the abdication crisis as a chance to probe 'the ultra-repressed condition of the British people'.[11] Writing in 1939 for a BBC programme about Mass Observation, *They Speak for Themselves*, Madge tried to explain both his motivations in establishing the organisation and his view of the 'observers' that he set out to recruit:

> What appalled me was the confusion at such times [times of crisis], not only in the minds of the masses, but among those who are supposed to be guiding the masses. I'd been thinking for some time about the possibility of studying these problems, objectively, scientifically, and this crisis crystallised my ideas… it immediately put us in touch with a section of people in the population who were at one and the same time ordinary, hard-working folk and also interested and intelligent enough to want to help us… We did *not* regard these people as being themselves scientists studying the mass, nor did we consider them as being a random sample of public opinion. Their position was something different. They were *Observers*, untrained but shrewd, placed at vantage points for seeing and describing in their own simple language what life looks like.[12]

Madge may have been interested in the lives and beliefs of 'the people', but it seems that he did not necessarily see himself as one of them.

Co-founder of Mass Observation, Humphrey Jennings was an emerging figure in the documentary-film movement, who worked with John Grierson's GPO Film Unit. Like the founders of Mass Observation, Grierson and the group of film-makers who worked with him wanted to represent and understand modern British life. Not for them melodramas set in the parlours and nightclubs of Mayfair. Instead their pieces documented the working life and leisure of the British working classes, with short films like *Coal Face* (1935) and

Night Mail (1936) becoming the best-known productions of the GPO Film Unit in the 1930s. Jennings's participation in Mass Observation was limited, and he went on to make widely viewed and respected wartime films for the Ministry of Information, including *London Can Take It!* (1940), *Fires Were Started* (1943) and *A Diary for Timothy* (1945). Before the war his best-known film was the fifteen-minute-long *Spare Time*, made for the World Fair in New York in 1939. *Spare Time* was, in its lyrical, almost wordless depiction of leisure time in three industrial areas, a long way away from the GPO's previous representations of working-class life, which had tended to focus on the heroic figure of the male worker, whether they were the coal miners of *Coal Face*, the railway workers of *Night Mail* or the trawler men of *North Sea* (1938). Jennings's workers were shown at leisure – eating dinner, cycling in the countryside and playing in brass and silver bands – and his attempts to build up a picture of 'everyday life' through observation and attention to detail harmonised with Mass Observation's practice of collecting and presenting richly detailed and wide-ranging material.

But the figure who was to dominate Mass Observation in its wartime years was Tom Harrisson, who had recently returned from two years living in the New Hebrides observing the life of the 'native' people there. He had been living in the Lancashire mill town of Bolton, where he was attempting to apply the same method to a study of the lives of the working-class inhabitants of the town. Participant observation was a new type of social research: one in which the researcher, far from distancing themselves from the subject of their study, instead immersed themselves in the lives, customs and habits of those they were examining. Writing in the same 1939 BBC programme about Mass Observation as Madge, Harrisson described Madge as a poet, but himself as an ornithologist and anthropologist, and claimed to apply the same principles to both:

> I started as an ornithologist, a bird watcher, and I went on to become an anthropologist, a man-watcher. My interest was to describe as accurately as possible how people behave.[13]

Harrisson observed and participated in the lives of Boltonians while working as a mill hand, shop assistant, lorry driver and ice-cream salesman, living with his team of 'investigators' in a terraced house, eating fish and chips and playing George Formby's 'When I'm Cleaning Windows' over and over again, as he attempted to immerse himself in the culture of the northern mill town.[14]

What these three men had in common was a desire to document everyday life in Britain. Mass Observation aimed to let the people speak for themselves, to move away from the journalism of George Orwell's *The Road to Wigan Pier* (1937) and J. B. Priestley's *English Journey* (1934), both based on the authors' observations of everyday life in the 1930s, but neither giving much space to the voices of the people they were observing. A short pamphlet issued by Mass Observation in 1937 to try and recruit new writers showed that the organisation's ambition was not only observational, but was also political. Mass Observation aimed to observe and record life, but also to extend and deepen democratic participation among 'ordinary' people:

> The Observer in this movement is the Man in the Street. He can tell us about mass behaviour because he knows – he is one

of the mass. The only time his opinion is consulted as a rule is at a General Election – but he should be given a vote on other things as well.[15]

This then was the age of 'the masses', exercising their new voting rights and enjoying new forms of popular culture, but also believed to be vulnerable to manipulation and exploitation. For evidence of this, Madge only had to look across the English Channel, where he saw these 'masses' participating in the parades and spectacles of the fascist regimes that had taken root in continental Europe, and which were being mimicked, albeit with less success, by the British Union of Fascists. Looking westwards he could see the emergence of a consumer society in the United States, where men like Edward Bernays, nephew of Sigmund Freud and pioneer of public relations, were finding ways to target and harness human desires in order to ensure the success of mass-marketed commodities. Both systems – consumer capitalism and fascism – seemed to be successfully manipulating 'the masses' into particular ways of behaving. Finding ways to understand how people lived, and how their opinions and beliefs were formed, was clearly urgently needed.

As soon as Mass Observation was established, its founders forged ahead with their different interests and methods for collecting material. While Harrisson established himself and a team of enthusiastic volunteers in Bolton – known as Worktown in Mass Observation publications – Madge got to work on the recruitment of volunteer writers and observers from across the country to form a 'National Panel'. These early volunteers were sent a list of questions to ask others, which was first drafted in December 1936. The questions are a mix of the sociological ('What is your class?', 'What is your father's profession, and your own?'), opinions on current affairs ('Do you want the King to marry Mrs Simpson, and if so, why?', 'Are you in favour of the Disestablishment of the Church of England?') and the strikingly personal ('Can you believe you are going to die?', 'How do you want to die?', 'Do you or did you hate your mother and if so, why?'). Unsurprisingly, the volunteers were urged to ask the questions 'at a speed that will prevent him [the interviewee] from taking refuge in a merely conventional and socially correct response'. If successful, they could take advantage of the situation by improvising their own supplementary questions 'as rapidly and spontaneously as possible', with suggestions including 'Do you avoid looking at street accidents' and 'What is the ugliest thing you can think of?' Sadly, the experiences of the volunteer observers, or the responses of their victims, are not recorded in the Archive.[16]

By the end of 1937 there were about 600 of these volunteer observers, although few responded to every request from Mass Observation. Their first regular written task was to keep a diary on the twelfth of every month, recording not only their activities and observations of those around them, but their thoughts, hopes and fears. The twelfth was chosen because Wednesday 12 May 1937 was to be the date of George VI's coronation. Mass Observation's first book-length publication, *May the Twelfth*, was an attempt to capture both national events and public mood and behaviour around the event. This included one observer's vivid description of London on the eve of the coronation:

> 11.45 p.m. Euston full of people staying the night on waiting room benches. Refreshment room and Enquiry Hall full.
> In waiting room drunk man knocks over chair, sits on floor,

Policeman says 'Hi, sit up' but leaves him to lie there. Man drinking beer and eating sandwiches in a telephone box. Rush of excursionists arriving from Macclesfield to reserve seats for their return journey.[17]

Around the country the vast majority of Mass Observers marked the coronation in some way or another; some by going to special church services, others by listening on the wireless, decorating their houses and taking part in street celebrations or, in one case, a village fete with 'races, sports, tugs of war'.[18] By late afternoon the day of celebrations was starting to descend, in some places, into a scene at least partially familiar to many British city dwellers at weekends today. An observer in Birmingham recounted a bus ride that:

> Passes through some meaner streets, past a council school playground full of middle aged men and women dressed in all types of costumes, hats and false noses, apparently playing some kind of game... A fantastically dressed couple of about 45 walk past wearing false noses and looking round to catch the approval of passers by. Further along a woman walks a little unsteadily along the pavement. She is wearing a long transparent mauve dress with some kind of diamante embroidery upon it... her face is old and haggard and she leers dreadfully at passers by. On the next corner we wait for traffic lights and I see two youths supporting between them a third youth who has evidently drunk more than is good for him... A youth of about 19 looking sorry for himself, lurches past me into a latrine.[19]

The anxieties diagnosed by Mass Observation in response to the abdication crisis just six months earlier had evidently been put aside, at least for the day. They would return with a vengeance during the Munich Crisis, just over a year later.

The diarists writing the following month, on Saturday 12 June 1937, were asked to begin by describing their own living conditions and background. These diaries give us a snapshot impression of life in late-1930s Britain. One of them, given the number A001 by Mass Observation, was written by an infant schoolteacher living in Barnsley, south Yorkshire. The introduction to her diary gives us a glimpse of life in pre-war Britain, and a flavour of Mass Observation writing:

> I live in digs. The house is pleasantly situated opposite to a big park. It has a nice front garden with a lawn, and inside a parlour and kitchen and cellar kitchen. I have a small back bedroom to myself and live with the family… The district is a working class district, or a 'dole district'. Quite 50% of the children's parents are on the 'dole'. A number of the others are miners and a few others in shops or offices. There are numerous rows of small gardenless houses – some of them are reported too bad to live in and the people are being gradually removed into estate houses… The life of the district consists for the majority of the people in working and 'pictures', shopping (on market days) and for the minority going to the park. On Sunday when a local band plays the majority of the people go to the park or for a stroll.[20]

The diarist herself spent her day planning her teaching, cutting and sewing a pair of shorts and cycling out to a rowing lake with friends. When it started to rain they cycled to a nearby farmhouse for tea, and in the evening she visited a friend for supper. Among the minority that were at work this Saturday was a coalminer, who described setting out for work at 5 a.m.:

> Secure my lamp (electric), test it, then proceed towards the pit. I am searched on the way for matches, cigarettes, but I have automatically done the same thing previously. This is a good habit. I meet my workmates (there are four of us) one has failed to turn up. Strange how quiet everyone is, while waiting for the cage. It is always the same… miners somehow cannot be aroused so early in the morning.[21]

Like many of the Day Diaries, and the later war diaries, that were carefully written and posted off to Mass Observation in London, nothing very exciting happened, but their attention to detail, their descriptions of how people lived, how they spent their time, what they thought and said and their reflections on their own feelings build up, layer by layer, into an intimate and complex portrait of the lives of 'ordinary people' in mid-twentieth-century Britain.

Occasionally the National Panel were asked to send in their views, and to record the views and actions of others around them, on a particular topic, such as royalty or Armistice Day. A smaller number of volunteer 'observers' were recruited to watch and record people's behaviour at public places like war memorials, and to note down interesting snippets of conversation that they heard, leading to the *New Statesman*'s vivid portrait of a Mass Observer as having 'a loping walk, elephant ears [and] an eye trained to keyholes'.[22] As the world edged towards war, Mass Observation grew more ambitious, conducting door-to-door surveys and questionnaires on street corners on a wide and eclectic range of topics, including cinema-going, co-operative stores and astrology. Some of the responses they collected might be surprising to anyone expecting the composed, unflappable people so familiar from the stories and films of wartime. For example, in November 1938, just two months after the Munich

Crisis and the distribution of gas masks to civilians on 'Gas Mask Sunday' in September 1938, Mass Observation sent some of its volunteers to ask people in west London how they had spent 11 November, Armistice Day, that year. Some of the replies take us a long way from the more familiar pictures of huge silent crowds gathered at war memorials, united in their remembrance of the dead. For one forty-year-old woman from Fulham, the impact of the Great War on her family and the threat of a coming war were almost too much to bear:

> My God, I lost my father and mother and three brothers… how can I ever forget it all (Cries)… On Armistice Day I take the children and we kneel down and pray… I tell them all about what it means… I tell them what an air raid was like… I went nearly mad when they told me there was no mask for the baby, that I should have to wrap it in a wet blanket, and he's bad with his chest… I told them they could have the gas masks back for all the family.[23]

Another woman, when asked 'What will you actually do if war breaks out?', was determined to avoid her family experiencing any coming war:

> I have been collecting poison for some time with guile and cunning. I have sufficient to give self, husband and all the children a lethal dose. I can remember the last war. I don't want to live through another, or the children either. I shan't tell them, I shall just do it.[24]

In London – the presumed target of the devastating air raids and gas attacks that were expected to begin any future war – it was fear of this possible, coming conflict that was uppermost in people's minds, not remembrance of the last war.

As war seemed increasingly imminent in September 1938, Mass Observation asked its writers to keep a 'Crisis Diary'. One volunteer writer, a woman from Glasgow whom we shall meet again as she waited for the war's end in 1945, described the anxiety that she felt, and that she observed in many of those around her:

> As a Mass Observer perhaps I should be writing daily reports detailing the crisis in Glasgow and the views of those with whom I live and work. That is beyond me. The situation distresses me intensely and I find it difficult to express my thoughts on paper… Whence comes my knowledge of the crisis? Not from the newspapers so much as might be thought. On Sundays I carefully study *The Observer* and *The Sunday Times*, but on weekdays I merely scan the dailies, in fact the last few days I have ceased to do that, even avoiding the illustrations. I am afraid to touch anything that might break the calm bearing that I am forcing myself to assume… I avoid discussing the situation for this heightens my distress, and as far as possible leave the room when I think someone is going to speak of it. Avoiding conversations is not difficult for many of my associates seem to be bent on doing likewise.[25]

A volunteer writer from Essex recorded how her sister, living in Streatham, south London, was planning to evacuate herself and her three children to Cornwall, while a neighbour described herself as 'feeling sick in her inside'.[26] A woman from Gerrards Cross in Buckinghamshire was volunteering as an air-raid warden and was distributing gas masks in her area. Although it was 'pouring with rain and a very wild night', she found that doing something to help in turn helped her:

I felt very strung up. It all seemed so horribly realistic. The continual movement and efforts to calm other people acted as a sedative, so that after an hour we were all acting mechanically, at least I was.[27]

The 'stiff upper lip' associated with the British at war was clearly hard won and could be as much a disguise for anxiety as it was a stoical response to danger and disaster.

As war grew ever closer, Mass Observation increased in both the numbers of its volunteer writers and in confidence. The organisation started to issue monthly 'Directives' in January 1939. These were open-ended questionnaires, which asked the National Panel to record their views on, and their feelings about, a varied assortment of topics, ranging from dreams to dances, from Poland to public houses, and from air-raid precautions to anti-Semitism. The first Directive was typically varied in its questions and wide-ranging in the answers it demanded, being divided into two sections, 'Saving' and 'Jazz'. Respondents were asked not only about whether and, if so, how much they saved each month, but how much cash they had on them at that moment, whether they knew this without looking, and to list their pet economies and indulgences. The section on jazz asked them to 'describe the part jazz plays in your home life' and whether they could record instances of 'people leaving the room when the radio is turned on because they hate it so much, or on the other hand of people dancing for joy with some particular band?' Unsurprisingly, the answers were rarely the kind of ones that we might expect to find in a more traditional survey of public opinion, which often asks questions needing simply a 'yes' or 'no' answer and does not expect, or desire, the more lengthy and detailed answers that Mass Observation tried to solicit. One of Mass Observation's younger writers, a woman born in 1917, described the kind of household tensions over music that might be familiar to many of us:

> I'm really crazy about jazz, especially swing. Father looks annoyed when I put it on unless it's Harry Hall's band... Mother once left the room while I was entranced by Duke Ellington's version of 'St Louis Blues'. She thought it a foul mix up and since that she won't even let me put this, my only jazz record, on the gramophone.[28]

The Directive for March 1939, which received more than 300 responses, asked the National Panel to 'find someone whose views you think are representative of public opinion' and ask them what they expected Hitler to do in the next few months, and whether anything in the recent news had prompted them to be more active in their preparation 'for a national emergency'.[29] The replies that were submitted provide a sense of the mixture of apathy, apprehension, uncertainty and unease among the public in the month that Hitler's armies marched unopposed into Czechoslovakia, occupying the capital, Prague, on 15 March. Some of the people whose views were recorded by a housewife observer from Gateshead (who was still writing for Mass Observation in 1945) were hopeful that the international outcry that followed the occupation would limit any further territorial ambitions on the part of Hitler:

> Hitler won't do much. He's got a fright with this many democracies against him.

> He will commit no further acts of aggression in the next few months.

> There'll be a revolution in Germany and that will settle Hitler.[30]

Further south in Kent, another housewife did not share this optimism. She believed that 'Hitler will proceed with his policy of so-called "peaceful penetration", which amounts to nothing more than an ultimatum of "stand and deliver or we bomb you to bits".'[31] Like the air-raid warden delivering gas masks in 1938, she had embraced activity as a way of coping with uncertainty and anxiety, and had already completed an 'anti-gas' course and trained as an air-raid warden. A student from Newport in Wales believed Hitler to be 'the antichrist' who would 'try to wreck the world', while a housewife from Chepstow, who remained confident that 'there will be no war', nonetheless 'reflected on how ideas had changed in six months'. 'Then I did not think it incumbent on me to mention any such thing as a gas mask to my little ones, and now think it as well to familiarise them with the whole idea.'[32] The fragile hope that peace could be maintained in Europe, which had been generated by Neville Chamberlain's promise of 'peace for our time' the previous year, was fracturing in the face of Hitler's continued aggression.

By August 1939 Mass Observation's confidence in its importance and ability to provide insights into morale in any coming war was checked only by its lack of regular income. Madge and Harrisson hoped that the planned Ministry of Information, which was to oversee the production of wartime propaganda and monitor its impact on the population, would recognise the organisation's value, so they asked their National Panel to begin keeping wartime diaries in August 1939. These diaries give us a picture of the war years in the words of the people who experienced them. They are a mixture of social history, with diaries cataloguing events such as 'Operation Pied Piper' – the evacuation of thousands of school children and the mothers of babies and toddlers from the major cities in the first days of September 1939 – and personal reflection, as the authors committed their thoughts, responses and – crucially – their feelings to the page. Some are typed, most are handwritten, with school exercise books, notebooks and jotting pads, and the fine, almost transparent letter paper of wartime, when the wood pulp needed to make paper was in high demand, all being pressed into use.

This was also the age of the letter, and at least one diarist assiduously filled an exercise book with copies of his almost daily letters to his parents, while a retired gas engineer and keen amateur poet copied out letters to his sister. Some (though a minority of diarists) wrote regularly throughout the war and beyond, with the most committed continuing to send Mass Observation regular instalments of their lives until the 1960s. Others began with great enthusiasm but tailed off after a few months. Some wrote animatedly, sending in long instalments every month, and then vanished for a year, only to reappear later with no explanation for the break. Military service could prevent people from writing during the war, as those in military uniform were not supposed to send material to Mass Observation in case they inadvertently gave away war secrets; however, some seem to have ignored this rule and continued to write whenever they could. Often they tell us of an imagined, but important, relationship between the diarist and Mass Observation, with diarists going out of their way to describe events, or responses to events, that they feel the reader will be interested in, and sometimes responding to letters from Mass Observation requesting particular information. But what they all have in common – with one another and with many of the Directive replies – is the generosity of the writers in committing moments of their wartime lives to paper, providing a window through which we can glimpse the 'people's war' through the eyes of some of 'the people'.

While the outbreak of war was, in many ways, the making of Mass Observation, encouraging a new wave of writers to join the National Panel, responding to Directives and sending in regular diary entries, and providing material that would prove useful to the new Ministry of Information, by 1940 all was not well at its headquarters. Jennings was busy working for the GPO Film Unit and then for the Crown Film Unit, for which he made classic documentary pictures of wartime life, such as *London Can Take It!*, about the first months of the Blitz, and *Listen to Britain* (1942), which produced a poetic picture of national unity. Meanwhile Madge and Harrisson were not getting on. Madge left Mass Observation in April 1940, when their first commission from the Ministry of Information meant that, for the first time, the organisation was on a stable financial footing. He was uncomfortable providing information for the government, seeing it as a 'sort of home front espionage'.[33] Perhaps too he was reminded of the *Daily Mirror*'s description of Mass Observation in 1938 as 'Public Busybody No.1', illustrated with a cartoon of Harrisson peering through a keyhole, notebook in hand.[34] Harrisson continued to run Mass Observation, with the help of a small number of volunteers and paid workers, until he was conscripted into the army in 1942. Even then he managed to continue overseeing the organisation from his army training camp in Yorkshire, until in 1943 he was recruited into Special Operations and parachuted into Japanese-occupied Borneo. Even Harrisson could not combine special operations behind enemy lines with running Mass Observation, and he handed over the reins to

H. A. 'Bob' Willcock, who ran it until the war's end. By the late 1940s Mass Observation had turned to market research in its search for financial stability, and for the next two decades the hundreds of thousands of wartime words sat in the damp basement of the organisation's London headquarters.

But back to the war. Mass Observation's first wartime book, *War Begins at Home* (1940), which provided a snapshot of the country in the first months of war, drew on these diaries alongside Directive replies, observations of public behaviour and vox-pops to reveal people's feelings at the end of August 1939, as they waited to see whether war would come:

> Thursday 31 August [the day after the public evacuation scheme, Operation Pied Piper, was announced]
>
> Woman, 49: Worried by 1 p.m. news. Collecting blankets.
>
> Man, 58: Taking it calmly, still betting on no war, but daughter anxious.
>
> Man, 30: War seems nearer after evacuation news. Sister asks cousin 'Will there be a war?' He says yes. She says she'd hoped he would say no.[35]

Worry, anxiety and stress seemed to be the most common feelings as people waited to see the outcome of events over which they had no control. There were, however, other reactions. Hitler would no doubt have been grateful not to be in Bolton, Lancashire, where Harrisson's Worktown project reported a conversation overheard between two women on 1 September:

> I would just like to get Hitler on this field at the top of the street just to give him some punishment. First thing I would

do, saw off his feet at the ankles, sharpen the shin bones and force him down into the earth, down into his shoulders, then I would just hammer the top of his head with my big saucepan until I'd driven him down out of sight.

To which the other woman replied:

I wouldn't give you that chance. I should take him on the same field, warn all the women of the estate to come and see the fun, then I would strip him naked and pluck every hair from his body, from head to toe.[36]

Imaginative though these fantasies might have been, they gave voice to the resentment provoked by Hitler as he dragged Europe towards its second war in a generation.

When Britain eventually went to war in September 1939, Mass Observation was uniquely poised to record the thoughts and feelings of at least some of the people. For many, the declaration of war itself was a relief – an end to the seemingly interminable period of anxiously watching and waiting. For others, it meant the end of hope that peace would, somehow, prevail. The housewife Nella Last, who was to become one of Mass Observation's longest-lasting contributors, sending in diary entries from her home in Barrow-in-Furness until two years before her death in 1968, joked that the announcement that children would be evacuated from major cities on 31 August would mean that 'everybody will soon be evacuating in another sense. Sales of Beecham's Pills [a popular remedy for constipation] will drop.'[37] A nineteen-year-old shop assistant from Essex recorded how 'I feel rather glad we are going to get it over with', while a shopkeeper from Leeds wrote:

So it was war; now the news had really come no one appeared bothered, only excited... We keep listening to the wireless news, hoping, I am afraid, for something sensational.[38]

One of Mass Observation's first wartime Directives was sent out in November 1939. The daunting list of questions and tasks for the panellists show us something of its ambition to understand how 'the masses' felt about the war, and thus to predict how they might act:

1. Give a list of what you yourself consider the six main inconveniences of wartime on the home front, in order of importance.
2. What are the wartime grouses you hear most often? If possible, give them in the words of the speaker, and give his or her age, sex and occupation.
3. Would you subscribe to a National Defence Loan, if one were issued now? Give your pros and cons for wartime saving.
4. If you are in a reception area, say what you think are the main problems between evacuees and hosts, and other evacuation problems. Try to give concrete examples rather than impressions, and verify the facts for yourself as far as possible.
5. What are your reactions to the black-out, and how does it affect your spirits?
6. How has the black-out modified your usual evening habits, if at all?
7. By what methods do you black-out your own home, and how long does it take each day?
8. What have been your experiences with ARP [Air Raid Precautions] wardens over the black-out?
9. What alterations, if any, do you suggest in present black-out regulations?[39]

Despite the length and complexity of the Directive, more than 200 people responded, showing the desire of many to have their voices heard, and perhaps also to complain about the changes that war had brought to everyday life.

Mass Observation's volunteer writers, whose voices are recorded in this book, were not necessarily representative of the British people as a whole: they were not what social scientists would call a 'representative sample', carefully recruited, calibrated, weighed and measured to reflect the make-up of the British population and organised by categories such as political belief, gender, age, social class, ethnicity and occupation. Instead the Mass Observation writers were self-selecting: largely (but not entirely) middle-class, often (but not always) living in the south of England, and tending (but not exclusively) towards liberal and left-wing political beliefs. When asked to describe their own social class in June 1939, only sixty-three of the 379 who replied identified themselves as working class, and only nine saw themselves as belonging to the upper class or gentry.[40] The miner who described his working day in the Day Diary for 12 June 1937 was certainly not typical of Mass Observers.

A map showing the geographic distribution of wartime diarists, many of whom also completed regular Directive replies, shows that the majority were living in London, its suburbs and the Home Counties. There were smaller concentrations around the industrial towns and great cities of northern England and the Midlands, and more diarists were scattered across Scotland's central belt between Glasgow and Edinburgh. Two lived in the West Highlands, and one each in the cities of north-east Scotland: Inverness and Aberdeen. Wales could lay claim to some nineteen diarists, mainly around Cardiff,

Newport and along the south coast; and Northern Ireland just three, two in Belfast and one in Armagh.[41] Penzance, in the far west of Cornwall, had one diarist, as did Blakeney on Norfolk's north-east coast.[42] They also tended to be younger than the general population, and had nearly double the number of male writers to female. Their writing is valuable not because it is necessarily 'typical', but because of its detail and its attention to feeling and individual responses to public events, as much as to the events themselves.

Some wrote faithfully every month, others more sporadically, and many just once or twice. Periods of crisis, like the Second World War, when people had a sense of 'living through history', attracted the largest number of participants, keen to have their experiences and opinions recorded for posterity. However frequently and for however long they wrote, these were people who wanted their voices, their thoughts and feelings and their lives to be recorded, and who often wrote down the most intimate details of these lives, recording their dreams, their romantic and sexual encounters, their private feelings, their hopes and fears alongside their thoughts on events of the day. The material collected by Mass Observation, always eclectic and wide-ranging in its interests, gives us an unparalleled glimpse into the interior lives of their writers. These writers were asked to consider themselves part of the new wave of documentary-making that focused on lives that had rarely been recorded. They were to be documentary cameras, observing both their own thoughts and feelings and those of others around them, in order to provide 'an invaluable insight into the WHY of what Britain is thinking'.[43]

Eccentric, unusual and unscientific as its methods and interests were, it was not long before the wartime government, in the form of the Ministry of Information, recognised that Mass Observation could be a valuable source of material on morale – that most elusive yet important element of wartime life. Long before 1939, civilian morale had been identified by strategists, psychologists and politicians as one of the key factors that could either secure victory or doom a country to wartime defeat. Without strong morale, it was predicted that democratic governments would struggle to motivate their people and enable them to subject themselves more or less willingly to the rigours and demands of total war. While authoritarian regimes like Nazi Germany and the Soviet Union could largely rely on coercion, democracies needed the consent and support of their populations in order to fight a war. Mass Observation's established methods of observing people's behaviour and asking them to reflect on, and record, their feelings offered a means of finding out what the people were thinking, and of keeping a weather eye on wartime morale.

The Ministry of Information employed Mass Observation throughout the darkest days of Britain's war in 1940–41, during which the organisation sent in regular reports on topics including fears of invasion, feelings regarding air raids, and thoughts about the government. Although this work – and the income from the Ministry – dried up as the immediate danger receded, Mass Observation continued to collect and amass material during the war, receiving reports from around 1,000 volunteer writers at its height.

By the time of VE Day in May 1945 the immediate danger of war for most on the home front had receded. The final V-2 rockets had fallen in March 1945, and in April the blackout began to be lifted. Men and women were starting to be released from their wartime service in the armed forces, in industry and in agriculture, and some of the lucky survivors of the war – including some of those who had been taken prisoner – were beginning to return home. People's thoughts were turning from winning the war to winning the peace and, just one month after VE Day, Parliament was dissolved and the political parties, which had formed a coalition government for the war years, began their General Election campaigns. VE Day itself did not mark the end of the 'people's war', but an important stage on the way to its end and to the rebuilding of the post-war world. The accounts collected by Mass Observation, and reproduced here, show us how some of the people of the 'people's war' marked the beginning of its end.

CHAPTER THREE

Mass Observers at War

'War Begins at Home'

Britain's Second World War started on Sunday 3 September 1939. Three days earlier Nazi Germany had invaded Poland on the pretence of defending ethnic Germans living in the country from persecution. Britain and France, which had guaranteed Polish sovereignty after the occupation of Czechoslovakia seven months earlier, decisively abandoned the policy of appeasement developed during the Munich Crisis of 1938 that had seen Nazi Germany first annex the Sudetenland and then occupy Czechoslovakia in its entirety. A year later the majority of the British people were expecting war: for the past twelve months Britain had been re-arming, building air-raid shelters, training volunteers for Air Raid Precautions work and finalising conscription plans. The blackout had been tested, with cities 'blacked out' while planes circled above, trying to identify targets; and the full blackout, which initially covered even the lighting of matches in the street after dark, had come into force on 1 September 1939. On the same day the BBC's new television service, broadcasting to a small number of viewers in London, was closed because of fears that its transmitter in Alexandra Palace, north London, would be a navigational aid for enemy aircraft. The evacuation of children, the mothers of infants and vulnerable adults from the cities had begun in earnest at the end of August. Six months' compulsory military training for young men had come into force in May 1939, and the expectation that this would be expanded in the event of war was strengthened by the creation of a complex schedule of reserved occupations, specifying the age at which workers could be conscripted into the military. On the declaration of war, all men aged between eighteen and forty-one who were not covered by this system found themselves subject to conscription. Women were to follow them in 1941, when the National Service Act was expanded to include all unmarried women between twenty and thirty.

Neville Chamberlain, the Conservative prime minister who had returned from Munich one year earlier with the promise of 'peace for our time', told the country it was now at war in a special radio broadcast that Sunday at 11.15 a.m. Many Mass Observation diarists recorded both their preparations for war and their responses to Chamberlain's announcement. The Soviet Union and Nazi Germany had signed a Non-Aggression Pact on 23 August 1939, opening the door to the occupation of Poland and followed swiftly by a full-scale Nazi invasion of that country on 1 September.* In the days afterwards people waited – some anxiously, some resigned, others hopefully – to see what would happen.

Dictators' dreams, fantasies of power and plans for conquest shaped people's everyday lives at home, in Britain as elsewhere. In neutral Sweden the children's author Astrid Lindgren described how 'a terrible despondency weighs on everything

---

* The Soviet Union invaded the east of Poland just two weeks later, on 17 September 1939, and the country was formally divided between the two powers at the end of the month.

and everyone'. Swedish neutrality offered no protection from fears of shortages and subsequent stockpiling, which were seen in Britain and elsewhere. Shopping for 'a fully legitimate quarter kilo of coffee', Lindgren found a notice on her coffee merchant's door: 'Closed. Sold out for today.'[1] Air-raid sirens had sounded for the first time in Berlin on 1 September 1939, and sheltering in the basement of her apartment block with her neighbours, Liselotte Purper, a young press photographer, wrote to her boyfriend Kurt Orgel of how the sirens frightened her, their wail 'arousing deep seated childhood terrors'.[2] Purper, who had established herself as a 'house photographer' with the Nazi women's organisation NS-Frauenschaft, went on to document women's lives behind the lines across territories occupied by, and countries allied to, the Third Reich during the war. Orgel, whom she married in 1943, was to die of his wounds in Copenhagen in 1945.

On the other side of the new battle lines the teenager Renia Spiegel, living in the south-eastern Polish city of Przemyśl, described in her diary how:

> We're all fighting, from young girls to soldiers. I've been taking part in female military training... In a word I'm fighting alongside the rest of the Polish nation. I'm fighting and I'll win![3]

Spiegel, who was Jewish, was murdered by Nazis in 1942 while in hiding. She was eighteen years old.

Back in Britain, a Directive of August 1939 asking the panellists to describe their dreams gives us some sense of the ways in which anxiety about the coming war bled into people's unconscious, as well as conscious, lives. A woman in her early thirties, living in north London, wrote that:

> The only nightmare I ever had which was caused by worry was a war nightmare. I dreamt I was caught in a cinema by an incendiary bomb. All the exits were blocked and the people all around didn't notice anything wrong. I woke up at the point where I was climbing on to the balcony.[4]

Another woman, a cookery demonstrator, dreamed that 'I was in the gas showroom surrounded by a Nazi crowd in uniform', while a librarian dreamed that she was sheltering with some children from an air raid. But 'they would press their noses against a French window. The windows were smashed in and the children slightly injured. I had to bind up their hands.'[5] This dream, she thought, was caused by a combination of war anxiety and going to see the film *Wuthering Heights* the previous week, in which Laurence Olivier's Heathcliff smashed his hand through a window.

The coming war intruded on the respondents' everyday lives as well as on their dreams. Watching events from Cardiff, a civil servant in his early thirties described his wife's 'anxiety' at the threat of air raids on the outbreak of war, as she was in the port city of Liverpool with their eldest daughter, who was receiving hospital treatment there. Nonetheless, she was going to wait until 'the last possible moment' to come home, a decision that he approved of as '[we] must not let normal activities be shaken by crisis'.[6] In Cambridge a twenty-five-year-old secretary, planning her wedding the following week, returned from a shopping expedition to the news that the German Air Force had bombed Warsaw on 1 September:

> We were stunned and incredulous. My fiancé refused to believe it. 'It's a fantastic rumour' he said. 'He'd never risk starting a raid on Warsaw in daylight. Besides, if he's done it he's done the one thing that gives our government no loophole at all. Well,

the news is on in five minutes, we shall soon hear.' We sat down to lunch without much appetite then we heard the news, and it was even worse than we had expected. We knew that now we were bound to go to war, I couldn't finish my lunch. We spent a miserable afternoon. All our plans for the future were shattered, everything in ruins… our married life might be at an end too.

She and her fiancé decided to bring their wedding forward to the next day, but they were clearly not the only couple to make the same decision and the Cambridge Registry Office 'could not fit us in, although they were working overtime'.[7] In Monmouth a young advertising salesman cycling home one evening watched a new anti-aircraft gunnery failing to spot a plane, although he could see it 'showing black against the moonlit sky. I thought that plane could have bombed the valley to pieces before those silly nitwits in the searchlights would find it.'[8]

In a pattern that was to be repeated as the war in Europe came to an end some six years later, people hunted for the necessities in shops that were rapidly emptying of them: our Cambridge secretary and her mother had spent much of 31 August shopping for preserving sugar and blackout material, with limited success, and a twenty-six-year-old Liverpool teacher added a torch to her usual shopping list.[9] A young journalist from Chelmsford in Essex noted a garage full of 'long trestle tables and tins of biscuits etc., and women volunteers obviously preparing snack meals for evacuees,' but had a rather more personal preoccupation and potential shopping list:

Now my worry is this: I've known girl and her family all my life. We've been in love two or three years. But although we've indulged in pretty extensive 'necking' or 'petting' (there seem to be no other words!) we haven't yet had intercourse (another horrible word!). What I am wondering is whether in view of the situation I shall broach the subject and suggest that we shall this weekend, and to that end, whether I shall buy contraceptives?[10]

As the percentage of babies born outside marriage more than doubled from 4.19 per cent in 1939 to 9.18 per cent by 1945, it's fair to assume that he wasn't the only person considering the impact of war on their actual or potential sex life.[11]

All the while, many continued to hope that war could be averted. A seventeen-year-old bank clerk from Sidcup, Kent reported that his customers were 'almost entirely optimistic' and that '"there will be no war" and such remarks [were] very prevalent', while a nineteen-year-old telephonist in Southampton described her aunt's hope that the astrology column in *The People* 'prophesying no war, was accurate'.[12] Both customers and aunt were, of course, to be disappointed. In Barrow-in-Furness Nella Last, Mass Observation's best-known diarist, was pondering 'if it was faith with a capital F or stubbornness which made those of us who thought "something will happen at the last minute" cling to their disbelief in the worst happening'. More poignantly she wondered 'if I should give my faithful old dog and my funny little comedian cat the "gift of sleep"'.[13] Amid concerns of food shortages and anxiety about air raids and the potential use of poison gas (no masks for pets!), some 400,000 cats and dogs were euthanised, on government advice, in the first days of the war.

Most of the diarists listened to Chamberlain's broadcast, some at home, some at church, where vicars dragged in heavy wireless sets so that their congregations could listen collectively, and others at work. Still others heard Chamberlain's words second-hand, or did their best to avoid hearing them. The schoolteacher from Liverpool had been working hard on her school's evacuation plans since the end of August, and the days immediately following the invasion of Poland, with no news from the British government, had been hard. On the evening of Saturday 2 September she had 'heard [the] news. Nothing much on it. Wish they would decide what to do, or have it decided for them.' The next morning she 'felt very upset about it all and had a good cry', leaving her rented rooms at eleven, 'specifically to avoid emotion at 11.15'. By lunchtime she was busy accompanying mothers and children on their evacuation train to Shrewsbury, where her heartfelt description of 'howling kids and smelly mothers' suggests that the declaration of war did not always prompt the instinctive national unity that we might perhaps imagine from tales of Britain's 'finest hour'.[14]

Further north, on the Carradale Estate on the Kintyre peninsula in Scotland, Naomi Mitchison – Mass Observation diarist, author, socialist, campaigner and landowner – was listening to Chamberlain's broadcast at home. This home, the large Carradale House, was full: Mitchison's five children were at home, accompanied by several of their friends, plus friends of Naomi's from England (the family also had a home in London) and a young Jewish refugee from Austria, while the cottages and farmhouse on the estate were providing a temporary shelter for evacuees from Glasgow. The household also employed several staff, including a cook and three maids, whom Mitchison had invited to listen to the wireless with the family and their friends. But:

> The maids hadn't wanted to come through. I told Annie [a maid] who was wonderfully cheery and said she remembered

the Boer War, and Bella [the cook] who said Isn't that heartbreaking. After a bit she began to cry, a saucepan in her hands, said Think of all our men going, then to me Of course you've got boys too. Dick [Mitchison's husband] said Think of all the women in Germany saying that too, but there was no response. Then she asked When will they send our men over? But none of us had much idea.

At lunch Mitchison and her friend, the writer Joan Rendell, were talking:

> Joan said she was on a small island of sand, with everything cut off before and behind. I said I had been feeling the future cut off for some time. We all agreed it was queer to feel the past so cut-off, everything had a different meaning now.[15]

The outbreak of war meant a break with the past – the end not only of peace, but also of waiting, hoping and wondering whether Europe would have to experience another conflict after the tragedy of the Great War. But it also meant an uncertain, perhaps unimaginable, future.

In London and the south of England, Chamberlain's announcement was followed just eight minutes later by the first air-raid warning of the war. Expectations that the outbreak of war would be marked by massive, devastating air raids were high: military strategists, politicians and popular writers of the 1930s were all agreed that attacks on cities and their inhabitants, by high explosive and poison gas, would be the defining feature of any coming war. Cinema audiences had been delighted and terrified in equal measure by Alexander Korda's 1936 *Things to Come*, based on H. G. Wells's 1933 novel *The Shape of Things to Come*, which showed the destruction of 'Everytown', a thinly disguised London at the start of a coming world war, while trainee air-raid wardens were given copies of Nevil Shute's *What Happened to the Corbetts* (1939), which described the impact of bombing raids on Southampton, with looting, cholera and martial law swiftly following the first, heavy raids. Top-secret Whitehall committees planned for a minimum of 7,000 daily dead in Greater London, while coverage of the Spanish Civil War – and in particular the bombing of the undefended market town of Guernica by the German Condor Legion in April 1937 – stood as a dreadful warning to civilians everywhere of the devastating potential of air raids. In Belfast, whose government mistakenly believed itself to be almost immune from air raids due to its position on the west of the British Isles, rumours circulated that London had been almost destroyed. Back in the south of England, the young bank clerk living with his parents in Sidcup carefully described their actions on hearing the air-raid siren:

> We rushed to the door to investigate our neighbour's reactions – the same as our own. We had made arrangements beforehand that in the case of air raids we were to go into my aunt's house next door. This we did, collecting our gas masks on our way and also taking inside a pail of thin mould [*sic*] in case of fire. We then put up our ARP curtains in order to prevent splintered glass from coming in. We also switched on the radio to hear any announcements which might be coming through. During the process we were running outside to see if anything was to be seen or done. This continued until we were ordered inside by some warden. The rest of the household continued with its business to await the arrival of the raiders. I read the paper. Sounds were heard which were interpreted as gun fire. Suddenly we heard the 'all-clear' signal. Rather dubious, we asked some air raid wardens if it was all right. Some said yes; others no. We decided it was all right… We had lunch at 1 p.m. – a lunch my parents did not enjoy, due to worry and nervousness.[16]

This first air-raid warning was a false alarm, but just one year later the wail of the air-raid siren was a familiar, and unwelcome, sound.

North of here, just outside Chelmsford in Essex, a woman in her early forties, who described herself as 'landed gentry', had welcomed four refugees from London the previous day: three children and one mother, whom, she was 'much relieved' to report, were 'quite nice looking and respectable'. Nonetheless she found herself alone, but for her dog, on the morning of 3 September when she settled down to listen to the wireless:

> I had been told by the gardener an important announcement would be given… It would either be peace or war and anxiety increased as the time drew near. Then it was the latter. I stood for God save the King and my little dog got out of her basket and stood beside me. I took her on my lap for comfort… After lunch I start the traditional war work of knitting socks.[17]

The journalist from Chelmsford, who had been preoccupied with whether or not to purchase contraceptives, was visiting his girlfriend's family in Tunbridge Wells that morning, where:

> We all sat and listened to Chamberlain's speech. I sat on the floor, back to back with girl, feeling rather analytical about [the] whole historical occasion; I'd never imagined I'd listen to news we were at war in such circumstances. It seemed rather ridiculous, comic, incongruous… that on a beautiful Sunday morning, blue sky, white clouds, green and beautiful garden, we should be having the war cloud, which we've so long regarded as a 'final horror' coming down on us.[18]

War may have been incongruous on such a beautiful morning, but the 'war cloud' was to cast its shadow for the next six years.

The declaration of war was a relief for some, after days of anxiously scanning the news and waiting for announcements that didn't arrive, but for others it was the culmination of a long period of fear and anxiety. The hospital telephonist in Southampton described her 'feeling of relief, almost of elation' when war was finally declared, while a thirty-one-year-old man from south London, who listened to the wireless with his wife while they waited for the car and driver they had hired to take them to the relative safety of New Milton in Hampshire, had a more mixed reaction:

> I felt suddenly rotten in the stomach. There was a sense of unreality about it all, listening to a declaration of war with our bags packed and waiting in the hall. It was at once worse and better than the last few days have been: a kind of perverted relief.[19]

For some, the knowledge that war had arrived didn't help. The diary of a thirty-five-year-old housewife and mother from Cambridge combined resignation and disbelief:

> Well, it is war! I feel it must all be some terrible nightmare from which I shall presently awake. I suppose it had to be. We could not go on with the fear of war over our heads indefinitely, which is what giving in to Hitler's demands would mean.[20]

Anxiety about the dangers and hardship that war would probably bring to her family were at the forefront of a forty-six-year-old teacher's mind as she listened to Chamberlain's broadcast after helping to organise housing and education for evacuees recently arrived from Birmingham:

> I listened to Chamberlain's speech being broadcast from a shop on my way home and my mind became occupied with thoughts

of my son in the first line of defence from air attack in the event of war. Hard work had kept me from thinking all day, and thoughtful friends had refrained from making enquiries. But now I realised that this was a thing I must do so I hurried home to send a cheery message to the one with whom I share him. I write telling her to 'keep smiling'. She is a plucky little thing and it is a shame for their married happiness to be marred by one stark maniac.[21]

Hard work, and anxiety, would become the lot of many millions over the next six years.

The mixture of relief, fear and anticipation that marked the announcement of war were soon replaced for many by boredom and resentment as the 'bore war' dragged on over the next nine months. There was comedy too, as people adjusted to wartime conditions. A diarist from Glasgow recorded that:

> There is a story going of a lady in London who went into her dug-out on hearing the signal. She failed to hear the all-clear, and sat there for three days. It was the longest air raid she had ever sat through.[22]

Humour permeated wartime Britain. It was both a necessary reaction to the multiple challenges and threats of wartime, a means of binding people together and a way to cope with changed circumstances. The Entertainment National Services Association (ENSA), founded in 1939 to provide entertainment for the troops, was affectionately known as 'Every Night Something Awful', and Humphrey Jennings and Harry Watt's short film about the London Blitz, *London Can Take It!*, told its viewers that while businesses remained open despite the raids, the bomb damage meant that some were 'more open than usual'.[23] Popular songs and sketches by wartime entertainers such as Flanagan and Allen, and Tommy Trinder, lampooned Nazi leaders, and amusement at their posturing and pronouncements helped to sustain wartime society.

Early in 1940 Mass Observation published *War Begins at Home*, its survey of the public mood and morale in the first months of war. Following the declaration of war, and in the absence of the expected calamitous air raids, rumour stepped in to fill the gap. Mass Observation reported on confident accounts of non-existent raids, including '35 dead' and 'twice as many injured' in Winchester, and the imminent introduction of a law stating that 'all women must use air raid shelters, immediately warning is sounded'.[24] In Portsmouth a newspaper salesman was given two months in prison for displaying a board declaring that 'Germany attacks Holland', claiming in his defence that he had simply forgotten to add the all-important 'If' at the start of the sentence.[25] For Mass Observation, the problem was not that – on the home front at least – little of any interest was happening, but that the government needed to work harder to communicate with and understand its people. Their aim in collecting and analysing the millions of words that were sent to them by their National Panel of volunteer writers throughout the war was to build a bridge of understanding between the people and their government.

This gap between people and government became evident in the public reaction to an early poster produced by the Ministry of Information and designed to boost morale. The first in a series of three that was to include the now-famous exhortation 'Keep Calm and Carry On', it was the only one of the series to be published. This attempt to 'win the nation's heart' was a vivid red, with large white letters telling passers-by that:

YOUR COURAGE

YOUR CHEERFULNESS

YOUR RESOLUTION

WILL BRING US VICTORY[26]

This message proved to be unpopular, with people feeling that it showed a divide between 'them' and 'us' rather than the hoped-for message of national unity. One housewife told Mass Observation:

> Be courageous, be calm, be something else; it will bring us victory. Who's Us I'd like to know? They don't say 'bring You victory'.

A young man thought he knew to whom 'Us' was referring:

> Your courage will bring Us victory. Yes, and feather the nests of the armament racketeers, the heavy industries and the politicians.[27]

The government's first big attempt to influence wartime morale was a failure and the posters were quietly withdrawn.

In fact it was wartime events, and the British response to them, that probably did the most to improve morale and bring people together in the first year of war. The German Blitzkrieg in the spring of 1940, which saw the swift and ruthless occupation and surrender of Denmark, the Netherlands, Luxembourg and Belgium, was followed with grim inevitability by the invasion of France, and the retreat of the British Expeditionary Forces who had been stationed there since September 1939 to the beaches in and around Dunkirk and Calais. The subsequent fall of France in June 1940, and the successful evacuation of the majority of the troops who made it to Dunkirk, was followed by the Battle of Britain, which was itself followed in September 1940 by the period of intensive air raids known as the Blitz. The war became myth as it happened, as commentators from across the political spectrum worked to shore up morale and reassure the British people that this was a war that would end, inevitably, in victory.

The rhetoric soared like the Spitfires and Hurricanes in the sky above southern England that summer. Winston Churchill, who had replaced Neville Chamberlain as leader of the Conservative Party and prime minister in May 1940, made his best-known wartime speeches during this period. He set out his war aims in his very first speech as prime minister on 13 May:

> You ask, what is our aim? I can answer in one word: it is victory, victory at all costs, victory in spite of all terror, victory no matter how long or hard the road may be, for without victory there is no survival.[28]

The single-minded determination of Churchill, who was cheered across the benches of the House of Commons, was also welcomed in the press, and in many homes. The leader writer for the *Daily Mail* thought he could discern a 'grimmer determination and a greater confidence' across the nation, while his counterpart at the *Daily Express* observed that 'the British people... recognize that the war of bombs is beginning and the war of pamphlets has ended'.[29] At home in Malvern, a journalist confided in his diary that 'we thought he was too fierce at the beginning of the war, but that is needed now', while a young mother and housewife in Portsmouth, expecting to be bombed at any moment, described 'being heartened and cheered by Churchill's speech', which she felt to be 'a spiritual challenge to which no man or woman with any pride in heritage could fail to respond'.[30] In Barrow-in-Furness, Nella Last reflected on the differences between Churchill and Chamberlain, concluding that 'if I had to spend my whole life with a man I'd choose Mr Chamberlain, but I think I would sooner have Mr Churchill if there was a storm and I was shipwrecked'.[31] The language of defiance and shared sacrifice that permeated Churchill's speeches, with their promise to 'fight on the beaches… the landing grounds… the fields… the streets [and] the hills' after the retreat from Dunkirk, and their assertion that in a thousand years' time 'men will still say "this was their finest hour"' created the mythology of the war as Britain's 'finest hour' at a moment that was understood by the people to be their time of greatest danger.[32]

But Churchill was not alone in the creation of this myth. Just two miles north of the Houses of Parliament sits the BBC's Broadcasting House, where the playwright, journalist and novelist J. B. – Jack – Priestley was broadcasting his *Postscripts* series of talks to the nation on Sunday evenings. Priestley and Churchill came from different ends of the political spectrum, but they shared a romantic sensibility and a talent for communicating this to an audience. While Churchill waxed lyrical about the British Empire, Priestley romanticised a version of the nation that was quintessentially English rather than British, and that was both egalitarian and nostalgic. It was Priestley who created the picture that still shapes our understanding of the 'little boats' at Dunkirk, talking in his first *Postscripts* broadcast on 5 June, at the height of the Dunkirk crisis, of 'another English epic', which was made domestic and knowable to his audience, gathered around the wireless at home, by his description of the 'fussy little steamers' that were part of the armada of small ships that set out from the coasts and harbours of southern England to help the Royal Navy in the evacuation. These were ships that his listeners could recognise and remember from seaside holidays, when 'we have watched them load and unload their crowds of holiday passengers – the gents full of high spirits and bottled beer, the ladies eating pork pies, the children sticky with peppermint rock'.[33] Mass Observation, reporting on the broadcast for the Ministry of Information, who were anxiously monitoring morale, found Priestley's broadcast to be 'slightly overdoing the sentiment'.[34] But like Churchill's 'finest hour', Priestley's 'little boats' came to sit at the heart of a story of Britain and its people that would 'go sailing proudly down the years'.

Between them, Churchill and Priestley helped to shape the myth of 1940: Churchill as belligerent and stubborn war leader, Priestley as the more whimsical storyteller, creating a version of the wartime nation and its people that was determined to see the war through to its end, and to eventual – and inevitable – victory. The flattering mirror that they held up to Britain, the stories they wove and the pictures they painted, were popular at the time and have remained so since, ensuring the centrality of the evacuation of Dunkirk, the Battle of Britain and the Blitz to our understanding of the war today. It is no coincidence that each of these episodes took place within, or close to, the British Isles and the home front. The soldiers rescued from Dunkirk returned to the ports and harbours of southern England and were sometimes brought home on fishing ships, yachts and leisure craft. The Battle of Britain was fought by 'the few', but they were cheered on by the people below, watching from the streets and gardens of southern England. And the Blitz on British towns and cities – like the bombing of towns and cities everywhere – targeted families and homes across the four nations alongside, and sometimes instead of, factories and wartime production. Unlike our shared understanding of the First World War, with its focus on the horrors of the trenches of the Western Front, we have come to recognise Britain's Second World War through the pictures, stories and people of the home front.

The war made multiple, and sometimes terrible, demands on these people: conscription and evacuation divided families, while the Blitz killed many thousands and destroyed or damaged more than one million homes in London alone. One in six Londoners was made homeless between September 1940 and May 1941. In Clydebank, a small industrial town west of Glasgow, more than 11,000 people lost their homes and more than 500 their lives over two nights of devastating raids in May 1941.[35] So many of those who were killed in the devastating raids on Belfast in April 1941 were unidentified that 250 bodies were laid out in the city's St George's Market in the hope that relatives would find their loved ones.[36] In the Blitz on Swansea in south-west Wales, 230 died and the city centre was destroyed in February 1941.[37]

Relatively few accounts of being 'blitzed' were written for Mass Observation. Perhaps those struggling to live under the bombs were simply too busy to put pen to paper. Some did manage, however. A female ambulance driver, stationed in London, reflected on how the war changed for those on the home front when the Blitz began: 'we have started using the phrase "since the war started", meaning since Saturday afternoon when the great raid set the skyline ablaze, and all the hilltops here were covered in sightseers between the first raid and the second'. She went on to describe how two of her colleagues had gone to help during the first great raid on the docklands of London that heralded the start of the London Blitz on Saturday 7 September:

> Manned by Matthewman (a little, elderly, charming creature) and Georgie (who has a sagging chin and vacant expression) it went down to Surrey docks, through flames meeting from each side of the road (where our next ambulance five minutes later could not get through) and picked up five casualties, including one woman who had just had a baby. Sparks and fragments kept falling on them, they beat them off their trousers and stamped out ropes that hold back curtains and came back another way, past a wall that collapsed just behind them.[38]

Just two months later her ambulance station was destroyed in an air raid and 'the ambulances blasted to bits'.[39] In nearby Eltham, one woman remembered these early days of the Blitz a year later, describing in her diary how she had spent the last hours of 7 September 1940:

> In amazed horror in our air raid shelter. That day, I know, I thought all was finished, as we looked at the fires all around us I thought nothing could save us and the next nights were equally horrible, bombs and more bombs.[40]

The bombing of London was to continue, night after endless night, with just a few welcome respites when the weather was too bad for the bombers to fly, until May 1941.

For one woman, a mother and housewife living with her young son and husband in Brockley, south-east London, the Blitz was a catalyst that started her writing for Mass Observation, as 'it should make very interesting personal reading in years to come when these days are a memory of a rather terrible but very vital time'.[41] That night was perhaps too 'interesting', as her diary for the next day recorded:

> After I had finished my recording of yesterday's events we had a real scare when at about 8.15 p.m. we heard the whizz of a bomb followed by crash after crash as a salvo was dropped and each one seemed nearer, as indeed they were. The last one finished the salvo at the bottom of the road and we thought it was this house for sure.

Horrified by the destruction of her neighbourhood the next morning, she started to ask herself whether she should take her young son out of London.[42] Meeting a neighbour in Hilly Fields park – a local beauty spot and viewpoint where, five years later, she would go to look at the lights of London on the eve of VE Day – she got talking about how and where they and their families took shelter from the bombs. While she went to her cellar, her neighbour had no shelter and instead she, her daughter and grandson 'just go to bed… and she says a little prayer, and if things get bad she trembles a bit and says another prayer'.[43] Two weeks later she met another young mother who had been sheltering with her children when an oil bomb was dropped on the flats where she lived. Three children in the shelter had been killed and 'her own toddler's clothes had been blown off the child whilst an older girl had both legs still bandaged with burns'.[44] Sheltering was no guarantee of safety, and at the end of November she finally decided to evacuate herself and her small son to Petworth in West Sussex, where she rented a small house with no running water, but blissfully distant from the continuous threat of air raids. The 'Blitz spirit', so beloved of politicians and journalists both during the war and since, often disguised individual fears and veiled the terrifying experience, for so many people in Britain and elsewhere, of trying to live beneath the bombs.

Britain's collective memory of the Blitz tends to focus on the experience of London, the most heavily and frequently bombed city in the country. But other cities, and their people, also had stories to tell. In Liverpool a chief assistant air-raid warden, who had spent much of his time in past months telling people how best to protect their houses, and themselves, from air raids, described some of the multiple difficulties, and dangers, now that they had arrived:

> I came down in my car this morning and picked up three people. By the way we had a hell of a night last night, at one moment I rushed out of my dining room where I was doing a spot of typing, this was at midnight, and into the hall under the stairs where my little girl was sleeping because I thought that a HE [high-explosive] would any moment drop, there was a terrible concussion that shook my house, Hans Buggerlugs [slang for German airmen] was certainly over in force last night and after three peaceful nights it sounded worse than ever... The talk in the car naturally turned on last night's raid. A lady whom I gathered is interested in Welfare work told me of an AFS [Auxiliary Fire Service] man who went off duty the other week and found that his house had been blown to hell, his wife and I believe she said three children killed, leaving him with one child. She said the man had asked them could they get him into the country, his nerve had gone. Can you wonder? I said to another young lady, and how do you react to these

bombings, what do you do? She said well we have a shelter in the garden but this past two weeks the weather has been much colder and wet so we have simply ignored the shelter and gone under the stairs because when all is said and done an Anderson is nothing more than a hole in the ground… we try and sleep but we can't. I know that the daily papers tell you to relax. I often wonder if the people who write those articles really relax themselves? If they do well they are either super men or women or they haven't got a lot of intelligence. We listen for the bombs dropping, we try not to, we play Ludo, sometimes we play the portable gramophone, but what we really do is WAIT FOR THE ALL CLEAR.[45]

While the Blitz is the best-remembered period of bombing, air raids continued throughout the war: the Baedeker Raids of spring 1942, named after the interwar guidebook, saw the attempted destruction of many ancient city centres such as Exeter, Bath and York; and the 'Little Blitz' in the cold winter and spring of 1944 saw further raids on London, Bristol, Hull and Cardiff. The 10,000 V-1 'pilotless plane' or 'Doodlebug' flying bombs that fell between June and August 1944 were to kill another 6,000 people, and the V-2 rockets that followed them took many more lives, among them 132 people killed when the last V-2 to hit London destroyed Hughes Mansions in Stepney, east London. Many of the dead that day were Jewish migrants from Eastern Europe. Neither rocket, however, was to kill as many as their production: an estimated 20,000 were to die in the making of the V-weapons by slave labour subjected to a pitiless regime of starvation, torture and execution. A Mass Observation survey of the impact on morale of the V-1 rockets during their first week's use against London found widespread relief that 'Hitler's Secret Weapon' (which was widely expected in the days after the D-Day landings) 'had not turned out to be as frightening as they had anticipated'. Indeed, for some people, their interest in this new turn of events outweighed any fear or anxiety, at least initially. One thirty-year-old man reported:

> I feel quite excited. Fancy this being the secret weapon – here's us living right in the middle of a sort of H. G. Wells-ian fantasy, pilotless planes and all, and yet it's just ordinary life! I don't mind them the way I used to. I feel now, if he's such a fool as to bomb London, instead of concentrating in France, well that's his funeral.

Others, though, were less keen. Lack of sleep was a common complaint and a seventy-year-old man was affronted by the rockets' novelty, complaining 'they're nasty things, you don't know where you are with them'. And not everyone displayed the kind of 'Blitz spirit' that has become so central to our mythology of Britain at war. As another thirty-year-old man explained:

> I didn't get to bed till 4 this morning and 5 the night before. Frightened? Good Lord no. I like walking around. I was round Kentish Town when that one dropped there. You should have seen bottles and wireless sets and things flying around. I saw people pinghing [stealing] stuff too. I wouldn't have minded doing the same myself – even though I'm an ex-Policeman – but you can't steal from these little people. They've a hard job to keep going anyway. Now, if it was a West End jeweller![46]

While some saw air raids as opportunities – after the air raids on Sheffield in December 1940 the Local Assizes had to set aside two days to deal with charges of looting – many people answered the call for Civil Defence volunteers, serving throughout the war as air-raid wardens and first-aid staff, and as members of heavy rescue and firefighting teams. Almost 7,000 of these workers would be killed while serving. Death, injury and the loss of homes were the most extreme ways that the war affected the lives of those on the home front, but other elements of the war effort (including rationing, family separation, the blackout and travel restrictions) all made wartime feel very different from – and often more miserable than – peacetime.

But alongside the multiple demands that war placed on people were war aims that became far wider than those of the First World War. Ideas about reconstruction – understood not only in terms of rebuilding housing and city centres, but also to be about rebuilding society along very different lines from those that shaped interwar Britain – began to circulate in the early years of the war. Priestley's *Postscripts* series contrasted the divisions and inequalities of the 1930s with the democratic impulse that he believed was being given voice by the necessities of wartime. In his broadcast of 21 July 1940 he suggested to his listeners that 'we must stop thinking in terms of property and power, and begin thinking in terms of community and co-operation', asking whether a house and garden left empty when its wealthy owners evacuated themselves to the United States for the duration of the war should be left vacant or put to use for the common good, with the garden planted for food and the house providing shelter for those who had lost theirs?[47]

The journalist and novelist George Orwell, himself of course an Old Etonian, writing in 1941, claimed patriotism for the 'common people', arguing that the country was 'a family with the wrong members in control' and assuring his readers that the war would 'wipe out most of the existing class privileges'. The demands of war, Orwell believed, had made existing social inequalities more visible and placed demands on the working class that they would meet, on condition that there was 'some kind of proof that a better life is ahead for themselves and their children'.[48] These ideas, revolutionary though they may have seemed, were not only being expressed by commentators on the political left. Just weeks after the fall of France that bastion of the establishment *The Times* published a leader column that set out to capture the public mood and to harness this to wider war aims:

> If we speak of democracy, we do not mean a democracy which maintains the right to vote, but forgets the right to work and the right to live. If we speak of freedom we do not mean a rugged individualism which excludes social organisation and economic planning. If we speak of equality we do not mean a political equality nullified by social and economic privilege. If we speak of economic reconstruction, we think less of maximum production (though this too will be required) than of equitable distribution.[49]

A return to the days of the Hunger Marches, the much-despised Means Test and levels of infant mortality that peaked at 105 per 1,000 in South Tyneside in the early 1930s were not to be contemplated. In their place a New Jerusalem was to be built, replacing the poet W. H. Auden's 'low, dishonest decade' of the 1930s with a modern, fairer and more equitable nation.[50] The reward for the terrible demands that war was making were to be found in the reconstruction of post-war British society.

People might have broadly agreed that something had to change, but exactly what, when, and how was more contentious. According to a 1941 report by Mass Observation, around half the people in London and Worcester who were questioned as part of a random survey about reconstruction thought that work needed to begin during the war, while the other half were equally certain that reconstruction should wait until the military war was won. Opinion on government plans for reconstruction was equally divided, and even more confused. Of those who thought the government had announced plans for reconstruction, there was no sense of what this might be: a forty-year-old man replied that 'there has been some muttering hasn't there', while a thirty-five-year-old woman thought the government wanted 'to build a better England. How they intend to do it, no one knows.'

People had plenty of their own ideas as to how a more equal post-war society could be achieved. One thirty-year-old woman thought that greater state intervention would be required, with 'production organized to meet needs', and a forty-year-old man agreed, demanding 'nationalisation of all industries'. A fifty-year-old man wanted to 'stop the cornering of everything. Stop all the carving up', while a twenty-year-old man argued for 'a change in the social system'. Still others saw Britain's problems, and its solutions, lying elsewhere: although a fifty-five-year-old woman wanted to 'send all the foreigners out', others believed that the Empire and better trading relations with other countries were the answer to Britain's woes, with one fifty-year-old man arguing that the nation should 'make more use of the colonies' and a thirty-year-old man wanting free trade, with 'an open market between all countries of the world'.[51] Although opinion about what kinds of reconstruction were needed, and how these should be achieved, was divided, the desire for post-war change was widespread. But it took a civil servant and academic, known for his tendency to meddle in government policy, to give shape to this desire.

Sir William Beveridge, who had been the director of the London School of Economics between the wars, had worked at Toynbee Hall in London's East End when he was a young man. Toynbee Hall had been founded in 1885 to bring future leaders into direct contact with the poverty found in the East End, and his time there had a profound impact on Beveridge, who became convinced that a state system of insurance was the only workable means of effectively alleviating want. His appointment as chairman of the Social Insurance Committee in 1941 gave him the opportunity to present his ideas to the government and, more importantly, to the public. After twelve months of research the Committee's Report on Social Insurance and Allied Services, almost universally known as the Beveridge Report, was published. It would be fair to say that its reception took the government, which had created the Committee as a convenient means of both keeping Beveridge busy and sidelining debates on reconstruction so that it could focus on the war's more immediate demands, by surprise.

The Report was enormously popular; 642,000 copies were sold in six months, and it was debated across the press, in pubs and in living rooms.[52] It even made it onto the much-loved radio comedy *It's That Man Again (ITMA)*, where in a reference to the popular historical epic *Gone with the Wind*, the comedian Tommy Trinder referred to it as 'Gone with the Want'. A man who had gone to the Stationery Office to buy a copy reported that 'there were queues of people buying it; and I was looking at it on the bus and the conductor said "I suppose you haven't got a spare copy of that?"' The Report was published on 1 December 1942; in a random survey the following day Mass Observation found that 92 per cent of those that they asked had heard of it. Two weeks later 88 per cent of those who replied to a national survey believed that the government should undertake its recommendations without delay.[53]

What were these recommendations? Fundamentally, Beveridge's Report had proposed replacing the piecemeal and patchwork system of social security that had developed with different authorities, agencies, charities and insurance companies providing different benefits and levels of support with a unified system of social security managed by the state. All of those who worked would pay into the scheme via a system of national insurance, and those who needed support would be able to draw on this in the form of pensions, sickness payments and unemployment benefits. Families would be entitled to maternity and child benefits and a funeral allowance would be available to all. A national health service, free at the point of access, would ensure that healthcare was no longer dependent on personal circumstances or local provision. The Report urged the government to provide a 'safety net' through which no one could fall. Beveridge had seized his opportunity to defeat the 'five giants' that he believed to be holding individuals, and the country, back: idleness, want, disease, ignorance and squalor.[54] Wartime conditions – and in particular the belief that the war had profoundly changed the country, strengthening a desire for social and economic reconstruction – provided the ideal environment for the Report's recommendations.

In the days after its publication, Mass Observation's writers were busy reading the Report and its summaries in the daily newspapers. One diarist, a housewife from Sutton Coldfield in the English Midlands, read about the Report in the highly critical *Daily Telegraph*, with which she found herself in profound disagreement:

> Some of us, far from feeling that 'the fires of genius are extinguished' are of [the] opinion that the fires would flare up nicely if there were a bit of social security behind us, and if we didn't always have the bogeys of illness, unemployment and old age staring us in the face.[55]

Just up the road in Birmingham another diarist heard the news on the wireless. He 'found it most exhilarating. What tremendous opportunities are offered, if only we can fight for them.'[56] In slightly more restrained terms, another woman felt that 'it contains many reforms that have been needed for a long time, if it comes into force it will solve many of the problems caused by present-day insurances', while an agricultural chemist from Barmouth in west Wales was more forthright, arguing it was '*Long overdue*... A country that preaches such high and noble ideals should adopt the Report *at once. Long overdue.*'[57] The organisation also sent its small number of paid and volunteer workers out into the streets of London to try and capture the public mood there in the days after the Report's publication. While the majority of those who stopped to answer questions were broadly in agreement with the 'charlady' who exclaimed, 'It is wonderful! To feel that one is secure from want and unemployment', not all found themselves in step with the public mood. One thirty-five-year-old woman had some heartfelt views that she wanted to share:

> I'm not an idealist. I'm selfish. I only think of myself. I know all is changing. I've been one of the lucky few and I want to remain so. I had a good life... I think we pamper the workers, especially in the factories, with their canteens and music. They ought to work harder.[58]

Clearly not all members of the wartime nation felt themselves to be fully signed-up members of the unified country imagined by both Churchill and Priestley.

As the war in Europe came to an end, some two and a half years after the publication of Beveridge's Report, the people of Britain began to regain some of the freedoms they had lost to the necessities of war. Not all were returned immediately: while many thousands of men and women were demobilised, many more were retained in the military services, some for the expected invasion of Japan, and Parliament voted to introduce an eighteen-month period of National Service (swiftly increased to two years during the Korean War in 1950) for young men in 1947. Shortages of food and raw materials meant that far from ending with the war, the rationing of some goods actually became stricter. Housing began to be rebuilt and a large programme of slum clearance saw much of the remaining urban slums that had not been destroyed by the Luftwaffe demolished, but in the short term there was a severe shortage of housing stock. Prefabricated houses, multiple occupancy of family houses and recently vacated army camps were all pressed into service to provide accommodation, while many newly reunited couples, sometimes with small children, found themselves beginning their post-war lives in their parental homes. Some people took the shortage of housing into their own hands. In August 1946 thousands of couples and young families simply moved into empty military camps around the country and, in the 'great Sunday squat' of September 1946, another 1,500 people took over empty flats in the London boroughs of Pimlico, Kensington and St John's Wood. The *Daily Mail* and the Communist Party of Great Britain agreed, for possibly the first and only time, that the squatters were in the right, the *Daily Mail* praising their 'robust common sense'.[59]

However, many others would never return to enjoy the gradual changes and reforms of post-war Britain, while some of those who did return could no longer live independently and were condemned to spend the rest of their days in residential homes and hospitals. The British Legion urged local authorities to build housing for disabled ex-servicemen and women, and in cash-strapped post-war Britain it became common to see adverts in local newspapers appealing to readers to contribute to the local authority's scheme for disabled ex-servicemen.[60] Housing, and other schemes that would benefit the public good, were also widely seen as an appropriate means of memorialising the war dead. When in 1944 Mass Observation asked its National Panel, 'What are your views on the form which memorials to the dead of this war should take?', the answers were almost unanimous: memorials 'must take the form of being useful to the living'.[61] Playing fields, parks, recreation grounds, community hall, bus shelters and hospital wings were all commonly suggested, alongside housing for disabled ex-servicemen and their families. Nella Last was typically eloquent in her answer. Describing her hatred of the Barrow-in-Furness First World War memorial, as 'I knew so many of the lads and men whose names were on it, warm, vital, laughing people – no connection with the lifeless, cold thing which commemorated them', she went on to reflect that:

> If I wanted to keep in memory a loved one, I'd choose a cot in a hospital, a garden of flowers, a holiday home for servicemen and their wives and children, and I'd care for those who came home sick in mind and body.[62]

For Last, as for others, the spirit of the 'people's war' could live on through its memorials. But as post-war austerity bit ever deeper, few of these grand schemes were to come to fruition, and the war dead came to be largely commemorated as another column of names on existing war memorials.

Despite constraints and complications, and no small anxiety about what the future might bring, the end of the war was eagerly anticipated by many. Equally anticipated was the country's first General Election since 1935. Just over a month after VE Day, Parliament was dissolved and Britain prepared for its first General Election in a decade. The result was a landslide victory for Attlee's Labour Party. Nonetheless, as the country went to the polls on 5 July 1945, the outcome had seemed far from settled. Mass Observation found that 39 per cent of first-time voters in London, of whom there were many, were undecided, and a sense of apathy, even exhaustion, dominated after almost six years of war.[63] Nevertheless, when the election results came in, they ensured that the welfare state conceived by Beveridge in the midst of war would become a peacetime reality. Back in 1939, the Mass Observation diarist from Essex who described herself as a member of the landed gentry and had stood with her dog for Chamberlain's speech on the outbreak of war, had recorded her feelings the next day:

> I packed away a fine favourite candelabra and wondered when, if ever, it would come out again for I feel this is the end of my class and way of life… (though) I don't feel for a moment that we could have done otherwise than declare war.[64]

After almost six long years of war, the British people had decisively voted to prove her right. In 1945 candelabras – and, indeed, the landed gentry – were to be packed away.

The diaries kept by Mass Observers on 7 and 8 May 1945 capture a moment towards the end of the war – if not the actual end, then at least, as Churchill suggested in his radio broadcast announcing victory in Europe, a pause in which 'we may allow ourselves a brief period of rejoicing'. And many *did* rejoice, finding different ways to mark the end of the European war and to celebrate their own, and loved ones', survival. Alongside street celebrations and tea parties, we find records of bonfires and bell-ringing, water fights and bicycle rides, quiet teas and solitary, contemplative walks. Not everyone felt like celebrating, though. Loss and uncertainty were everywhere. Many were still waiting for news of family members who had vanished in the fog of war. Thousands of Allied civilians (mostly Dutch, but many British) had been interned in the Far East, while around 130,000 British and Commonwealth forces had been captured during the fall of Malaya and Singapore. A large number had died in captivity, and pressures on shipping meant that many of the survivors would not return home until 1946. These returns were not always easy, and many women were wondering what married life might be like with someone they hadn't seen for years. Others were waiting anxiously for news of those listed as 'missing in action', while for still more there was the certainty that there would be no return, and that their post-war lives would be scarred by the kind of loss felt by the woman whose son had been killed in 1943 and who wrote to Clement Attlee, the new prime minister, in 1945 to protest at the re-introduction of the two-minute silence, commenting bitterly that, for her, 'life has been completely silent for two years'.[65]

As they headed into a General Election, people's thoughts were full of hope, and fear, for the future. Depending on their political allegiances, these could include hope that the end of the war would see the beginning of a 'New Jerusalem', and the more general hope that 'when all the young people come back from the war, there'll be a better world for them to come back to, and a better way of living altogether'. Fears included it 'being the same bad old world it was before the war', or that the promised changes would mean that it was *their* property that would be redistributed – like the man who believed the Labour Party would take his car away from him, or the man who owned five houses and 'was afraid that the Labour Government would take four houses away from him'.[66] Mass Observation writers recorded their expectations, hopes and fears at this point in the war, alongside the ways in which they spent the two days that together made up VE Day. Together, their feelings and experiences show us something of the togetherness *and* the differences of the British people at war.

CHAPTER FOUR

1–6 May 1945

'A Week of Confusion and Fluctuating Emotions'

When the end of the war in Europe finally arrived, it came wrapped in confusion, chaos and rumour. Allied victory had been widely anticipated and expected for months, if not for years. The collapse of the Nazi regime had been confidently predicted since 1941, when Hitler's Operation Barbarossa, the attempted invasion of the Soviet Union, brought that power into the war on the Allied side; and confidence grew again in December of that year when the Japanese attack on the US Navy at Pearl Harbor finally brought the United States decisively into the war against the Axis powers. Writing in his Mass Observation diary for December 1941, one young Air Raid Precautions volunteer and food worker from Surrey had described his feelings after Germany and Italy declared war on the United States:

> To me this joint action of the dictators will ultimately bring such retribution over their heads that December 7, 1941 will be a day which is cursed wherever German and Italian is spoken. This declaration will in due course bring American troops to Europe… [In the First World War] their arrival spelt relief for our sorely tried forces, and in six months Germany asked for an Armistice. Will history be repeated?[1]

Overall, Mass Observers were pleased that the United States was now at war. One fifty-one-year-old man from rural East Sussex thought that although the Japanese attack on Pearl Harbor had been 'rather a shock to us all', it meant that 'the USA is in all the way at least', although a shorthand typist from Liverpool was worried that 'we shall not get as much to eat as we have been doing as the United States reserved its resources for its own war effort', rather than shipping food and fuel to Britain in the Atlantic convoys.[2] Luckily for Britain, her fears came to nothing and the amount of foodstuffs arriving from the United States under the Lend-Lease Scheme in fact increased from 1,073 to 1,427 thousand tons between 1941 and 1942.*

While Churchill is said to have 'slept the sleep of the saved' after the attack on Pearl Harbor, it took another three and a half years for Hitler's regime to finally fall.[3] The battles of Stalingrad and Kursk on the Eastern Front had drained the German army of men and materiel, while the Allied bombing of German towns and cities decimated civilian life and cityscapes alike. In the West, the Allied victory in North Africa led to the invasion and subsequent surrender of Italy in 1943, which in turn was followed by the June 1944 Allied landings of D-Day, and the liberation of France two months later. The Soviet troops moving rapidly west and Allied troops fighting their way north and east through the Low Countries and western Germany finally met on the banks of the River Elbe, in north-west Saxony, on 25 April 1945. By the spring of 1945 the Nazi regime found itself caught in a pincer movement from which there was to be no escape.

---

* Lend-Lease was the scheme by which the United States 'lent' or 'leased' weapons, food and raw materials to countries fighting the Axis powers.

By April of that year the Red Army was closing in on Berlin, the capital of Hitler's planned Thousand-Year Reich. Soviet troops had crossed the German border in October 1944, their progress west preceded by millions of refugees desperate to escape the Red Army, which was becoming notorious for acts of brutality against civilians, including rape. Some four million ethnic Germans who had settled in the east fled west by foot or by boat, accompanied on the road by the surviving inmates of concentration camps who were forced to march towards Germany as the Nazis attempted to destroy the camps to remove evidence of their crimes. They were part of the largest movement of peoples seen in twentieth-century Europe, as millions tried to make their way home – from camps, from refuges and from armies – while others sought a place of safety in countries far from their homeland. The Canadian historian Modris Eksteins, whose family were part of this mass migration, left Latvia when he was a child, living first in a camp for displaced persons before emigrating to Canada. Eksteins describes this movement of peoples as the war ended:

> People going, coming, pushing, selling, sighing – above all scurrying. Scurrying to survive. Never had so many people been on the move at once. Prisoners of war, slave labourers, concentration camp survivors, ex-soldiers, Germans expelled from eastern Europe, and refugees who had fled the Russian advance.[4]

The architect of this chaos and misery had made his last public appearance on his birthday, 20 April, to the background noise of heavy artillery as Soviet troops fought their way through the Berlin suburbs. Footage shows Hitler in the gardens of the Chancellery, awarding medals to the young members of the Hitler Youth who had been drafted into the defence of the city. After this last appearance he retreated to his underground bunker beneath the Chancellery in the centre of the city, now the headquarters of the Nazi government. Realising that his German Reich was crumbling, Hitler killed himself on 30 April. His body, and that of Eva Braun, whom he had married on 29 April, was carried to the Chancellery garden and set alight by SS troops, following the orders of a man whose desire not to be humiliated in defeat outlived him. His death was followed the next day by that of the Minister for Public Enlightenment and Propaganda, Joseph Goebbels, and his wife Magda, who killed themselves after first murdering their six young children. Hitler's last message to the world combined self-pity with poison, blaming his generals for Germany's defeat and urging the continued persecution of Europe's remaining Jews.

Meanwhile Berlin itself had become a city that lived largely below ground. People sheltered in basements, cellars and underground stations as they sought refuge from both Soviet artillery and soldiers, and from the SS troops rounding up 'volunteers' to defend the city, often murdering those who refused, or those to whom they took a dislike. Children and teenagers of the Hitler Youth were recruited for the futile defence of the city with the poorly trained Volkssturm, a militia made up of men previously considered unfit for military service. The anonymous author of *A Woman in Berlin*, then living in an apartment block in the east of the city, records what life was like for some ordinary Berliners as Hitler made his last public appearance. Listening to his final speech was by no means a priority:

Friday, 20 April

11 p.m. by the light of an oil lamp in the basement, my notebook on my knees. Around 10 p.m. there was a series of three or four bombs. The air-raid siren started screaming. Apparently it has to be worked manually now. No light. Running downstairs in the dark, the way we've been doing ever since Tuesday. We slip and stumble... Then down some more stairs, through more doors and corridors. Finally we're in our shelter, behind an iron door that weighs a hundred pounds, with rubber seals around the edges and two levers to lock it. The official term is air raid shelter. We call it cave, underworld, catacomb of fear, mass grave.[5]

Seven days later the Red Army arrived in her quarter of the city, and three days after that Hitler was dead. His Thousand-Year Reich had lasted just twelve years.

Although the war in Europe was effectively over following Hitler's death, its ending was chaotic and confused. News of the Führer's death was announced in a German radio broadcast on 1 May. Christabel Bielenberg, a British woman whose German husband had been part of the German resistance involved in the Stauffenberg plot to assassinate Hitler in 1944, heard the news on the wireless from their village in the Black Forest, which was by then occupied by French troops:

This time the wireless seemed certain of its message. (There had been plenty of rumours but this was a certainty.) It gave no details as to where, how and when, but just crackled out something about Hitler (the Führer), having first appointed Admiral Doenitz to be his successor, had made up his mind to die a hero's death and had done so... So that was it; he was dead. Although bombers still droned occasionally overhead, reminding us that some parts of Germany still had to pass through the final ordeal, he, Hitler, was gone... But we, Peter and I and our three sons and the good friends around us were alive, we had outlived him. He had not managed to drag us off with him to some preposterous make-believe Valhalla. So perhaps it was for that reason the silence was suddenly broken and we found ourselves glancing at each other, pushing back our stools, starting to our feet and moving eagerly from one to another in order to hold hands, to embrace, to celebrate, one survivor with another.[6]

German resistance swiftly collapsed. Soviet troops occupied the centre of Berlin, raising the Soviet flag over the Reichstag on 2 May 1945 as the city's defenders surrendered. Fighting continued sporadically in some areas for a few more days, largely in south-west Germany, Czechoslovakia and around Breslau, a besieged city on the Eastern Front. German troops in Italy, low on arms, ammunition and morale, had been the first to surrender unconditionally to Allied forces on 29 April. On 4 May German forces in north-west Europe surrendered to Field Marshal Montgomery, commander of the 21st Army Group, and the following day the final pockets of German forces in Bohemia and Bavaria surrendered to the commander of the US Sixth Army. An officer in the Coastal Command wing of the RAF had been ordered to fly over the Kattegat, the stretch of sea separating Denmark from Sweden, to observe German naval vessels that had been ordered to return to port. 'Crossing Denmark,' he wrote, 'we were surprised to see so many Danish flags flying from houses and farms... we saw many people who waved to us. We answered with a wing wave.' As he flew on, he saw one U-boat being abandoned and another heading to Aarhus to surrender.[7]

The next day, Sunday 6 May, German forces in Breslau surrendered to the Soviet forces that had besieged the city since February. Fighting continued in Prague, the capital of Czechoslovakia, until 9 May, when the city was occupied by Soviet fighters. Josef Chalupsky had been a child in the city at the time:

> Half the houses in our street were in flames and the other ones were set on fire. With groups of other inhabitants we were guided to another quarter of rented houses, a kilometre away. We were crammed like sardines into these flats, about 10–15 to a room. Why they did this we could only guess… We could hear incessant shooting during our transportation to the rented houses. And we heard from the radio the atrocities being carried out on the civilians of Prague. While we were crammed into these houses we prayed to God thinking our last hours had come.[8]

At 2.41 in the morning of 7 May the Chief of Staff of the German Army signed Germany's unconditional surrender in Reims, France, the headquarters of the Allied forces in the west of Europe. The next day German military leaders travelled to Berlin to sign the surrender for the second time – this time in the presence of Marshal Zhukov, who had commanded Soviet troops in the Battle of Berlin. The war in Europe ended officially at one minute to midnight on Tuesday 8 May.

In Britain people had been anxiously following the news, waiting daily to hear of the capitulation of Nazi Germany following the proclamation of Hitler's death on 1 May. The fighting had moved away from almost all of the British Isles earlier that year; the one exception was the Channel Islands, just off the coast of the Cherbourg Peninsula in France. German forces who had occupied the Channel Islands since 1940 surrendered on 8 May, but remained until 9 May, when naval ships arrived in Jersey and Guernsey, with tiny Alderney –

home of two concentration camps, and the graveyard of many prisoners – waiting until 16 May for its formal liberation.

The wider German surrender was expected for at least a week before it was finally confirmed, but expectations of what this would mean, and how it would be marked in Britain, varied widely. While most people avidly followed the news from the continent, listening to the regular bulletins on the wireless and asking one another if they had heard anything more, many of those writing for Mass Observation were also following events elsewhere. The surrender of the remaining German and Italian fascist troops at Caserta in Italy came into force on 2 May, and in Argyll in the west of Scotland Mass Observation diarist Naomi Mitchison thought 'the Italian news is grand', while a forty-year-old office worker from south London was almost overcome: 'Wonderful news from Italy over a million German troops have surrendered unconditionally to the Allies there... to think that the war in Italy is over is almost too much for us to take in.'[9] In Bolton-le-Sands, Lancashire, a young secretary, whose husband was away in the forces, was cheered by the news, which showed, she thought, that 'things are moving fast!' She was also following events in Burma, where Allied troops were advancing on Rangoon, though they had been slowed by the monsoon rains, as well as attempts to relieve the famine in the Netherlands, commenting that 'Rangoon is rather a sidelight, but none the less satisfactory, and so is the fact that we are getting food to Holland and Denmark.'[10] The last months of the war had seen growing hunger in the western Netherlands, as a combination of a harsh winter, a Nazi blockade of food shipments to towns and cities, Allied bombing of occupied ports and the flooding of farmland to prevent Allied advances combined to produce a critical shortage of food in the winter of 1944–5. The Swedish Red Cross had started to import flour in January 1945, and in the early spring Allied air forces began to deliver food to the starving via air drops.

In San Francisco on America's Pacific coast, delegates from forty-six Allied countries were meeting at the United Nations Conference on International Organization. The United Nations, which was formed at this conference, seemed to offer the world's best hope for avoiding further global wars, and several Mass Observers were following events there. The difficulties of achieving meaningful cooperation and lasting peace between the world powers were clear to some commentators, even if the problems they predicted were not always those that have stymied the United Nations in subsequent years:

> Argentina is admitted to the San Francisco Conference, despite the opposition of Soviet Russia – opposition which I think is justified. It is a grim thought that the South American countries by joining themselves together are so strong that they can dominate the Conference.[11]

But rather than South American countries forming a voting bloc, it was to be the fault lines of the emerging Cold War that would demarcate the post-war world and limit the work of the United Nations in the coming decades.

Many people, though, were preoccupied by more personal concerns. Sevenoaks in Kent had been at the centre of 'bomb alley', directly in the path of Luftwaffe bombing raids on London and of the V-1 'doodlebug' and V-2 rockets in 1944 and 1945. A Sevenoaks housewife in her fifties was finding the end of the conflict, with all of its dangers and demands, an unexpected personal challenge. At the beginning of the week she had travelled to London to visit her optician and noticed that the city was more crowded than it had been for a long time, 'the bomb-shy people now coming out I suppose'. On the train home she listened to other passengers discussing how their offices were starting to collect money to pay for victory parties. The confused news from the continent left the door open for multiple rumours, and by 3 May her cook and home help was explaining how 'Himmler has surrendered to the Italians', a story that she recounted with some scepticism. By 4 May she was becoming fed up with the lack of certainty and its impact on her plans:

> Damn V Day say I. Want to keep appointment with oculist in London on Monday (being bullied into it by optician), also want to meet Mrs R. with whom I have been corresponding for a year on Wednesday, and am in doubt whether travelling possible. Much housework and ironing.

On 7 May she had been told, definitively, that victory would be announced, first at 3 p.m. and then at 6 p.m., and decided to cancel her appointment in London with Mrs R. She had volunteered during the war for the Red Cross and was now unsure about a future that seemed to be filled with the drudgery of managing a home. She confided to Mass Observation that she felt:

> Deeply depressed and… as if [I] were floating in nothingness. The background of life in the last 5½ years has suddenly gone – not that I wish one moment of it back – and it's going to need a lot of guts to pick oneself up again. If there were something someone wanted one to do, and one could just go and do it… Personally, I must pull out of this vague, negative existence of

lonely housekeeping, which during the war I felt was my duty, though I frequently had to go away from it. It's all been very futile looking back; have done nothing useful as far as I can see.[12]

In common with many other women, she found that any sense of purpose and value that she had achieved during the war – when simply 'carrying on' with housework and domestic duties could be understood as patriotic and a part of the war effort – was in danger of evaporating, with the declaration of victory.

In County Durham in the north of England, well away from the recent dangers of V-2 rockets, a teacher found equally little to be excited about at the European war's end:

Surely the war in Europe cannot be long? Seems that the peace celebrations are to be such a flop that they will not provide the outlet for the dangerously pent up emotions. No pulling down of blackouts, switching on of lights. I don't know what there will be to mark the day.

By 2 May she was in Richmond, North Yorkshire, where she found '*no one* mentioned death of Hitler. Everyone seems just weary. The only ones who mentioned peace thought the government would release the news at the weekend and we would be done out of some victory holidays! Was peace ever such a flop?'[13] While many were waiting to celebrate, others were concerned and anxious, not just about when the war in Europe would end and how this would be marked, but also about what the post-war world would bring.

Mass Observation described the final week before victory in Europe was declared as 'a week of confusion and fluctuating emotions', in which 'the news was changing hourly, rumours were rife, and peace was held to be imminent for at least a week before it became a fact'.[14] The headlines in the *Daily Express* for the final days of the war in Europe show how information was at a premium, being recorded and reported to an audience eager for some definitive news of the war's end in Europe in the week preceding VE Day:

> Tuesday 1 May 1945: 'Nazis Radio "Good-bye"'
>
> Wednesday 2 May 1945: 'Hitler is Dead!'
>
> Thursday 3 May 1945: 'Army of 1,000,000 Surrenders'
>
> Friday 4 May 1945: 'British Enter Denmark'
>
> Saturday 5 May 1945: 'Germans Surrender Inside Monty's Tent'
>
> Monday 7 May 1945: 'The Last Hours'[15]

Throughout this period of uncertainty, rumour and counter-rumour, Mass Observation was busy capturing the thoughts and expectations of people as they waited, and hoped, for peace and victory in Europe.

The BBC first heard of Hitler's death when it was announced over the German radio service on the evening of 1 May. The German Department of the BBC's Monitoring Service, based in Caversham Park near Reading, was staffed largely by exiles and refugees from Germany and Austria who spent their days listening to and translating German broadcasts. When news came through, the whole building erupted in cheers. The news was quickly passed on to the Cabinet Office and to BBC newsrooms, which interrupted their scheduled programming to announce the news to Britain and the world. While some people immediately started to celebrate, others received the news with a degree of scepticism. Some believed that it was part of an elaborate plot, designed to let Hitler escape justice and to plan for some future return to power. In south-east London one diarist captured this sense of disbelief in her writing:

> Hitler is dead – words we longed to hear five years ago, are almost unimportant now, and people don't seem interested. Admiral Doenitz has become fuerer [*sic*] in his place, and has said that Hitler died at his headquarters defending Berlin against the Russians, but that is probably merely a tale. Opinion here seems to think that a) he has been murdered, and b) that he has gone into hiding and will appear again at a later date. I am inclined to think that latter is true.[16]

This sense of Hitler as immortal – immune to the normal challenges and dangers – was perhaps driven by his longevity as German leader (he had come to power twelve years earlier in 1933) and by his inescapable presence in British wartime culture. His easily and widely caricatured face was familiar from cartoons and propaganda posters, where he had been pictured (variously) as a 'squanderbug', urging British housewives to waste food; as a spy, eavesdropping on careless conversations on buses and trains; and as a spectre, providing ghostly encouragement to a mother thinking of keeping her children at home, rather than evacuating them. He had entertained wartime cinema-goers by being punched by George Formby in *Let George Do It!* (1940), impersonated by The Crazy Gang in *Gasbags* (1941) and satirised as the fascist dictator Adenoid Hynkel in Charlie Chaplin's *The Great Dictator* (1940). Hitler's face, as well as his distinctive, harsh oratory style, was as familiar to most people as Churchill was.

It could be difficult, after so long, to realise that this omnipresent embodiment of the Nazi enemy was gone. One diarist recorded how the *Daily Chronicle* newspaper was encouraging its readers to think of the Nazi leaders as mortal, publishing 'a voting form in which you can record your guess of the probable fate of six of the Nazi leaders', perceptively noting that 'I should think suicide is the most sensible thing.'[17] A retired Electricity Board Inspector from south-east London, who had no doubt that Hitler was dead and wondered in his regular letters to his sister Nora, which he carefully copied out for Mass Observation, 'what kind of reception [Hitler's] astral form has received on the other side', was in a minority. So convinced of Hitler's death was he that he wrote a lengthy poem to mark the occasion, imagining Hitler's arrival in the afterlife:

> I can imagine when he came
> And when his victims heard his name
> They gathered round him not to miss
> So good a chance to hoot and hiss...
>
> But those on earth may all agree
> From torture he must not go free
> That God almighty has some plan
> To punish such a naughty man.[18]

But many of those who responded to Mass Observation's National Panel, which had asked passers-by what they thought about Hitler's death, recorded a distrust not only of Nazi Germany, but also of British information:

> I think it's all a take about Hitler. I think he's escaped from the country weeks and weeks ago.

I don't believe he's dead at all. He's hidden away in the mountains and he'll come out again in a few years' time and start another war… He'll find a way, he's cunning. We haven't heard the last of him, you'll see.

He's not dead; don't you believe it. They've got him hidden away somewhere, to bring him out in 10 years' time, when they think we'll have forgotten about it, and start the business all over again.[19]

A young shop assistant living in Essex, who had kept a Mass Observation diary throughout the war, describing himself early in the war as a 'semi-pacifist', recorded the suspicions of two of his landlady's friends:

One of them said [Hitler] might have had his face altered by plastic surgery so that he wouldn't be recognised. Another said no, he'd escape in a coffin.[20]

The diarist himself thought that 'Hitler's death might be announced as a subterfuge to help him escape.' In Sevenoaks the discontented housewife wrote in her Mass Observation diary that 'Hitler may or may *not* be dead, as convenient to the Nazis', while a teacher from Essex, who privately believed that Hitler 'has been dead for a long time', passed several groups of people in Leytonstone 'all smiling and discussing his death. Surely there can never have been such great rejoicing over the death of anyone?'[21] A diarist and keen member of the Women's Institute in Coventry, however, was sceptical, writing:

Hitler has committed suicide. Good luck to him! Or so the latest story goes. So has Goebbels. But quite a lot of salt is being taken with any story that comes from Germany from any source.[22]

Long years of war, censorship, propaganda and the ever-present image of Hitler in British culture had combined to create an atmosphere friendly to rumour and mistrustful of official information.

In the absence of any clear and final announcement of the war's end, frustration and disappointment grew. For one forty-year-old woman, the lack of a definitive announcement following Hitler's death reminded her of the end of the blackout, which although it had been formally lifted in April 1945, had been preceded by a 'dim-out' in areas well away from potential final bombing raids.

> The mess they're making of it! First they've surrendered, then they haven't. Then peace will be declared in a few hours, then it won't… It's tearing people's nerves to shreds… It's just like the ending of the blackout… then the dim-out, then more muddles. They miss the dramatic moment every time.[23]

Writing from Penzance in west Cornwall, a sixty-year-old man who described himself as 'a cripple', having been 'knocked out of the war by [an] army lorry on December 17, 1943', shared the general sense that the end of the war in Europe – or at least the sharing of this news with the public – was being mismanaged, leading to confusion and muddle:

> At last it has come to an end in Europe. What a relief! But nobody seems very excited. One little boy with a red, white and blue rosette, and even he was not very excited.[24]

A sense that the government was procrastinating and failing to give people the news that so many longed for might have been unfair, but it did reflect a more widespread 'war fatigue' and a frustration with the many rules, regulations and restraints of wartime.

Others were concerned with wider issues. Nella Last was worried that the focus on victory, and on the end of the Nazi regime, meant that people were not seeing:

> The horror that is Germany. Millions of homeless are 'adrift' in the very essence of the word, no home, no work, sanitation, water, light or cooking facilities, and untold dead to bury... We cannot draw a circle or [as her husband argued] 'build a wall' around Germany and let them stew in their own juice. The poison will spread.[25]

While Nella empathised with those struggling to survive in Germany's broken cities and worried about the legacies of this struggle, others were preoccupied by the news of the concentration camps that was starting to emerge from the continent. Bergen-Belsen concentration camp, some miles north of Hanover in Lower Saxony, had been liberated by troops of the British Second Army on 15 April. There they had found some 60,000 sick and starving prisoners, at least 14,000 of whom could not be saved. Some of those in Belsen were survivors of the 'death marches' from camps further east, from where Nazi guards and the SS had evacuated their prisoners ahead of the Soviet advance, planning to continue their murderous regimes within Nazi Germany. Corpses in Bergen-Belsen lay unburied, and soldiers could have difficulty distinguishing the living from the dead. The eminent BBC journalist Richard Dimbleby had accompanied the troops into the camp and recorded a ten-minute radio report, which the BBC did not broadcast for several days, so shocking did the news editors find his description of a 'world of a nightmare' where 'dead bodies, some of them in decay lay strewn around the road' while 'inside the huts it was even worse'. In this camp, where Anne Frank and her sister Margot had died of typhus just two months earlier, Dimbleby found 'a girl... a living skeleton impossible to gauge her age for she had practically no hair left on her head and her face was only a yellow parchment sheet with two holes in it for eyes'. He reported that 'I have never seen soldiers so moved to cold fury as the men who opened the Belsen camp this week.'[26] This fury was shared by many of those who heard his broadcast.

Members of the No. 5 Army Film and Photographic Unit documented the camp and its liberation, and their footage was released as a newsreel, shown in cinemas across the country in the first week of May. Among the many to view the film this week was the shop assistant from Essex who had recorded people's suspicions about Hitler faking his own death. He was shocked by what he saw, finding the footage 'horribly gruesome'. 'Still,' he thought, 'everybody should see it, fully to appreciate the sickening reality' of the Nazi regime.[27] Some of those who watched the film, heard the broadcast or read accounts in the newspapers felt Germany and its people could not be punished enough:

> Do you know, I keep seeing them in my sleep and dreaming about them. I don't know what you can do with a nation like that, they ought to be wiped clean off the map, they're not human, they're devils. Some people talk about teaching them different. But I don't see how you can teach devils any different.[28]

The retired Electricity Board Inspector from south-east London, who had written the poem to mark Hitler's death, saw the film with his wife when they went to the cinema on 5 May. He was shocked by the images on the big screen:

The German prison camp was shown. It was not very clear but
it was clear enough to make me want to put our Nazi prisoners
in under the same conditions; nothing else will make those
subhuman beasts realise that it is wrong to torture other folk in
such cruel ways.[29]

In his argument that 'all [Germans] under 25 should go to a lethal chamber for the future peace of the world', his response uncannily echoed the Nazi policy of genocide formalised in the Wannsee Conference of January 1942, which had implemented plans for the 'Final Solution' – the systematic annihilation of European Jews.[30] He was far from the only person to believe that the German people were beyond redemption. Mass Observation sent an investigator to record responses to the newsreel outside a cinema in Kilburn, north London, on 3 May. One woman was overheard describing the film to a friend:

I don't think we could ever be hard enough on the Germans;
their behaviour is more like animals. Why, savages wouldn't
behave that way, yet the Germans are supposed to be a
highly cultured race. What I can't understand is why we send
missionaries out to Africa and such places to civilise tribes,
when we've got such a lot to learn from them.[31]

The *Daily Express* held an exhibition of photographs from the camps at Belsen, Buchenwald and Nordhausen in Trafalgar Square, and two days later the busy investigator was there, interviewing people as they left. Many of those who replied unconsciously echoed the beliefs and prejudices that had enabled the Holocaust:

After seeing the exhibition I feel we ought to shoot every
German. There's not a good one amongst them. We're too soft.

We oughtn't to take so many live prisoners.

I'd like to do the same to the Germans. I'd like to give them a taste of their own medicine.

They're a most horrible and cruel race. They think nothing of murder and brutality.

I think the German people are as much as their leaders to blame for the atrocities committed, and those participating in such crime should be meted out the same kind of death.

One interviewee in particular failed to see the similarity between their solution to the 'problem' of the German people and the Nazi regime's answers to its own 'problem' population:

The Germans have a sadistic trait in them and delight in the sufferings of other races… The only way to punish them is to castrate every prisoner of war before he's released. Destroy the German race once and for all. Every healthy German citizen, man, woman and child, is a potential breeder of a future army in the making.[32]

For many people this was their first glimpse of the horrors of the Holocaust, and after almost six years of war these visions of hell validated their beliefs not only about Nazism, but about Germany more widely.

But others were less convinced of Nazi crimes, and had less sympathy for their victims. In Hampstead one forty-year-old man thought the Allied policy of bombing German towns and cities since 1943 was probably to blame for the dreadful images coming out of the country:

I think it's been rather an unfair trick of the government to have fastened on these horror camps like this. I don't say that it wasn't a dreadful thing, but I do think they should tell us the other side of the picture – the dreadful disorganisation of

Germany during the last few months, due to our bombing largely. Well I ask you *would* the Germans deliberately establish focal points of dysentery and typhus all over Germany if they could help it?... I don't say they were run like the Ritz before all this, but I do think it's gross misrepresentation to suggest that the prisoners have been treated like that all along.[33]

A thirty-year-old woman seemed hardened by the war and almost desensitised to human suffering:

I'm beginning to get fed up with all these pictures in the papers. I know it's very terrible, and I was as horrified as anyone in the beginning, but honestly, you can't keep on feeling emotional about it... I feel quite hardened. I mean, you keep on looking at pictures of dead bodies heaped on top of each other – well, you just get used to it. Just as we've had to get used to the idea of death all through the war.

Another woman, who had seen the film that afternoon, found that she had little sympathy for the camp victims:

It was so horrible, I just couldn't go on looking. But I didn't feel pity or the sort of righteous horror you are supposed to feel. I just felt disgusted. Not even with the Germans but with the people themselves. They looked so horrible and disgusting, their cracked faces and their skinniness and sloppiness and horribleness. I know I shouldn't have felt like that but I just do.[34]

The Nazi policy of dehumanisation, so central to the 'Final Solution', continued to do its work even after the Reich had collapsed.

Some of those interviewed by Mass Observation in this peculiar week of waiting had more personal concerns, which prevented any pleasurable anticipation of victory. One woman, asked by Mass Observation how she intended to mark the coming victory, replied:

> I have no plans for VE Day. It can't mean much to us as my daughter's husband is a prisoner, and we have heard nothing since December.

Another woman responded:

> I shall stay at home – there is no point in our celebrating, we have nothing special to celebrate in our family.[35]

For a fifty-eight-year-old housewife from Coventry, active in the life of her local Women's Institute, pleasure in the liberation of Europe was countered by the piecemeal nature of surrender and liberation, which compared poorly for her with the excitement and heroism of the summer of 1940:

> Tomorrow at 8 a.m. Denmark and Holland will be free! But all this marvellous news is falling on numb ears. Victory has been so certain for so long now that it is getting familiar. Life goes on as usual and we actually forget to turn on the news... The one thing that still thrills me speechless is June 1940, little boats of Dunkirk, and August 15, September 15, 1940, Battle of Britain...[36]

But even as she reminisced about Britain's 'finest hour', she also recognised that for some people, including a widowed friend, there was little cause for rejoicing at the defeat of Nazi Germany:

> Peace won't bring back her husband, killed in [the] Coventry blitz, nor her house, destroyed [at the] same time.[37]

In Essex the young shop assistant asked his landlady what she would do when peace in Europe was declared:

She said 'I shan't do anything. Some'll go mad. Others will just heave a sigh of relief, like myself. I don't think there's much sense in celebrating while we're still at war with Japan. There's been too much tragedy in this war, for civilians as well; there's not much to celebrate… I might have a drink.'[38]

A retired schoolteacher from London was contemplating the post-war world and the multiple legacies of the conflict. She too found little to celebrate:

Of course I feel relieved that the war in Europe is so nearly over, but not elated. I think my feelings have been more or less stunned by the overwhelming nature of events – and the sinister thought of the aftermath deepens with victory. Especially just now, I think of the thousands of young men who will spend their lives as invalids, laid aside for ever.[39]

In Bolton-le-Sands the young secretary was listening in to the conversations of those around her. On the evening of 1 May, shortly before the news of Hitler's death broke, she overheard the following:

I'm not going to celebrate the end of the war. Everything is going to be far worse. You can't expect a woman who has a husband or son in Burma to celebrate because the war in Europe is over. What's going to happen when the lads come home? Look at my young brother. He was a boy when he joined up, but he's a man now, and he won't be content with a 30 shilling a week job.[40]

The imminent end of the war in Europe inspired a range of feelings, among them empathy for its victims and anxiety about what was to come.

Reunions with family members, made possible by the liberation of prisoner-of-war camps in continental Europe, gave many personal reasons to celebrate the coming end of the war there. In beautiful Tayvallich, Argyll, a housewife described meeting three neighbours who were '"walking on air" because a son or a nephew was back home after being a prisoner of war – in one case since the Dunkirk times. I have seldom seen such genuine happiness on people's faces.'[41] Further south on the Argyll peninsula, Naomi Mitchison was attending an agricultural fair where, although 'there was hardly any talk about the war', she also found reason to celebrate, as 'Douna was there and her husband, who looks awfully nice, back from his prison camp and not looking too bad at all.'[42] A nurse in Blackburn, Lancashire found herself listing between hope and anxiety as she waited for news of her fiancé, a prisoner. Informed that 'Berlin has fallen' on 2 May, she reflected on her feelings: 'pleased as I am at all the good news, how much more pleased I could be if at the same time I knew my fiancé was safe'.[43] Four days later she was cheered by:

> A girl I know whose fiancé is also a POW [who told her] that there were several local boys in Stalag VIII-B who had not as yet been heard of. One who is back from that camp fell out of the ranks as they were being marched South somewhere near the spot where the Yanks and Russians first met. So there is still hope that he may be alive amongst them.[44]

A bus ride home the following day, however, was a reminder of the continued uncertainty facing so many:

> I know the conductor on the bus and I asked him about his son, also a POW but he had heard nothing. Then someone asked him with ill-timed levity whether he had got his flags out. He said that unless the boy came home his wife could not bear to put any decorations up. They lost their only other son

on the Anzio beachhead. At this moment another man got on the bus and the conductor turned to him and said briefly 'heard anything Joe?' and 'Joe' shook his head. His son was also in Stalag Luft VIII-B and Joe told me that the last letter they had from him was last July, and the one before that January. There is always someone worse off than yourself.[45]

By 25 May she had given up hope of her fiancé returning, writing:

As it seems most unlikely that my fiancé is still alive I have been thinking over very seriously what I intend to do and have decided that if possible I shall join the Colonial Nursing Service and see something of the world before I settle down to a staid middle age.[46]

A year later, in one of her final diary entries, she was to describe 'the gradual realisation that he was amongst the few that would not come back', a realisation that was strengthened by receiving official confirmation that he was amongst those categorised as 'missing'.[47] Stalag Luft VIII-B was in Prussia and was one of the camps from which prisoners were sent on the infamous 'death marches' deeper into Germany as Soviet forces advanced from the east. According to a letter she had received from a fellow prisoner at the camp, her fiancé had tried to escape, heading back towards Soviet lines, where he disappeared from history, and from her life.

As the week turned into the weekend, people's initial excitement at the war's imminent end slid further into confusion and disappointment. In the absence of an unconditional surrender by the rump of the Nazi state, and the subsequent lack of a confirmed date on which victory would be celebrated, rumours proliferated. Mass Observation attempted to summarise the different moods that were sweeping the country:

> Every anti-climax added a little to people's slowly increasing apathy and confusion. Their hopes were raised and dashed so often, disappointments were so frequent, that it became safer to feel nothing at all.[48]

An architect from Slough compared these days with August 1939, describing 'tension of a different kind, expectancy, preparations being made for a change in our way of living. But the tempo is slower – we wait, without anxiety, for the official announcement.'[49] The secretary from Bolton-le-Sands recorded her fluctuating emotions, and those of the people around her, in her Mass Observation diary:

> 1 May
> People tend to be slightly hysterical in my office. I don't mean that they are over-elated, but their moods change very rapidly, from depression to high spirits, and tempers are on edge. I'm very tired.
>
> 5 May
> It has poured with rain all day and I have felt depressed. Now that victory is assured, and the end of the war in Europe only a matter of weeks or days, I find that I am more interested in my two days holiday, and getting away to spend them with Nan, than I am in the actual event… I am increasingly longing to have my husband back, and increasingly restless.[50]

In London the proprietor of a small school was feeling 'lonely, depressed and in a "wander mood"', but also had 'an urge to be in the heart of events' and so took herself off for a walk around central London:

10 a.m. Went to Charing Cross, walked along the river (the tide was high, so it was as I like to see it), to Westminster, on to Trafalgar Square, into St James' Park, sat on seat. Heard one clock after another strike 11, and also the church bells. I think it was the 'Sundayish' sound of the church bells that seemed to smooth out the strain and stress of the war years, and that spoke of a different future.[51]

Cheered and reinvigorated by the calmness of the city that Sunday morning, she returned home and listened, hopefully, for news of the peace, which was not yet to be announced.

The diarist and teacher from Essex, who had noted people celebrating the death of Hitler just three days earlier, was feeling equally subdued by the weekend:

It is queer how flat I feel considering that the war is almost over. I suppose it is because the whole thing is not happening at once, but it may also be due to the weather. It rained all day today without stopping.[52]

Early May 1945 had been unusually cold and wet, with snow in parts of southern England, and the weather, together with the slow pace of events on the continent, was taking its toll on the feelings of many. For a housewife from Oxfordshire, writing on the same day, happiness outweighed frustration at the slow pace that events seemed to be taking:

It will be hard to get very excited when VE Day comes if it goes on much longer, felt rather the day after the party all day, but wonderful inward peace and happiness.[53]

After the excitement and hope of the week, by the weekend many people had given up predicting the date of VE Day and were, instead, simply watching and waiting, bystanders to the news in these final days and hours of the war in Europe.

Excitement, confusion, apathy, anger and frustration were all common feelings described by Mass Observers in the week between the announcement of Hitler's death and the final confirmation of victory in Europe. Nevertheless, many confirmed that they had some plans, however vague, for how they wanted to mark the end of the European war. As in Plymouth, much of this involved alcohol. One young soldier had given his plans careful consideration:

> They tell us that on V Day we will be confined to camp for 48 hours. Most of us know plenty of ways out. Myself, I'm going to get tight and stay that way as long as the money lasts.

And a window cleaner from south London had a similar idea:

> For some time now I've been putting a bit by every week so that on V Day I can get really blind drunk. What with getting bombed out in Balham, and business worries I want to forget it all at least for a bit.[54]

A twenty-year-old member of the Women's Auxiliary Air Force was expecting a more restrained celebration:

> The Group [Captain] has said that he will lock the gates. Still, there will be organised 'amusements', and an issue of one bottle of beer each. Be funny to see what some of the lads do with one bottle.[55]

Sadly, she didn't record the form these 'amusements' took, or exactly how well the issue of one bottle of beer per person was received.

Others had spent the week preoccupied with both the problems that a national holiday might cause for shopping and cooking, and with trying to buy flags and bunting, both of which were in short supply as VE Day approached. Those who were organised had begun to lay in supplies of flags in April, when the news of the Italian surrender and capitulation by individual German soldiers and commanders to the Allies had begun to filter through. Big department stores, smaller shops like Woolworths and street vendors were all doing a roaring trade, not only in flags but also in bunting, photos of Allied leaders, 'victory bows, victory rosettes, hairslides, victory flower sprays, and victory scarves', alongside 'red, white and blue ribbon for making rosettes or streamers', as a Mass Observation investigator, visiting Woolworths, recorded. By early May such items were scarce. An investigator visiting West End stores just before VE Day found the following scenes:

> Inside Derry and Toms, about 20 people were standing round the flag counter. Nothing to buy except gilt cardboard crests in two sizes... no flags of any kind.
> Barkers are selling flags in the basement. The assistants in this store seem to sense what you're going to ask for before the words come out of your mouth.
> Assistant: Flags are in the basement in the Turnery Department.
> Inv: How did you know I wanted to know where the flags were?
> Assistant: That's all we're selling today, that and victory ribbon.

The intrepid investigator followed the crowds to the basement, where they found a queue of 150–200 people, mainly women, overflowing into the china department. It was a good-natured queue, and many were no doubt used to waiting in line after almost six years of rationing and shortages. Gradually the flags went up, until 'London was vivid with red, white and blue'.[56]

At 6 p.m. on Sunday 6 May this peculiar week of waiting and wondering concluded with an official statement that VE Day would be confirmed by Thursday 10 May at the latest. The forty-year-old office worker from south London was holidaying with a friend and her aunt in Essex and had rather more prosaic, and personal, preoccupations:

> We didn't hear the news this morning because the Aunt won't have the radio on because it wastes electricity – nor could we have toast because that is extravagant with gas. We took our meat (ration) with us because Dorothy said her aunt wouldn't be able to manage if we didn't, and the old woman said 'I don't know what I shall do with all this meat.' Surely a good idea would be to knock her over the head and drop her into the river or something.[57]

Meanwhile, a twenty-year-old ATS clerk with somewhat happier domestic circumstances recorded her mother's frustration:

> Mother met me at the bus stop tonight, she having been out for a walk. I asked if there had been any fresh developments, but she had been out for the 6 o'clock news. On getting home we turned on the radio for the 7 p.m. Forces news; it was announced that VE Day, and Churchill's official declaration, could be expected in a matter of days. The first broadcast Mother has missed for days, and it has to be the first with any concrete news![58]

Some diarists were concerned with the other news of the weekend – the uprising in the Czech capital of Prague, where civilians, partisans and Russian soldiers fought the city's German occupiers in the war's last European battle. A civil servant recently returned to London, after her office had been evacuated to Morecambe, Lancashire for the war, was following the news closely:

> The most exciting news… has been of a Czech partisan rising in Prague. It has been a real life thriller… They say most of Prague is now held by the patriots.[59]

For another diarist, a teacher from rural Sussex, the fighting in Prague raised memories of the Warsaw uprising of 1944, which had ended with the defeat of the rebels and the destruction of much of the city when the Soviet troops paused on Warsaw's outskirts, allowing its Nazi occupiers to decimate the supporters of an independent Polish post-war state:

> I feel really worked up about Prague all day. Are the allies answering those radio calls for help with speed and imagination? I think the Czechs are fine. May it not be another Warsaw. Tanks 70 miles away still leave the Germans free to butcher. The wireless is so maddening, it records the calls for planes, paratroops, but doesn't say whether they have been sent.[60]

Prague's calls for help were not to be answered by the western Allies. While SS units entered the city, the US Third Army waited fifty miles to the west, as Eisenhower submitted to Stalin's demands that the Red Army liberate the Czech capital. Sporadic fighting continued in the city until 9 May; as Britain prepared to celebrate peace and victory in Europe, people were being massacred on the streets of Prague.

A film-strip producer from south London found that the news from Germany prompted memories of a walking holiday in the years before the war:

Berchtesgarden [*sic*] captured. Whenever I hear the name I see in my mind's eye the sign-post leading there, as I saw it once on a tramp from Partenkirschen [*sic*] before the war. H., my stepson and I, explored there a bit. Went quite a fair way up the Zugspitze, and came down, without knowing it, on the wrong side of the frontier, too late for train back so had an 18 mile walk back, past the Eibsee. We had come via Augsburg and Munich, returning by way of Innsbruck and Nurnberg. When I hear the news I always have a map in my head, but when these places are mentioned they form pictures as well. How futile all the eyrie fortress talk seems now.[61]

Hitler's Thousand-Year Reich, planned and dreamed of from the Eagle's Nest – the Nazi palace overlooking Berchtesgaden from the slopes of the Kehlstein – had ended in blood and ruins. Between fifteen and twenty million Europeans were dead, including at least six million murdered in the Holocaust and five and a half million German combatants. The task of rebuilding the ruined continent lay ahead, but first the people of the 'people's war' were going to mark their victory.

PROLOGUE

7 May 1945
The Funeral of Germany

In the early hours of Monday 7 May a sleep-deprived General Alfred Jodl, Chief of the Operations Staff of the German Armed Forces High Command, signed the German Instrument of Surrender in Reims, France, the headquarters of the western Allies. The previous week had seen the surrender of German forces in Italy (2 May), north-west Europe (5 May) and southern Germany (6 May). The final surrender of all German military forces to the western Allies was to come into force one minute after midnight, British time, the following day.

Across Europe, and across the world, very few people had any idea of the momentous events unfolding in Reims. Indeed, for those waiting for and expecting news of the end of the war in Europe, Monday 7 May was to be another day of confusion and disappointment. Fierce fighting between occupying German forces and Czech resisters continued in Prague, despite hopes of relief from General Patton's US Third Army, based some fifty miles west of the city. Texel, one of the Dutch Wadden Islands just off the coast of the Netherlands, was to see fighting between German and Georgian forces – men who had originally volunteered to serve with the Wehrmacht, but had revolted on 5 April. This fighting continued until 20 May with the loss of almost 1,500 lives. The war also continued in British waters: that night a U-boat sank two ships, one a Canadian cargo ship, the other a Norwegian minesweeper, in the Firth of Forth. Another Norwegian minesweeper was sunk off the coast of Dorset. Nine crewmen died in the Firth of Forth, and twenty-two off the coast of Dorset.

Although millions of German soldiers were laying down their arms and hoping to return to what was left of their homes and families, Stalin's refusal to recognise Jodl's surrender, at which no representatives of the Soviet Union had been present, stymied plans for a coordinated announcement of victory. Arguing – in one of many telegrams flying between Moscow, London and Washington that day – that Soviet radio intercepts had picked up messages from German troops who were planning on ignoring the surrender, Stalin insisted that there could be no formal peace in Europe until a second surrender document had been signed, this time in Berlin and in the presence of Marshal Zhukov, leader of the Soviet troops occupying the German capital. Before this could be signed, however, sporadic fighting continued between retreating German and advancing Soviet troops.

For many of these German troops, and the many thousands of civilians who accompanied them on their flight west, avoiding capture by the Red Army, which was keen on vengeance after years of fighting, was the priority. Others joined them on the road: concentration-camp prisoners, prisoners of war and some of the multitudes displaced by war who were trying to get home or simply find a place of greater safety. A journalist reporting from the Baltic for the *News Chronicle* described this exodus:

Down the road come the endless trail of covered wagons, pails and household utensils dangling from the axles, children long since weary of the adventure of sleeping with heads bouncing against furniture and crates stored in the back.

Mothers, bleary-eyed and frightened, are walking behind the wagons, shrinking back at the curt summons to clear the road as military vehicles roar by.

Thousands upon thousands of German soldiers are making their way westward, the trail of discarded equipment and personal gear along the roads marking the rising tide of exhaustion and demoralisation.

Then there are the great crowds of the liberated – British, Americans, Canadians, French, Russians, Poles, Belgians – they are all there by the multitude – and sometimes through this great multitude… there sometimes walks the skeleton figure of a political prisoner from one of the horror camps, unmistakable in his hunger and his weird striped-flannel prison garb.[1]

South of here, at the small Hanseatic city of Tangermünde on the banks of the River Elbe some seventy miles west of Berlin, a tragedy was unfolding. The British journalist James Wellard, covering the last days of the war in Europe while attached to Patton's Third Army, was there to witness it. The *Daily Express* published his account of German combatants and civilians attempting to cross the river ahead of Soviet troops.

Russian mortar shells burst in the midst of German soldiers and civilians waiting to cross the Tangermünde bridge to the American side of the Elbe, scores of women and children were killed or wounded. German soldiers pushed old women out of the boats in which they were trying to cross the river. German officers, stripped naked, paddled a rubber boat loaded with German soldiers and three women, with their baggage and bicycles. A German girl drowned in mid-stream after screaming for help. German soldiers swam the river in their vests, climbed up the west bank and were sent straight to the prisoners' cages, still in their vests. German soldiers panicked and rushed in waves towards the river as Russian tanks burst out from the woods... I stood at the broken bridge and watched paratroopers, generals, high-ranking staff officers, nurses, tankmen and Luftwaffe men run across wild-eyed.[2]

Those guilty of heinous war crimes, those who had closed their eyes and ears to the crimes committed in their name, those who had merely tried to survive the Nazi years and those who had, in different ways, tried to resist: all were simply Germans as they tried to cross the river and avoid the wrath of the Red Army.

A similar tale of defeat and despair greeted the readers of the *Daily Express* on its front page that morning. 'Funeral March of Germany', by the Australian war correspondent Alan Moorehead, described the pitiful state of the country after twelve years of Nazi rule:

> Adolf Hitler wanted Germany to go down with him in utter ruin, a colossal sacrifice to a colossal vanity. He has done it. Here today we attended the funeral of Germany.
>
> All around us things are too monstrous to grasp. Starvation. Fifty great cities in ruins. Ten, 20, perhaps 30 million people roaming helplessly through the countryside without homes, their relatives lost and all normal hope gone out of their lives... Greater Germany is extinct. The Third Reich is simply a dead carcass and there is no need for any of our generation to think that we may be hurt by it in our lifetimes.[3]

Daily Express readers, perhaps reading Moorehead's article over their breakfast or on their daily commute that morning, may not have known exactly *when* the final victory in Europe would be declared, but his words and the picture of chaos and defeat at Tangermünde on the inside pages would have reassured them that victory was inevitable.

Readers of broadsheet newspapers could feel similarly relieved that morning. The headline in the *Daily Telegraph* was 'Germany's Final Surrender is Imminent', while *The Times* reassured its readers that 'the confusion and uncertainty, the hesitations and divided counsels, are a measure of the magnitude of the German defeat. These are the maladies of vanquished nations and armies.'[4] There was darkness and light for readers of the *Manchester Guardian*, where an account of 'prominent Nazis in Ohligs, near Dusseldorf' being made to 'dig up the bodies of seventy-one murdered political prisoners' sat side-by-side with a description of how France was planning to celebrate VE Day with 'Sirens, church bells, and floodlighting of public monuments… full-page newspapers, one day's holiday for schools and an extra ration of a litre of wine per head.'[5]

Copenhagen, the newly liberated capital of Denmark, was a city where celebration and vengeance sat alongside one another. While cheering crowds packed into the city centre, the Danish Resistance, distinguished by their red, white and blue armbands and tin hats, was rounding up suspected informers and collaborators; at least 22,000 were detained in the days following Denmark's liberation on 5 May.[6] Among these were members of the 'HIPO Corps', an auxiliary police organisation established by the Gestapo in 1944 after the Danish police force had been disbanded. Unsurprisingly, its members now feared retribution. Ralph Hewins covered their desperate battles for the *Daily Mail*:

> Shooting began when the Patriot resistance forces... were rounding up informers and 'Hipo' men... even at lunch beside a bay window in the heart of Copenhagen I had often to take cover. The Hipo men were firing back, knowing that they were doomed anyway... By 6 p.m. there was serious fighting in the Christianshaven, free harbour and other districts. By that time 34 Danes had been killed and 200 wounded. The Germans and traitors suffered much more heavily... One had frequently to dive to the ground, face down, with the rest of the huge crowd in the streets as volleys suddenly swept the main thoroughfares. But the Danes could not be persuaded to stay at home. This was their historic day and they were out to make the most of it.[7]

Forty-six of Denmark's German occupiers were eventually executed, and seventy-seven Danes were imprisoned as war criminals. They were outnumbered, however, by the German prisoners of war, who were forced in Denmark – as in the Netherlands and France – to clear mines from former battlefields and beaches. In Denmark around 20 per cent of all of those employed on this dangerous work were killed or injured; in France 1,709 were killed and 3,000 injured.[8]

News of the end of the war in Europe, announced over the German radio that afternoon, gradually spread and was greeted with excitement and relief in many places, not just in occupied or combatant Europe. In neutral Dublin, however, an impromptu celebration at Trinity College chapel had degenerated into scuffles and fighting by the evening; an impromptu Thanksgiving Service was being held there when news of the surrender was received:

The chapel was crowded to the doors with students and members of the Faculties. Eire, British, American, French and Russian flags were hoisted over the main gate of Trinity College by students who sang Rule Britannia when standing on the roof over the gate. A large crowd collected and police intervened when scuffles started.

Later, after a street meeting, another group marched to Trinity College and tried to take down the flags. Police then resorted to batons to clear the crowds which blocked the traffic.[9]

In Palestine the young flying officer Anthony Wedgwood Benn, later better known simply as Tony Benn, Labour MP, wrote home to describe how he and two friends celebrated on hearing the news after a rowing trip on the Sea of Galilee:

> We solemnly celebrated with an orange squash and an ice cream each – hardly believing it could be true. Hardly thinking of it, it seemed so remote.

Returning that evening to the Sha'ar HaGolan kibbutz at the foot of the Golan Heights, they found that the news had reached the settlement:

> Outside on the grass an effigy of the swastika was burned, and the settlement crowded into the eating hall, where a little wine and lots of biscuits and nuts were laid along tables. I asked for an orange squash and was given one, however one old boy emptied half a cupful of wine into it and I drank it up – it was practically communion wine – rather an appropriate beverage with which to celebrate peace. Then the national dances began, Germans, Czechs, Poles, Turks, Yugoslavs, all did their national dances. Then there was a pause and an announcement in Hebrew. Everyone looked at us and it was explained that the three RAF Officers would do an English national dance.

> Hurriedly deciding to do the boomps-a-daisy two of us took to the floor. It was an instantaneous success and everybody joined in.[10]

Benn resigned his commission three months later and in 1950 began his parliamentary career as Labour MP for Bristol South East. The celebrations of 7 May were a brief moment of peace in Palestine, as the Jewish insurgency opposing the British Mandate for Palestine, led by the paramilitary group Irgun, saw increased attacks and fighting as the war in Europe ended. Britain finally left Palestine in 1948. The Israeli war of independence that followed, which included the ethnic cleansing of Palestinian Arabs known as the Nakba, was to see more than 10,000 Israeli Jews and 20,000 Palestinian Arabs killed and more than half a million Palestinians become refugees.

The developing conflict in the Middle East as the war in Europe came to an end was not the only site of crisis and tension becoming visible as the world reshaped itself. Chief among these were the rapidly deteriorating relations between the 'Big Three' Allied powers of the United States, the Soviet Union and the United Kingdom. Disquiet at the 'disappearance' of sixteen Polish politicians, all members of the Polish Underground State, which was opposed to both Nazi and Soviet occupation of that country, was another precursor of the reordering of world power as the wartime victors positioned themselves to win the peace. Although the men had disappeared in March, while attending a meeting to discuss the future of Poland, discussions at the United Nations conference in San Francisco had concentrated people's minds on the matter. On 5 May the Soviet Union finally announced that the men had been arrested on a charge of sabotage. A statement released by Tass, the Soviet news agency, claimed that the group arrested had been led by General Okulicki, a commander in the Polish Home Army, and was charged with 'preparing diversionary acts in the rear of the Red Army', leading to the deaths of more than 100 officers and men.[11] *The Times* worried – with good reason – that emerging divisions between the Allies could threaten the coming peace:

> It has long been apparent that the last hope of Germany in defeat is to drive a wedge between eastern and western allies. This purpose has dominated Nazi propaganda for months and years, and in the past week the moment has come to translate it into action… The Germans know well the jealousies and rivalries which are liable to spring up between allies in the hour of victory, and will neglect no opportunity of creating and exploiting them.[12]

These divisions may have done little to hold up the end of the European war in 1945, but they did go on to shape the history of the continent for the next four decades as the 'Iron Curtain' that Churchill was to warn of in 1946 divided Europe between West and East, with post-war Poland very firmly 'behind' the curtain and part of the Soviet world. A taste of what this might be like for its citizens, and for any who dared to oppose Stalin, was seen over the next few months. In a trial in Moscow that summer twelve of the sixteen Polish men were found guilty, and Okulicki and Jan Stanisław Jankowski, deputy prime minister of the Polish Underground State, were both to die in Soviet prisons. Political opposition to communist rule in Poland was thus swiftly beheaded and, conscious of their desire that the Soviet Union join the fight against Japan, Britain and the United States quietly acquiesced.

So as the war against fascism in Europe limped to its close, a new war – between the Soviet-occupied and led Eastern Bloc and a West dominated by a newly resurgent, outward-looking and internationally powerful United States – was beginning to take shape. This conflict would shape the world for the next forty-five years. In Britain, while many people were aware of, and worried about, these new, emerging alliances and divisions, more personal and workaday concerns were at the forefront of most people's minds. When would they get their long-anticipated Victory holiday? Would they be able to buy bread and milk, or should they try to stock up in preparation of shops being closed? And, most of all, *when* would victory in Europe finally be announced?

CHAPTER FIVE

Daytime, Monday 7 May
'The Most Unsettling Day of All'

As the second week after the announcement of Hitler's death dawned, on Monday 7 May, expectations that victory in Europe was about to be announced were high. But it was not until that evening that the BBC would interrupt its scheduled programming to announce that the next day, Tuesday 8 May, would be celebrated as Victory in Europe Day. Thus, for many, it was a day of combined expectation, frustration and disappointment. For one Birmingham clerical worker, faithfully writing for Mass Observation since 1941, 'Monday was the most unsettling day of all.'[1] After the official statement of the preceding day, people were keen not to miss any announcement of the end of the war in Europe and – perhaps even higher in many minds – which days would be holidays.

> The BBC had told us that the Announcement would probably be before Thursday, and everybody was 'phoning everybody else about the time of the news broadcasts to say 'Let us know if you hear anything'. We listened to the three o'clock news on the Forces programme and learned that the German radio had said that the terms of unconditional surrender had been signed that morning… I 'phoned this through to the people at my morning's office, who have no access to radio, and later

they 'phoned through to me to say would I let them know what happened at the six o'clock bulletin. Which I did, but that took us no further. However, it seemed so certain Tuesday would be The Day that everyone went home prepared for a holiday.[2]

Despite her attentive listening, she missed the BBC's early-evening newsflash, but her neighbour told her the much-awaited news as she left her home in the evening to attend a party at the air-raid wardens' post where she had been volunteering.

North of Birmingham, in Sheffield, an accountant and auxiliary policeman who had been paying equal attention to the news all day was not so lucky. Both his colleagues and a tram conductress had confidently predicted that 'peace would be pronounced at four p.m.' and the office boy 'brought in an evening paper which announced that VE Day would be tomorrow'. He recounted how at work 'we listened for the church bells', which were expected to ring in the peace, 'but they did not come'. Back at home and disappointed, he and his wife decided to visit the cinema, 'hoping to see a news film', but:

> They did not show even a newsflash, the whole time being taken up with *The Adventures of Mark Twain*. We were thoroughly disgusted. Arriving home, we switched on the 10.58 news and were relieved to hear confirmation that VE Day is to be celebrated tomorrow. The suspense is over at last.[3]

The suspense, anticipation, disappointment and confusion felt by so many Mass Observers that Monday was a shadow of the diplomatic drama being played out in London, Washington and Moscow. Eisenhower had telephoned Churchill's Chief of Staff, General Sir Hastings 'Pug' Ismay, shortly after Jodl had signed the German surrender early that morning at Reims. Informed of the news when he woke, Churchill wanted to announce victory in Europe as soon as possible, but was convinced that a time would have to be found that also suited Washington and Moscow, in order that the 'Big Three' could make the announcement simultaneously. Meanwhile in Moscow, Stalin insisted that the war in Europe could not be considered to be over until the sporadic fighting that continued, as retreating German troops tried to avoid capture by the Red Army, had ceased and the surrender was formally ratified in Soviet-occupied, and hard-fought-for, Berlin. Telephone calls and telegrams passed backwards and forwards between Moscow, London and Washington DC, where Harry S. Truman had succeeded Roosevelt as President of the United States after the latter's death the previous month. Frustrated, Churchill postponed his planned announcement, first until midday, then until four o'clock and then until six. Finally, he reluctantly agreed not to speak until the following day. Minutes of the War Cabinet meeting that day, at which Churchill informed his ministers that 'all hostilities would formally cease one minute after midnight on 8/9 May', capture something of the day's frustrations:

> Truman and Stalin had originally agreed that announcement should be made on 8 May 1945 at 3 p.m. in this country, at 9 a.m. in Washington and at 4 p.m. in Moscow... PM [Prime Minister] proposed 6 p.m. here on 7 May (12 noon in Washington and 7 p.m. in Moscow). During the course of the day he had several telephone conversations with Washington. President Truman had been unwilling to agree to the proposed change in the time of the announcement unless Marshal Stalin concurred... as Marshal Stalin did not concur in the

> change proposed, President Truman would not make any announcement in Washington until 3 p.m. on 8 May even though the PM should decide to make his announcement at 6 p.m. on 7 May… In view of the numerous reports that were being broadcast around the world he (PM) thought it unfortunate that the official announcement should be delayed and he thought it a matter for special regret that the public in this country should be deprived of the opportunity for spontaneous celebration of the victory; but on balance he had thought it preferable to avoid the risk of a reproach from Marshal Stalin for having departed from the arrangements previously agreed between the three Powers.[4]

Stalin's insistence on delaying the formal announcement until the German surrender had been signed in Berlin was to lead to confusion and resentment, both in the War Cabinet and in the country more widely.

Other news did emerge, however. That afternoon Count Schwerin von Krosigk – a Nazi official who was the current German leading minister and who had been finance minister, overseeing a department that managed the theft of property, money and belongings from Germany's Jewish population – had broadcast to his country from the remains of its government, then in Flensburg, close to the Danish border. The war, he told them, was over: Germany had 'succumbed to the overwhelming might of our enemies'.[5] The BBC picked up the speech from its Monitoring Centre in Caversham and reported it on the 3 p.m. news that afternoon in a broadcast that was heard by many Mass Observers. Still, though, there was no word from Churchill or the King; no official announcement of the victory in Britain. The war in Europe was clearly over, but without formal confirmation, public celebration – and a much-anticipated holiday – would have to wait. This official affirmation would eventually arrive in the form of a brief, dry statement by the Ministry of Information, broadcast by the BBC at 7.40 p.m.

While people wondered and waited, the working day went on. A young clerk serving with the ATS, living in Grays, Essex and working in London, had returned to her unit that morning with an unusual goodbye for her family:

> I said goodbye to my mother and brother and 'See you after the war!' At last I am beginning to feel fluttery inside. There is an atmosphere of exhilaration in the office with everyone cracking feeble jokes and laughing enormously at each other's efforts. I have just bought a couple of yards of red, white and blue ribbon, a paper Union Jack and a tawdry Stars and Stripes on a stick – the latter price 3/9 [three shillings and ninepence, equivalent to about £6.67 today] from Harrods!

As the day went on she recorded the mood in her office:

> What a day!... There has been a steady crescendo of excitement, and the lack of any official announcement only added to the chaotic conditions. At the 3 p.m. news broadcast there was a report from the German radio that they surrendered unconditionally this morning, but SHAEF [the Supreme Headquarters of the Allied Expeditionary Force in Reims, where the surrender had been signed early that morning] has said nothing. Now this really is something; the office is buzzing with excited facetious chatter. A woman clerk comes in and we tell her the news. 'Six years I've sat in this chair waiting to hear that news, and now, when it comes, I have to be out of the room!'
> At 4 and 5 we listen to news headlines, but still nothing official; in-between times we half-heartedly toy with the work on

our desks. It is impossible to concentrate. At 5.15 the evening papers come in, and are scanned for concrete news. The war is over – that's obvious – but when is Churchill going to say so?[6]

It seems that little work was done that day, as people in offices all over the country worked with half an ear, and much of their minds, on the long-hoped-for announcement of victory.

On the Wirral in Cheshire, uncertainty, expectation and excitement combined in the diary of a young woman working as a clerk in the offices of a local factory. News of the German surrender, reported on the BBC news at 3 p.m., came to her and her colleagues at first through the reaction of the factory workers:

> At 3.30 p.m. this afternoon, Monday, we in the works office heard cheering from the direction of the factory.
> 'What's that?' we asked, and rushed to the window.
> 'The wireless is on in the factory. It must be a news bulletin.'
> But we didn't believe, even then, that it was THE NEWS. 'It must be just the kids in the Parish hall playground.'
> 'It's probably the usual cheer that goes up when the factory tea arrives.'
> Five minutes later the 'phone rang in the next room. Mrs V., a middle-aged typist, put her head around the door of our room.
> 'The war's over' she announced simply, and went back to her work.
> An excited young girl messenger came scampering up the stairs. I went out of the room to hear what news she brought. The Boss was talking to her and to Mrs V.
> 'Mr Churchill won't be speaking for some hours yet, so it can't be regarded as official' he was saying.
> 'Yes, they're still fighting in Prague and even if the German

navy's been handed over to us there's still the U Boats. There was a pack of them waiting outside the Mersey last week and they sunk some ships in a convoy.'

We all felt restless yet no-one showed much excitement openly.

'I feel sick, my stomach's gone queer. It must be the reaction' said Miss S. the cashier.

There was singing now, from the direction of the factory. A large ensign floated above its wide roofs.

A girl messenger said 'Mr H. has sent Daphne to Liverpool with two guineas to buy a large Union Jack. He's tickled to death because nobody in the factory is doing any work now they have heard the news.'

'I don't know what to think. I don't trust Stalin' said a (single) girl clerk.

'Don't you say anything against Stalin or I'll do you' said the girl messenger.

The middle-aged typist was singing last-war songs 'How're you going to keep them down on the farm?'

'See you Thursday!' we joked, as we left the office at 5.30 p.m. The streets were deserted. Shops and banks were hung with flags and big V's were in the windows. A man was taking his dog for a stroll, a red-white-blue ribbon on its collar. As yet, nobody was rejoicing in Heswall.[7]

The uncertainty and anticipation recorded by the adult Mass Observation writers on 7 May were shared by children who, even if they were not aware of all the complexities and confusion that so marked the war's end in Europe, were well aware that *something* was happening and that this something was a cause for excitement. The boys of Abbotsholme boarding school in Derbyshire heard the news of the German surrender at 3 p.m. and were, their teacher wrote, 'very much distracted for the rest of the day's classes'.[8] A teacher in rural Sussex was surprised by the degree of knowledge shown by most, if not all, of the children in her care:

> While the senior boys garden they wonder if V Day will be announced today. Various opinions. One boy says 'I'm going to get drunk on a bottle of milk'. In school I ask my infants. They seem to know about the end of the war and the holiday. They tell me of flags they've bought. Several small girls assure me solemnly that they're going to wear red, white and blue hair ribbons. I ask who will announce the end and someone answers Churchill and that he's PM and that we'll still be at war with Japan.

However, not all the children had such a grasp of events, or personalities. She described how 'a five year old from a neglectful uninterested home' said, 'And then we'll kill Churchill.' The teacher gave him the benefit of the doubt and assumed that he had simply confused Churchill with Hitler.[9]

Without official word – preferably from Churchill, whose speeches had been so central to the war years – people were unsure whether or not to begin celebrating, and rumours filled the space left by firm news. Across Britain, Mass Observers recorded both the anticipation of people working that day and widespread worries that a long-anticipated day's holiday would be lost if the much-desired announcement was not made soon. The London school owner who had so enjoyed her solitary walk around central London the previous day bravely decided that as 'no one felt like work' and 'some of the older children should "sense" events', she would take a small group of them to the West End for the afternoon. The children clamoured to see Big Ben and the Houses of Parliament and arrived there at 5 p.m., 'just as HE struck five'. There she saw news of Germany's surrender on the evening editions of the newspapers and met an older woman, 'sitting at the top of Boadicea steps – picture of a Londoner'. This Londoner was quietly rejoicing:

> I'm just sitting. It's wonderful. I'm just sitting – I've been in London all the time – It's wonderful.[10]

Like the school owner and her charges, and so many others who had been a part of London's long war, she was drawn to its centre to share the news of peace and victory.

A social worker, living and working in north London, was finding it difficult to concentrate on work. She described her day:

> Go to the office as usual, but we all find it difficult to concentrate on work, as we keep on wondering when peace is going to 'break out'. There seem to be so many conflicting rumours. One of the men from the Divisional Office comes up to say that peace will probably be proclaimed at 3 p.m. today, in which case we are to go home. The afternoon wears on however and nothing happens… A man from the Divisional Office comes up with two large flags to be hung from our office window – the Chinese and the French. The Special Officers in the next room have the British and the American flags while the Red Flag is suspended from the window of the ladies lavatory.[11]

Even without the distraction of a Red Flag hanging from the bathroom window, a sergeant in the WAAF (Women's Auxiliary Air Force) and her colleagues felt similarly unenthusiastic about work that day:

> We all felt restless and disinclined for work. Bets were being made as to which day would be declared VE Day, and

rumours ran wildly around the camp. I felt woefully depressed and didn't want VE Day to be Tuesday because I was on night-duty on Monday and was afraid that I should sleep and miss the fun.[12]

Rumours were also rife at RAF Cardington, in Bedfordshire, which one Mass Observer, a young man who had been writing for the organisation throughout the war, was visiting to discuss the design of a new anti-aircraft device with Balloon Command, which had one of its headquarters at Cardington. The last air raid on Britain, by V-2 rocket, had been on 27 March, and protection against such raids seemed less important than it had done throughout the war, as German forces collapsed and surrendered:

> No one was working seriously, they all had their ears to the news bulletins, listening for the PM's announcement. Various rumours emanated supposedly from Station Commander. He was in touch with high ops because Allied thanksgiving service was being broadcast from the station and had to follow PM's announcement immediately. Everyone assumed the announcement would be made today and were ready to dash off to get most of the day off, as tomorrow would be last holiday. Remarks such as 'well the war's as good as over chaps' was common.[13]

Military or civilian – most felt sure that the war in Europe was as good as over; none knew when this would be made official.

A young army clerk writing for Mass Observation was travelling from his Scottish army base to nearby Edinburgh, and from there to London, on 7 May, hoping to be home on leave in time for the anticipated public holiday. He recorded that he:

First heard the news of unconditional surrender at about four o'clock, as we were boarding the train at North Berwick, on our way home on leave. Various stories were drifting about.
1. It was all over. 2. It was a neutral report. 3. A German radio report 4. Didn't [know] where it had come from.

While waiting for a train repaired to the Bodega in Edinburgh – a few glasses to make sure in case anything was on… people were in a very expectant mood and the general opinion was that it was as good as over.[14]

Also travelling to London that day, though far less happy about it, was Naomi Mitchison, journeying south from her home in her beloved Argyll, where she had hoped to celebrate victory. She found herself sharing part of that journey with fellow passengers who did nothing to improve her mood:

At Wemyss Bay we got into a carriage with two American and two low grade floozies. One of the Americans spotted my Cross of Lorraine and said 'Oh French'. I was constrained to talk French for a bit! Later they began to talk to two other people in the carriage, finally asked if Scotland was civilised! I began talking, trying to be nice and not lose my temper. They couldn't stand Sunday and the general absence of means to a 'good time'. They kept on saying a good time is not possible without money, and one must be able to 'celebrate'. I said English pubs were nicer to which one of the floozies said she had been in Wolverhampton and none of the English had been nice to her… There was some discussion as to whether V Day had come, as one of the Americans said that someone on the boat had said it had… discovered it wasn't V Day yet, though people didn't seem to be quite sure. There were a lot of saltires and lions but less stars and stripes than hammers and sickles.[15]

With the dearth of definite news, the presence – or absence – of flags had to serve as an indicator of events.

And flags *were* starting to appear outside people's homes, workplaces and on the streets. Mass Observation was busy watching these preparations from its headquarters in central London. Westminster, the seat of government and the one place aware of the ongoing squabbles over the formal announcement of victory between Moscow, London and Washington, was noticeably slow to put out flags:

> At about 3 p.m. flags seemed to be coming out from West to East along Victoria Street. The end near Victoria was beflagged but nearer Westminster none had yet appeared. The only flag to be seen from Parliament Square at 4 p.m. was one hung from the first floor of the Express Dairy. A disreputable little coffee stall called the 'Sanctuary Shack Bar' near the end of Tothill Street was gay with flags and bunting.[16]

As shops, snack bars and offices started to hang out flags in celebration, more and more 'ordinary' people followed suit. The presence of some flags encouraged others to appear. Mass Observation recorded an overheard conversation between two working-class women in Chelsea, west London:

> F45D: I don't know whether to start putting out me flags or not. I don't want to be the first and make a fool of myself.
>
> F40C: Just look opposite. (Indicates block of working class flats with flags hung across the courtyard.)
>
> F45D: Ooh, I'll go home and get mine up right away.[17]

Gradually at first, and then more quickly, flags and bunting spread across the city until London was 'vivid with red, white and blue'.[18]

For some, though, the question of whether or not to hang flags was more complex, and more personal. One woman had been visiting her sister in the small Midlands town of Barnt Green. This sister had recently been bereaved, losing her son the previous month, and the pleasure at victory was tempered by their loss. They decided to try and find a way to both celebrate the end of war and commemorate the young man who had died:

> My sister asked me to pick a huge bouquet of flowers, all colours, and we listened in at 4 p.m. – still no Churchill announcement, but that unconditional surrender had been made. So I ran up the flag at the top of the pole, and we put the flowers at the bottom in memory of her son who had died a month ago.[19]

Over the next few days many more would find their pleasure in victory similarly shaped by thoughts of those who had not survived, or had not yet returned from the war.

Mixed feelings – joy and relief at the end of the European war, combined with an awareness of the sorrow that war had brought, the knowledge that the conflict was not (yet) over and anxiety about the future – shaped many people's feelings on the eve of VE Day. The Birmingham clerical worker whose diary opened this chapter was also thinking of the future, and considering how her wartime experiences and observations had shaped her political views:

> It is true that there are a few noodles about who love to say 'we shall have to fight the Russians next' but I don't believe for a moment that any government we are likely to have in the next ten years – perhaps twenty – would dare to attempt to lead this country into a war against Russia. Because we all know what

Russia has saved Europe from (with American and British help, certainly), and even the Blimpiest Blimp in the Athenaeum [a reference to the 1943 film *The Life and Death of Colonel Blimp*, itself based on David Low's long-running cartoon character] can't now pretend that there is any horror in Bolshevism for fear of saying the same thing as the perpetrators of Belsen, Buchenwald and Dachau. At least they ought not to dare… There was a time when I thought there wasn't much to choose between the Russian and German totalitarianism (vile word) and indeed I still am cautious about the Dictatorship of the Bureaucracy. But actually Belsen and Buchenwald have done something to me – have completed my journey from the middle to the Left, though that is more picturesque than accurate, and if anyone says anything to me about the horrors of a Red revolution I shall say 'Would you rather have Nazism or Fascism?'[20]

A social worker from Bury St Edmunds in Suffolk was feeling far less optimistic, arguing that there would be another war within twenty years, as 'we shall be quarrelling with Russia and [the] USA before many months, or even weeks'.[21] As the second global conflict in three decades came to an end in Europe, some were already sceptical about the potential for a lasting peace.

For those bereaved by the war, thoughts of their loss inevitably shaped their feelings about peace, and about celebrations of peace. The clerk from the Wirral, who had heard of the German surrender while at work, passed a local shopkeeper on her way home that day: Mrs G., who had lost a son in Burma, was standing in her shop doorway talking to neighbours. 'I don't think people should go mad until it's properly over. There's many a lad will get killed before it's finished.'[22] A schoolteacher and young mother who had been scrupulously reporting for Mass Observation since 1940 recorded an overheard conversation between two women waiting at a bus stop:

> I'll be glad when it's all over. My boy's out in Italy. I hope he'll be home soon now. Your Harry's out in Burma isn't he?
> Yes. Oh I wish it were all over out there as well. You'd feel like celebrating then.[23]

Another diarist, a retired teacher from Brighton, described the mixed feelings of one woman she spoke to in the street:

> People in streets very cheerful. We stopped to speak to utter strangers. One girl said 'this glorious sunny day and the glorious news come together. But my sister is sad because she has not heard since Christmas of her fiancé in a camp in Silesia. No one can give her news. Boys from the same camp say they know nothing of him. They refuse to talk of their experiences, whether because it was so hateful or because they've been ordered not to.'[24]

Older people sometimes remembered the combination of joy and grief that had greeted the Armistice in 1918. One man, a caretaker in his sixties living near Rochdale, interviewed by a Mass Observation writer who was keen to discover his plans for VE Day, had this to say:

> I wouldn't mind working a' th' time if that would help them to get it all over. An' this is how I looks at it – it's not over when this is done wi'. There's Japan and then there is all the problems after. In any case it's like that last time – we was celebratin' when a neighbour comes in and says 'My son won't come back'. You see?

The author did see. She shared his mixed emotions and was sensitive not only to her own feelings, but to those of the people around her. She described her reaction to the news of the German surrender at 3 p.m.:

> I went off to town in a dream, doped with aspirin and the feeling of excitement abroad – not wild excitement but the deep emotion which chokes one with its movements. It was a tense journey – flashes of flags being waved by children and bunting fluttering. A glimpse of 'Welcome Home' on a mean little fanlight and a tinsel gaudy crown over a narrow grimy doorway... as we ran into the square we could see the little bunches of people clustered round the paper sellers and the splashed headlines 'German War Over'. But there was no thrill of stupendous exhilaration as I had imagined. Instead – a feeling of remote sadness and a fear of what is to come now.[25]

Others, however, were caught up in the excitement of the day and were uninterested in either looking forward or in the wider ongoing war. The civil-defence worker who had been visiting RAF Cardington in the morning had returned to his London offices in the afternoon, determined to carry on working. This desire was not widely shared:

> Returned to office where I was told there would not be much work done for me this week... Went down to workshop where manager was very surprised to see me. 'You're not working today, are you? It's V Day.' I said that it hadn't been announced yet and that I was carrying on as usual. The girls had gathered round the loudspeakers and were disappointed when there was no announcement on the three o'clock news. I erected a new device prototype in the middle of the floor and I heard one of the girls say 'You won't be wanting that now.' They had completely forgotten there was a Far East war on.[26]

In contrast, a Mass Observer in Bolton – Tom Harrisson's 'Worktown' of the 1930s – found themselves unable to stop thinking of, and worrying about, the future, the ongoing war and its multiple legacies:

> I realised that the war had not solved anything except 'might is right' (in peacetime at any rate). Poland, the country that caused us to enter into war, was being occupied by Russia and being forced to have a Russian-inspired government, and there is dissatisfaction and chaos in most countries. I felt sorry for the chaps who had to continue fighting against Japan. I felt sorry for the vanquished too.[27]

Although some were anxious about the continued fighting in Burma and the Pacific, and others were worried about the growing division between the Soviet Union and Britain and the United States, or about 'what was to be done' with Germany, the concerns of many others were more personal. What would become of them, and their friends and family, in the post-war world? Mass Observation had asked its National Panel to record both how they expected to spend VE Day and what others were planning.

One woman from Sheffield, who had been loyally writing for Mass Observation since 1939, asked a cross-section of people in her workplace, and on her way to work, about their hopes and anxieties for the future. Their answers tell us of the ways in which world events and personal concerns intersected after almost six years of war. One woman, a middle-aged telephonist, was concerned with her husband's job prospects and the ways that his current discontent impacted on their family life. She said, 'I want Charlie (husband) to get a new job. He doesn't like it where he is. He doesn't say much but he's irritable. The money is not worth it – he ought to have something better. That's why I want to keep this job on for a bit, for the money.' A caretaker's wife was similarly looking forward with some anxiety, wondering where her son and daughter-in-law would find to live, and what her daughter would do when her war work ended: 'There'll be our George coming back and he and Joyce'll have to get somewhere to live. I expect they'll be with us for a bit. Then Doris'll want a new job when she comes off the trains.' While a man about to leave service with the RAF was considering a fresh start in Canada with his wife and new baby, two younger women were thinking about the novel freedoms that they hoped the post-war world would offer:

> Typist, 24: I want to get a decent job and get out of here as soon as possible – foreign correspondent or something with a bit of scope.
>
> Typist, 33: I want to get a new job. I'm fed up with this stuffy place.[28]

Figures for women's work in post-war Britain show that, statistically at least, they were likely to be disappointed. Women's work, both paid and unpaid, had been vital to the war effort, with women being subject to conscription into the forces, fields and factories since 1941, and by 1942 more than 90 per cent of able-bodied single women were engaged in some kind of war work or military service. Any gains, however, were short-lived. Although there wasn't the same widespread dismissal of women from war work as there had been at the end of the First World War, when half a million women had lost their jobs within six months of the Armistice, officials overseeing demobilisation and employment assumed that the majority of women who had been 'mobile' during the war would want to return home; and that home-making, marriage and motherhood constituted the ideal, desired occupation for most women. Some women simply found themselves unable to carry on working, as the workplace nurseries that had enabled those with small children to work in factories and other areas of industry during the war swiftly closed. Although many women continued to work in post-war Britain, which needed labour to rebuild and recover from the war, much of this work was low-paid and often part-time. The Marriage Bar, which forced women to leave employment on marriage, was lifted for most public services in 1946, but remained in place in many private industries. By the time of the 1951 census only 25.2 per cent of young married women (aged between twenty-five and thirty-four) were recorded as being employed.[29]

Then, of course, there were more pressing and immediate worries. After the widespread concerns about exactly when a national holiday would be announced, and for how long, came the question of food. By 1945 people were well used to queuing, to rationing and to intermittent shortages of food and other consumer goods. At the outbreak of war Britain imported much of its food, making it especially vulnerable to the kinds of shortages that wartime disruption to global supply chains could bring. Civil servants and politicians in the Board of Trade were well aware of the impact of food shortages on the wartime population, and preparations for the supply and control of food and other vital goods started as early as 1936. By 1939 some fifty million ration books were printed, ready to meet the demands of wartime and to try and ensure that what food there was would be fairly distributed, and a Ministry of Food was established to oversee the nutrition of the British people.

The first commodity to be rationed, however, was not food, but petrol, just three weeks after the outbreak of war, on 22 September 1939. In January 1940 a range of foodstuffs, including sugar, butter and bacon, was rationed. Tea, the nation's favourite drink, followed in July 1940, and clothing started to be rationed in 1941. More food, including milk, cheese and eggs, was rationed in 1942. Shoppers had to register at a specific store, which was the only place where they could buy these rationed goods. As the war went on and shortages became more frequent, long queues outside shops became more and more commonplace, with women often spending hours each day trying to feed their families. By 1942 Mass Observation was reporting on 'grumbles about the amount of time wasted in shopping' and the ways in which shortages and suspicion that others were not suffering could result in rumour and resentment, as in Kilburn, where 'nobody… has had any eggs for several weeks, while it was believed in Golders Green there are plenty'.[30]

Although people were used to queuing and to shortages, the lack of information about VE Day, and how long the expected public holiday would last, meant that many were keen to stock up on food while the shops were still open. Indeed, they were expected to: as early as 2 May the *News Chronicle* reported the official advice that 'housewives are requested to lay in an extra supply of bread'.[31] The young mother and schoolteacher from Swansea, who had overheard the bus-stop conversation between two women with family overseas, spent much of her morning shopping for food, as did her mother and many others:

Since just before nine she [mother] has been in the local shops buying bread, vegetables, spam and biscuits. It's a most unusual time for her to shop. She says the shops are packed with people buying their rations... There are crowds in all the food shops and around the food counters in Marks and Spencer's and Woolworths. In the latter I buy a tin of peas... Most of the people in the bus were women with full shopping bags and baskets... The houses have a few flags out. So far they seem to be centred around houses with 'Welcome home' and 'Welcome home Danny' etc. notices. The town is still crowded. In Liptons and Maypole branches in the High Street the people are crowded out to the doorsteps... I lay the table for lunch while mother dishes up the carrots and potatoes and heats the peas I've brought home. We have cold mutton assisted by a slice of the spam.[32]

In Claverham, close to Bristol, a diarist and nurse-companion had heard that 'the shops are unlikely to be open tomorrow', so she 'hurried to the grocers for the rations and oddments that we usually fetch on Tuesday'.[33] Like the young mother, she had also had cold mutton for lunch – a common meal that day, made of leftover meat from the traditional Sunday roast.

In Forest Hill, south London, the retired Electricity Board engineer decided to follow 'the French Queen's advice' and 'buy cake for tea', because by late afternoon there was no bread to be had anywhere.[34] For a retired nurse in Steyning, West Sussex, concerns about shopping over the expected holidays were shared with her neighbours, causing her to reflect on the sense of community that had helped to sustain her during the war years:

At 3 p.m. the grocer's girl came for my weekly order. I asked her in to listen to the 3 p.m. Forces news. When it came it said that the Germans had broadcast that all hostilities were at an end with unconditional surrender. We both shook hands. She told me that her shop would not be open tomorrow (though a food shop). After she had gone, I went to tell my neighbour. She wondered if the baker would come and then decided to go to High Street and get some bread. We also shook hands, and I told her how it had helped me to know I had neighbours like her and the one on the other side all through this terrible time. I had not felt alone because, when there was a raid on in the night, if I went out some of them were always up and out. Her husband, who is a Warden, once even called through the letter-box to know if I was alright.[35]

Concerns about food for the holiday, and whether or not shops would be open, were shared by women across the country. On the Essex–London border a teacher recorded that there was 'no bread to be bought in Ilford, but a notice outside one shop said bread tomorrow, 8.30–10.00'.[36] The clerk from Glasgow explained that the shortage of bread and the 'enormous queue outside Colquhuon's the bakers at 8.45' on Saturday convinced her that 'hundreds of people must expect VE Day on Monday or Tuesday', while a shop assistant in Dewsbury, West Yorkshire was wondering how she would supply her customers, as 'the baker told me he is coming at VD but not for two days after. He is bringing no extra so that we are in a queer position.'[37]

As day slipped into evening there was still no official confirmation from the British government of the end of the war in Europe. Despite the BBC's coverage of the German declaration of surrender at 3 p.m., it was difficult to be sure that the fighting in Europe was really over. It was hard for many people to sustain the mood of expectancy and joy that had greeted so much of the news almost every day of the previous week. While some nonetheless continued to feel a sense of excitement and anticipation, waiting eagerly for the news that many of them still expected to be delivered over the wireless by Churchill, others were surprised by their own lack of enthusiasm, and irritated by the lack of official confirmation from the government. The shopkeeper from Dewsbury wrote that:

> The strain of wondering when it will be is getting on people's nerves. 'Why can't they tell us without all this mystery? They know well enough when it will be. Having folk wondering what to do' is the note.[38]

An office worker from Birmingham found that Monday had been 'a queer and confusing day' with 'no excitement in town', while in the East Midlands a civil engineer felt that 'the delay in signing the surrender, drawing out the expectation of it at home made it "flatter" than it would otherwise have been'.[39] A timber merchant from Leeds complained that 'keeping people in suspense from hour to hour' meant that the news was 'more of a farce than a feast'.[40] One forty-four-year-old chemist attempted to explain his feelings to Mass Observation in more detail:

> I approached V Day with a growing sense of anti-climax. I had imagined that if ever the war got to that stage where decisive victory for the allies seems certain I should be conscious of a growing sense of excitement. As it was I found it difficult to work up any enthusiasm at all as did those with whom I came into contact. I even found it difficult to join in speculative discussions of when the expected declaration would come... A lunchtime rumour that Churchill was making a statement at 3 p.m. caused some little excitement and I turned on the

radio in the fire-watching room. The carefully worded report of Germany's capitulation was *so* carefully worded that it meant little to me and when I reported it verbally to the rest of the staff their attitude was one which would have been adequately expressed by Jack Warner's 'di da di da'.[41]

Warner, who went on to be best known in British households for playing the title role in the long-running BBC series *Dixon of Dock Green* (1955–76), had starred in the BBC variety show *Garrison Theatre* in 1939 and 'di da di da' was one of his catchphrases, communicating the very lack of communication for which the Ministry of Information was becoming known. It seemed that, for some, the combination of drawn-out expectation and a lack of official confirmation of peace in Europe drew them back to the early days of the war and the widespread belief that news was being deliberately withheld from the public.

In London, Mass Observation was doing its best to map the shifting moods of the city over this long and perplexing day. They found that 'a rather unexcited expectancy was the dominant mood, coupled with the usual uncertainty and confusion'. Much of this, they felt, was due to the drawn-out nature of the news – not only on Monday 7 May, but in the preceding week, when 'uncertainties and rumours' had combined with a 'sense of an imminent announcement of peace', which was to be frustrated again and again. By mid-afternoon people were starting to gather in Whitehall, hoping to see or hear someone or something that would tell them that the war in Europe was over, and that they could – officially – begin to celebrate. One Mass Observer went along there and painted a detailed picture of the mood around Westminster as the afternoon went by:

At about 3 p.m. Inv[estigator] goes to Parliament Square and hangs about. There is a queue of people for evening papers at the end of Parliament Street; all the seats in the square are occupied and a few groups are sitting round the stone coping round the grass. Each time Big Ben strikes a ripple of expectation goes through the waiting people, and each time they sink back into themselves when nothing happens. They are fairly silent, but the numbers grow from minute to minute, till the pavements at the end of Parliament Street are solid with people.

In the absence of news, rumours circulated among the gathering crowds:

At about 3.30 M45C is overheard to say 'Churchill's left Downing Street and gone over to the House, so we may expect to hear something any minute.' Inv. goes and sits on seat in Parliament Square, opposite St Margaret's. F55D remarks 'I've not got an evening paper. Mine was out just before lunch. It says that after his speech he'll go to St Margaret's to give thanks with some of the MPs. Well, I hope it's true. They shouldn't keep people hanging about waiting like this. They'll lose all their interest. The government shouldn't be afraid of people going mad. Everyone's very sober about it.'[42]

Westminster may have been the centre of government – and the centre of the Empire at war – but those gathering there in the hope and expectation of news knew no more than anyone else.

By about four o'clock the Mass Observer went off in search of tea and refreshments, eventually finding a café open, where one waitress was saying to another:

They say it's 5 o'clock now. Before that it was 4 and before that it was half past three and before that it was Sunday.

Returning to Parliament Square just before five o'clock, the observer found that:

> Most people seem to have got dispirited and bored. Most of the seats on the west side, by the shelters, are deserted, and so is the grass plot... At 4.55 Inv. asks a Special [Constable] if he has heard anything. He says 'It won't be today now. May be tomorrow'. The Special Police were all called out to Buckingham Palace, but they've all gone home again. Five o'clock strikes. A more intense stir of expectation runs through the waiting crowd. A minute or two passes and they begin to move restlessly. Some go towards the tube. Here and there a few murmurs are overheard about 'Fed up with all this waiting' 'Let's go home' 'Too bad – going on like this – you get browned off.'[43]

Despite, or perhaps because of, spending the afternoon watching and waiting outside Parliament, some people had simply had enough and, disgruntled, set off home for their tea.

Just north of here, in Trafalgar Square at the top of Whitehall, loudspeakers had been set up and another crowd had gathered. Mass Observation sent another investigator to record the late-afternoon mood there. They found:

> Few people... no more than would normally assemble on any sunny Sunday afternoon, and they are far from excited. People are sitting round the fountain, but there's plenty of room for others. About fifty to seventy stand in a circle watching or feeding the pigeons. Small groups scattered all over the Square, and there's not much talk. Mostly people are looking around to see what others are doing... At six o'clock the numbers increase, but not to any appreciable extent. The same people seem to be walking backwards and forwards, as if unable to keep still. Aeroplanes pass overhead in V formation and everyone looks skywards. Young people climb on the plinth of

Nelson's monument but the policeman quickly orders them off. Big Ben strikes six. People flock round the loudspeakers and listen to the news. But as no official peace announcement comes through, nor mention of Mr Churchill broadcasting to the nation, people begin to walk away.

Just after six o'clock, though, there was a ripple of excitement in the square:

> In the distance a rumbling resembling native war cries is heard. Very soon the rumbling rises in crescendo and people sitting round the fountain or hanging about the square scramble across the road in the direction of The Strand, where a procession of 200 students from University College comes into full view. A youth about 20 heads the procession, carrying Phineas, the college mascot, and marching five abreast they chant 'Oh why are we waiting, oh why, oh why' sung to the tune of 'Oh Come All Ye Faithful'. Still chanting their college cry they march in the direction of Whitehall.[44]

Waves of excitement and mounting expectation, followed by disappointment and a decision to either hang on and wait for the next event or cut one's losses and head for home, seem to have been the lot of those who gathered in Westminster that afternoon.

Back in Parliament Square, the original investigator had had enough and met up with a friend [described as M35B] to head to a nearby pub. There the addition of alcohol had made the mood more hopeful, and the crowds more enthusiastic and determined to have a good time:

> There is an air of mild hilarity, still mixed with a certain amount of tension and disappointment. But the noise is terrific… A group of Australian privates come in, already rather drunk and happy. One gets out a pen-knife and slowly and

solemnly cuts off the ends of the tie of another. All roar with laughter. Presently the one attacked does the same with perfect good humour to his attacker. Inv. does not see all that happens but in a few more minutes the six or seven are all shrieking with laughter and all have ragged ends below the knot of their ties.[45]

London, for many years a diverse city, had become even more cosmopolitan in wartime as troops, workers and refugees from the Empire and from occupied Europe filled its streets. By late afternoon some in this multinational city had clearly decided that – official announcement or not – it was time to celebrate.

CHAPTER SIX

Evening, Monday 7 May
'I Still Rejoiced with All My Heart'

When the great news was eventually announced, it came wrapped not in the oratory of Churchill, but in the dry and dispassionate words of the Ministry of Information via a BBC newsreader. At 7.40 p.m. the BBC interrupted a piano concerto with a brief and somewhat low-key confirmation that the war in Europe was over:

> It is understood that, in accordance with arrangements between the three great powers, an official announcement will be broadcast by the Prime Minister at three o'clock tomorrow, Tuesday afternoon, 8 May. In view of this fact, tomorrow, Tuesday, will be treated as Victory in Europe Day and will be regarded as a holiday. The day following, Wednesday 9 May, will also be a holiday. His Majesty the King will broadcast to the people of the Empire and Commonwealth, tomorrow, Tuesday, at 9 p.m.[1]

And that was that. The culmination of six years of fighting, separation, death, hardship and sacrifice was marked by the somewhat terse instruction that the following day should be 'treated as Victory in Europe Day' and thus could be 'regarded as a holiday'. The language chosen did not really rise to the occasion.

Indeed, it seemed that the anxiety expressed by the *Daily Mail* earlier that day about how the country would communicate and celebrate the news of victory in Europe had been justified. The newspaper's editorial had warned against understatement by the British state, arguing that:

> VE Day will be one of the great occasions of the century. A full programme of permitted celebrations and festivities, mainly of the 'garden fete' variety has been announced by the government, but something on a grander plane is needed to impress this day on our memories.
>
> We suggest that there should be salvos of guns fired in London and other large centres, followed by a prolonged sounding of the All Clear.
>
> Moscow has its big gun salutes after every victorious battle. London, the only city in the world to have endured enemy attacks for five years is certainly entitled to the traditional salutes after a victorious war.
>
> The sounding of the all clear would be one of those imaginative touches which have been so conspicuously absent from all public arrangements during the war. Without it the end will be prosaic. The great moment will be dulled by the hand of the bureaucrat.[2]

But the 'hand of the bureaucrat' – so apparent during the war, with its endless rules and regulations governing everyday life, and so evident in the announcement of the end of the war in Europe – would not have everything its own way that evening.

This was not for want of trying. Whitehall had been planning for VE Day for several months, and an Interdepartmental Conference to agree arrangements for marking the end of the European war was held in October 1944. The main aim of the conference was to allow for some celebration, but also to ensure that 'there should be no relaxation of the national effort until the war in the Far East has been won'. Those present 'doubted whether… the mood of the country will be one of universal noisy rejoicing'. They felt that the impact on civilians, particularly London with its:

> 75,000 casualties and 2,450,000 damaged houses, has been too long and too prominently in the front line to experience the sort of outburst of feeling normally found only in those who have taken a passionate interest in war but not a personal part in it. It may well be that a large proportion of the people will be only too thankful to stay at home rather than to crowd into the streets. On the other hand there will undoubtedly be many who will not want, or will be unable, to resist the temptation to make merry. In any case the special programme which the BBC propose to broadcast will provide an attraction indoors.

Bonfires were a special concern, as 'in the past the lighting of them in inappropriate places by the irresponsible few has sometimes caused disturbance and danger'.[3] Local authorities were urged to announce official bonfires, to be lit after the planned King's speech as a way of avoiding people taking matters into their own hands. A circular to local authorities in April further explained their hopes for restrained celebrations. Church attendance was to play a large part in the day:

> The general feeling of the nation will, no doubt, be one of thankfulness for victory, and it is expected that churches of all denominations will be open for services and for private prayer on VE Day. It is hoped that churches will be able to arrange for church bells to be rung throughout the country.[4]

Churches were open, and many did attend them, and church bells – silenced for the duration of the war, except to notify people of a mainland invasion that never came – did peal the peace. But pubs were also open, even though alcohol was often in short supply, and any plans for municipal bonfires were often eclipsed by more spontaneous community bonfires as neighbours celebrated victory, and survival, together.

The Birmingham clerical worker, whose account of her day spent trying to catch the news opened the last chapter, missed the announcement on the BBC because she had just left her house to go to a party at her air-raid warden's post. Luckily for her, her neighbour had heard the bulletin:

> I set out just before eight o'clock for the small Warden's party which we had arranged at the Post, and just as I got outside the front door the next-door-neighbour was rigging a flag out of his front window. He said 'It's come – they've just broken the news to say it's tomorrow.' I dashed back into the house and switched on our radio, trying both stations in turn but everything seemed normal. However, we decided to rig our own flag as we fully expected to hear by nine o'clock. Then I went over to the Post again and there was a solitary Warden standing outside and wondering if he had made a mistake about the date of the party. I wondered the same so we went in to see if there was a message about postponement. No. We dawdled about outside again and presently two more Wardens joined us. We called out as they approached 'have you heard anything?' and one said 'Yes, there was a newsflash about ten minutes ago.' Eventually we were joined by the Head Warden, who went into the Post and did some telephoning and then the five of us set out for the local; a most sober and restricted party.[5]

Also in Birmingham was an eighteen-year-old chemist and student who had 'visibly quivered' with excitement when he had heard the news of the German surrender at work that afternoon. At home in the early evening he had eagerly tuned into both the six o'clock and seven o'clock news, but heard nothing, 'finding the radio silence rather mystifying and inexplicable'. However, he heard the BBC newsflash at 7.40 p.m., although its rather half-hearted tone 'mystifies me even more'. Nonetheless, he was reassured that 'we know more or less where we are now'.[6]

The shop assistant from Dewsbury in West Yorkshire was feeling rather less reassured. Having kept the wireless on all afternoon and evening 'for fear of missing something', she found that the BBC's newsflash left her feeling 'quite exasperated'. She continued:

> Why couldn't they have said earlier instead of all this caution? If anyone was feeling gay and 'celebratory' this business would knock all the joy out of them.[7]

She was not alone. A little way north of Dewsbury, a school medical officer in Northallerton was also rather underwhelmed. That evening she was playing bridge with friends in a local café. The café manager came to tell them the news, but 'this seemed a bit of an anti-climax after having expected the announcement so long'.[8] This feeling of let-down, or flatness, was recorded by many that evening.

A Mass Observer living just outside London with his parents was also unimpressed with the announcement, or perhaps was simply overwhelmed by the rapidly moving events of the past few days:

Quietly, my father said 'It's over'.

Personally, I was unmoved, and I think I'm right when I say the other members of my family were also unmoved to[o]. It was obvious a week, a month, or more that V Day was on the way. I could not get thrilled or excited to save my life. After the news in the past few weeks, I feel that I will never show undue enthusiasm again. My brain is past comprehending such titanic moves that have and are going on around me.[9]

Such a reaction was common among those describing their feelings for Mass Observation. On the Wirral the office worker who had described her excitement that afternoon at work in such detail explained in the evening that 'I am writing this with a feeling of spent energy – a sort of bitter reaction after being keyed up for what turned out to be a damp firework.'[10] In Finchley, north London, a young married woman told Mass Observation that 'immediately I heard the radio announcement of V Day I felt "flat". More than that I felt in some indescribable way cheated.' She and her husband had visited the West End in the late afternoon to see the decorations and heard the news when they returned home:

> Until that moment we had been quietly excited like most of the people around us, waiting anxiously for those vital words. When they were read to us it was as if all the excitement, all the bottled up feeling and tension evaporated without so much as a spontaneous 'hurrah'. I went to the kitchen and fetched orangeade. We clinked our glasses and endeavoured to be bright, but it was forced because we were alone and those vital words had come to us quietly and casually as if of no significance.[11]

After so many years of war, and so many days of expectation, the final, muted announcement of victory and peace in Europe left many feeling 'cheated' and unsure how to react.

For some of those listening to the wireless that evening there was little personal reason to celebrate. The war had seen so many casualties. In addition to the more than six million who had vanished into the obscenity that was the Holocaust, over five million German combatants were killed and at least 600,000 German civilians perished. Around twenty-seven million citizens of the Soviet Union had died, and at least seven and a half million Chinese. In India between two and three million people starved in the Bengal famine of 1943, and by the war's end more than two and a half million Japanese would be dead. In Britain the damage the war was leaving in its wake was less cataclysmic, but nevertheless profound: more than 264,000 combatants had been killed and at least 60,000 civilians. More than 170,000 British men had spent at least part of the war in German or Italian POW camps, and of the almost 140,000 Allied combatants taken prisoner by Japanese forces, around 30,000 would die. Many others would eventually return broken in body, mind or spirit.

Those who had lost loved ones, or who were waiting to see if they would return from POW camps or from the continued fighting in Asia, were of course less interested in celebrating victory in Europe. One Mass Observer recounted how she had given a children's ballet class in Finsbury Park that evening and, talking to one of her young pupils afterwards, discovered that she wouldn't be celebrating because her father was still in India.[12] An office worker in Birmingham spent the evening digging his allotment and found himself in opposition to the idea of celebrating the victory. His reasons for this were both political and personal:

> We shall not be putting any [flags] out... I am not in sympathy with the idea. After all, with my views, I can't countenance this display which is allied so closely, solely really, with military sentiment... I don't think that it is a proper way to celebrate the part ending of the most destructive war in the world's history. The problems facing us call more for calm and contemplation. And yet another reason: how upsetting it must be for those who still have relations in the far east. We have two close to us and the one fellow is now back in the Burma fighting. I fancy that his wife will not be too pleased with all the junketing and celebrating while she still has this worry on her mind.[13]

The continued fighting in Burma (now Myanmar) was also on the mind of a young shorthand typist from Middlesex, whose boyfriend was there, and in that of a teacher from Watford in Hertfordshire whose sister had a son there and 'was not interested in the news'.[14] Just outside the peaceful village of Rottingdean on the Sussex coast the mood in an Anglican convent – home to nuns, retired single women and girls 'who have got into trouble of various kinds and are here for the training', and who 'object to being here at the best of times, and especially so just now' – was subdued, not only because they lacked a wireless, but because 'our dear old Chaplain lost a son, killed in Italy, last October'.[15] The teacher at Abbotsholme boarding school in Derbyshire, who described her daytime feelings of excitement in the last chapter, was feeling 'ecstatic' by the evening, but tempered her feelings of happiness:

> In the presence of the Head Master and his wife because they had lost one of their sons in this war. Our second master

too had lost his only son; and our music master is a Jewish refugee from Oberammergau, having spent three weeks in a concentration camp.

She concluded, though, that 'I thought of the Japanese war, and the tasks of peace ahead; and I still rejoiced with all my heart.'[16]

Although many were missing loved ones, although the war went on in Asia and although the Ministry of Information may have done its utmost to dispel any excitement, many people shared this feeling of jubilation, and others were still determined to make the most of the evening. The chemist from Manchester who had earlier described the 'quiet air' in his mill found that by later afternoon the atmosphere was starting to change. The mill was full of nervous energy, with everyone 'working faster and singing', and an enforced pause in the work while they waited for some material to finish dying was filled with 'the "girls" dancing, jogging and singing'. As they left for home, still without confirmation of the war in Europe's end, he heard two women saying goodnight: 'Don't get too drunk,' said one, and the other replied, 'How can I enjoy myself without getting drunk?'[17] On his commute home across the city he was caught up in the general enthusiasm, finding himself stopping at a crowded draper's to buy 'two flags, a [Union] Jack for 2/11 and a Red Ensign for 2/9' (two shillings and elevenpence and two shillings and ninepence respectively). As he continued his journey he saw more evidence that people were preparing to celebrate, regardless of both the lack of official confirmation and the long-standing war regulations on waste:

> As I was passing the flats in West Gorton I saw some boys had already lit a huge bonfire, and were not obeying the Waste

Paper Order. They were burning cardboard cartons. People were putting out flags and bunting; 60% of the Jacks were upside down.[18]

Just across the Pennines in Sheffield another diarist was feeling rather subdued, but was 'trying to show some enthusiasm' for her son's sake. As in Manchester, her children and their neighbours were equally intent on having a bonfire, topped with an appropriate figure:

> The children commissioned our next door neighbour to model Hitler's face for their effigy. Our neighbour is an artist and he modelled it out of a great lump of clay. In a few minutes a great crowd had collected to see him work. It was a great joy to watch him. Finally it was finished and painted and the children gathered hay and stuffed the clothes and complete with swastika arm band and iron cross trundled it off in a wheelbarrow and lashed it to the top of the bonfire.[19]

Across the country, bonfires were being built and flags and bunting were appearing as people prepared, with varying levels of enthusiasm, to mark the end of the war in Europe.

For those unable to hear the evening's announcement of victory on the BBC, the presence of flags and bonfires could serve as evidence that the war in Europe must, finally, be over. For a young army clerk and his friends travelling from Edinburgh for leave in London, seeing these from their train window confirmed their belief that victory over Nazism had been officially verified:

> While we were on our journey down we noticed flags hanging out and when it got dark we saw bonfires burning all over the place. Thinking the announcement might have been made we asked a bloke at Darlington who then told us that the official

announcement would be three o'clock Tuesday. So our gang decided to celebrate by opening some bottles of beer we had with us.[20]

Naomi Mitchison, who was also heading south, though in considerably more comfort on the sleeper train from Glasgow, had heard the news before her train left, and although her diary doesn't tell us of her reaction, she does describe that of the crowd at Glasgow's Central Station, listening to the nine o'clock news, who were 'disappointed that there was nothing much, a kind of annoyance and frustration at its being dragged out, and irritation with Churchill for not speaking'. Mitchison's own feelings were mixed; on the one hand, she felt that 'now the trouble begins', as peace in Europe would deepen the divide between the Allies; but at the same time 'it was a most peculiar feeling, to be coming South, coming to London, and yet not coming into danger'.[21]

And London itself was most definitely getting ready to celebrate. Few of those who had crowded into Westminster and the West End, and who had doggedly stayed there throughout the delays and disappointments of the afternoon, were willing simply to go home and wait to celebrate the next day. By seven o'clock Mass Observation's investigator in Parliament Square had moved to a milk bar on Charing Cross Road:

> Wireless is on, and when the pips come on there is absolute silence. The milk bar is full, that is, the counter has people standing all down it, but only one deep. Headlines that it is expected that Churchill will not make his announcement until tomorrow. Immediate spontaneous 'oohs' of disappointment. No one pays much attention to the rest of the broadcast.

Writing up their report on VE Day, Mass Observation felt that in the early evening there were few spontaneous celebrations, and instead what there was 'seemed to be an effort rather than a need'. For example:

> 6 p.m. Regent Street. People beginning to anticipate celebrations. It is still unusual to see people in paper hats, two F20Cs and American GIs all wearing paper hats, walking along arm in arm in Regent Street, were stared at briefly by the passengers in a bus.

The presence of photographers, keen to capture images of the city in a carnival mood, reinforced Mass Observation's belief that the celebrations of the early evening were more of a performance than spontaneous outbursts of joy:

> Press photographers hold the attention of the crowds. One mounted on the plinth of Nelson's monument beckons to the vast crowd below to wave their flags while he photographs them. They not only wave their flags, but blow trumpets and blowers and rattles and generally make an uproar… After a while the photographer makes the V for Victory sign, Churchill style, and the crowd catch on. They fling their arms high into the air V fashion, fingers making the V sign. He takes many such photographs and each time the crowd get more and more excited… a rival photographer comes onto the scene. This time a military man, his camera mounted on an army lorry standing in the roadway. This time the crowd need no coaching, they fling their arms V fashion in the air and blow trumpets and rattles and look very jolly indeed.[22]

A desire to be a part of history, to be recorded for ever as having 'been there' at the moment of victory? A longing to lose oneself in the multitude and to be part of something bigger than the individual? A hope that the spontaneous excitement that Mass Observation found so lacking in the early evening could be found in the crowd? Or a simple desire to celebrate on the streets of the capital with others? All of these, and more, drew people to the streets and sites of the city centre early that evening.

One of those present in London at this time was the young ATS clerk who had left her family that morning with the words 'see you after the war!' By early evening she and her comrades were becoming exasperated with the lack of firm news and worried about their evening:

> Feeling frustrated, we ATS trickle back to the billet; it is our CB [confined to barracks] night – it would be! We are determined however that when the balloon does go up we will break out and see the fun. Knightsbridge is beginning to blossom with balloons and bunting, and it is a lovely sunny afternoon. The conductress ignores our outstretched bus-fares but collects it from civilian passengers.
>
> We have an egg and boiled bacon for tea; in our rooms we grouse at the way the public has been built up to this point only to be let down by lack of official news. Suddenly, one of the girls, leaping out of the window yells 'Hey – something about three o'clock tomorrow!' With one accord we race round to the Rec[reation] room where the radio is, but it is turned off. At this moment the bell rings for Parade. We troop into the Concert Hall, all talking at once. I realise that I have my bedroom slippers on and have to dash back to put my shoes on! Then, the Company Commander announces that tomorrow is VE Day, Churchill will speak at 3 p.m., gives out a few other items, then 'any questions?' The shout goes up – can we go out? Smiling broadly, she gives us permission, but we must be in by midnight...

> We rush back for our hats, and jump on a bus to Hyde Park Corner. The western end of Piccadilly is no more crowded than usual, just milling people, mostly in uniform, strolling in either direction. 'I thought there'd be *millions* more people out' remarks K. Nearer Piccadilly Circus there are more, and we stop to buy red, white and blue favours for exorbitant prices from hawkers, who already line the pavements and are doing a roaring trade. By an entrance to the Tube, a soldier is being helped along, a white cloth round his forehead, his hand to his face and blood pouring from it. M. says 'I don't think I'm going to like this' but as it happened this was the only distressing sight we were to see all evening.[23]

We will re-join her and her friends later that night.

A Mass Observer on his way home from work in Cricklewood to south London was watching the same crowds around Piccadilly from the top floor of his bus:

> In Piccadilly Circus there were great crowds of people on the pavements and on the roadway. Nobody seemed quite to know why they were there, although of course it was obvious they were all just waiting for the 'word' to start 'celebrations.'[24]

They were luckier than the City worker who had spent much of the day in anticipation of the announcement, walking to Mansion House in the late afternoon, where he found there was 'already a crowd… with flags being unfurled and planes overhead'. Travelling on to the West End, he was perplexed to find that despite 'Surrender' being the headline in the evening papers, and 'crowds everywhere', there was still no news at six o'clock, at which point he gave up and went home to south London.[25] A twenty-nine-year-old soldier, on leave and shopping in London with his fiancée, also found himself in the West End that evening, where they had gone to the Pavilion Cinema on Piccadilly to see the film *The Fifth Chair*, a comedy starring the American comedian Fred Allen as a ringmaster searching for his inheritance, which is hidden, for some reason, within the seat of one of five chairs. Waiting on Piccadilly to meet a friend at six o'clock, they watched the crowds that were building:

> There were noticeable crowds at Piccadilly Circus, along the pavements and around Eros [the statue at the centre of Piccadilly, which had, until recently, been covered to protect it from bombs]. An unemployed band played 'Does Your Mother Come From Ireland' and 'Little Grey Home in the West'… There was much standing and waiting and speculating. Three bombers flew back and forth over the Circus.[26]

These crowds would continue to grow as more and more people were drawn towards Westminster and the West End, the heart of government and of the city's nightlife, and the place where people had gathered to party, protest and celebrate for centuries.

The desire to be part of a larger, joyful crowd was widespread. While some Mass Observers reflected on their personal feelings and responses to global events, others – perhaps remembering the original Mass Observation desire that their observers be 'meteorological stations from whose reports a weather-map of popular feeling can be compiled' – were keen to record what other people were thinking or planning.[27] One diarist had asked a young woman in his office if she was planning to celebrate:

> Celebrate? I don't know how yet, but I shall celebrate all right. I think I shall go into town and look around until I find a crowd doing what I want to do, and then I shall join in with them.[28]

Another diarist from Great Baddow, just outside Chelmsford in Essex, had asked his office junior what she wanted to do; she replied, 'I want to go up to town and go mad.'[29] In Kilburn, north London, one Mass Observer noticed that, after news of the victory had been confirmed, 'a sudden push began, to the public houses, the West End and the main streets'. The pull of the city centre was strong, 'and the general tendency was to walk south, i.e. towards the West End, though most won't get further than the next public house'.[30] Individually people may not have been sure of exactly how they should mark the news, but the pull of being with others, who might just have a better plan, was recorded in diaries across the country.

And it was not only city centres, but local pubs – the traditional space for community gatherings, whether in celebration or commiseration – that were starting to get crowded. Not just in London, but in towns and cities all over the country people looked for others to confirm the news, and to celebrate with. The social worker from west London, who had described hanging the Soviet Union's flag out of the lavatory window earlier that day, had visited central London in the early evening for a meeting of the Socialist Medical Association, founded in the 1930s to campaign for a national health service, before heading back to her home in Ealing. There she, her landlady and their neighbours decided to go 'in search of a drink to "celebrate"'. Many others had the same idea, and in a manner that would no doubt have pleased the bureaucrats planning for VE Day the previous year, the local pubs were starting to run out of drinks:

> We try one pub, where there is nothing but beer and ginger wine. We then try another, where there is a livelier atmosphere,

plenty of decorations up, and we succeed in getting some port... On our way home we go to yet another pub – very full of people, but again nothing to be had but beer and ginger wine... Plenty of people are wandering about the roads, and there are plenty of decorations about. The local fire-station is floodlit, quite early in the evening.[31]

Some had more luck than others. The pub eventually chosen by the Birmingham office worker and air-raid warden and her colleagues that evening was initially 'as quiet as a church'. As the evening went on, though, more and more people came to celebrate and the pub became 'very noisy and smoky', with 'people singing songs of the last war... but in rather a laboured and not very spontaneous round'. She and her friends moved to a quieter corner, where 'our eyes got pricky and our heads just a shade muzzy'. As air-raid wardens, she and her comrades had been at the heart of the Blitz on Birmingham, a centre for armaments production and one of the most-bombed cities in the country. Killing more than 2,000 people and injuring thousands more, the raids had been described in a letter to Tom Harrisson as 'a moonlight massacre'.[32] By 1945 these raids were a memory, but in Birmingham, as elsewhere, their legacy remained. Walking home later that night she 'enjoyed coming home "over the crater"... through the derelict gardens at the back where it was cool and quiet and smelt fresh'.[33] The city itself seemed initially unsure about how to mark the news, the *Birmingham Gazette* describing the reception as 'doubtful at first, but later joy was let loose' as:

> The news spread like wildfire. It got into the bars, the smoke rooms, and the dancehalls. The crowds rushed into the streets.

The newspaper sellers were almost mobbed, somebody started singing... and soon everybody was at it, irrespective of tune or anything else.

In the city's factories, however, 'the night shift workers received the news with an initial outburst of excitement, and then calmly carried on... determined to finish the job at hand'.[34] The continuing war in Asia may not have been at the front of many minds that evening, but it was still driving the munitions factories of the West Midlands.

Just over forty miles away another Mass Observer was trying to mark the victory in a Leicester suburb. As their neighbours drifted home from work in the early evening, 'flags began to appear at windows and in gardens and occasional streamers could be seen'. The suburb seemed 'determined to mark the occasion but also to be very dignified about it'. The writer wondered somewhat wistfully whether perhaps 'there were scenes of wild hilarity' elsewhere.[35] According to the *Leicester Evening Mail*, this was relatively unlikely in the city, where local magistrates had approved an extension of pub opening hours from 10 p.m. to 11 p.m. on VE Day, but 'in order to avoid any misunderstanding... VE Day is the day on which the Prime Minister announces the termination of hostilities in Europe'.[36]

Such scenes could, however, sometimes be found in the most unexpected places. Facing each other across the River Thames in Berkshire were the historic, but perhaps rather staid, towns of Windsor and Eton, the former home to the Royal Family throughout the war, the latter the site of Eton College, public school to the ruling elite and producer of religious, military and political leaders since its foundation in the fifteenth century. But as an Eton master reported, both towns let their hair down on the evening of 7 May:

> After 8 p.m. there was continuous hooting, flag-waving, throwing of water, squirting everything with mini-maxes, stirrup pumps, and buckets; there were large scale mobs, traffic was stopped in the streets until about 11 p.m., when things got quieter, and most people went home. Shouting and singing continued all night intermittently.

Far from disapproving of the lack of restraint shown by the good citizens of these two Berkshire towns, the schoolmaster recorded that as well as observing the revelry, he 'joined in it'.[37]

Reports of such civic abandon were, however, the exception rather than the rule among that evening's Mass Observers. Most spent the evening alone or with family and friends, often reflecting on the turbulence and changes of the past extraordinary five and a half years. In Southend-on-Sea one young woman, living with her parents after travelling abroad with the ATS before being invalided out of the service, was wishing that she could be part of larger celebrations. She and her parents went to the local pub, where they:

> Met several friends, but generally speaking nobody was particularly excited. I should very much liked to have gone up to the West End where all the fun and games really does go on, but it was impossible for me of course to risk the crowds.

On the way home she noticed several bonfires and was struck by the floodlights lighting up the local Odeon cinema – 'we stared at it almost as though we were visitants from another planet'. Her thoughts were quickly brought back to the war years, though, as Southend celebrated with fireworks and 'hooters and sirens from the boats on the Thames and in the docks'. In bed she:

> Thought how strange it was that I should have started off the war in my own bed in this room, and I had finished up there, despite the blitz, joining the ATS, going abroad, and being in six different hospitals, not to mention the buzz bombs and rockets.

She hadn't been asleep for long when she was woken by:

> A terrific flash and noise and for the moment I completely forgot that it was all over and I waited for the crumbling roar of falling masonry – but of course 'there was a Peace on' at last! It was a thunderstorm.[38]

In nearby Brentwood a teacher was similarly confused by the storm, when she and a friend went for a walk later that evening:

> May arrived to say there was a glow over London. It seemed very queer to see it and realise what it was due to – we have seen so many glows in that direction but due to quite different causes. We walked up to the brickfields a while where we heard the nightingale. Then brilliant flashes began and bangs. At first we thought they were fireworks, but gradually it dawned on us that they were thunder and lightning. As we came home a searchlight began to flash the V sign, and I realised it was after midnight.[39]

For some people, gratitude for the coming European peace was accompanied by something else: a sense of imminent individual changes, and the personal impact of the conflict, alongside the social and political ones. A civil servant in

Harrogate, Yorkshire, who had been just seventeen when the war started, was spending a quiet evening at home, doing her mending, when she heard the nine o'clock news on the BBC. Feeling 'very limp', she hung out the landlady's flag and went to bed early. First, though, she wrote a letter to her mother, trying to explain, perhaps to herself, her reaction:

> When war was declared I had just left school... all my growing up years had been spent under wartime conditions. It is impossible for me to conceive [of] life being very different from what it has been during the past wartime years... I thought of what all these years had brought me in experience, the numerous yet passing friends, extensive travelling over the country... I could not fully grasp the situation.[40]

In Berkshire a poultry farmer was feeling a similar sense of melancholy:

> For some reason that I find hard to analyse, I felt a profound depression. Was glad, naturally, that the guns had ceased, that no more lives in Europe at any rate were being lost, but could not get up any sense of rejoicing. Compared my feelings with those on the outbreak of war... Then I felt a sober sense of, what? Relief that the tension of 'peace' was ending, a determination to face whatever came with what courage I might, a mounting tide of excitement. As for 1940, those were exhilarating days, I was carried on a wave of exultation. Why, on the eve of V Day, could I feel nothing but a dull depression? Perhaps it was reaction after so many years of war, more probably it was the memory of those frightful camps... still more it was disappointment at the farce of San Francisco [the United Nations Conference on International Organization]... Those 16 arrested Poles by Russia has had a profoundly depressing effect on me.

After a warm day in the south of England the storm that was to wake the diarist in Southend was building and she went out into her garden to watch:

> I stood in the silent garden and looked at the silent sky – the thunder was only lowering, the storm had not yet broken – and said aloud 'it's over, there will be no more guns, no more destruction, no more dead', and I burst into tears.[41]

Perhaps she was crying for the end of the 'excitement' and 'exhilaration' of the war years, when the combined anxiety and tedium of daily life could be accompanied by a heightened sense of consequence, of living 'through history' and being a part of something bigger than oneself. Perhaps it was the realisation that although the war in Europe was over, the world was still dangerously divided, and the ruptures that had been knitted over by the necessities of wartime were coming apart again. And perhaps they were simply tears of relief, a response to the heightened stress and tension of the past six years, and of recent days of waiting and wondering. The European war that had destroyed so much, taken so many lives, changing the world for ever, but shattering lives, relationships, cities and entire countries as it did so, was finally over.

One of the changes that the war had brought to Britain was the presence of refugees and volunteer combatants and workers from around the world. The Polish government-in-exile, based first in France and then, from 1940, in London, meant that there was a sizeable Polish presence in Britain throughout the war, including some 17,000 troops and many civilian refugees. Among them were a mother and son who were lodging with a family in the comfortable suburban town of Bearsden, on the north-west edge of Glasgow. The daughter of the family was a social worker and a Mass Observer, invalided and living with her parents while her husband was fighting in Burma, and she carefully recorded the thoughts and preoccupations of their lodgers that evening. As elsewhere, there was some confusion over whether or not the next day would be a holiday:

> Her son, aged 16, said that he wasn't going to school anyway whether it was a holiday or not, and added in the next breath that there shouldn't be a holiday till Russia was smashed. He then proceeded to give us a long account of how well we were equipped for war against Russia, and how soon the Russians might be expected to collapse.[42]

Divided between Germany and the Soviet Union in 1939 and subsequently occupied by Nazi Germany, Poland had been at the epicentre of the war in Europe – as the site of the Nazi extermination camps, including Auschwitz-Birkenau and Treblinka, and with its capital city destroyed in the aftermath of the Warsaw Rising. Britain and France had gone to war, at least in part, to defend the right of Poland to self-determination, and the Yalta Conference of February 1945 had seen Stalin promise free and fair elections in Poland. However, the establishment the previous year of a Soviet-backed provisional government in the east of Poland, in opposition to the government-in-exile in Britain, suggested that his word might not have been his bond. Polish exiles were right to be nervous: by 1947 a communist government, loyal to Moscow, was in control of the country, and Poland was to spend the next four decades as a key member of the Eastern Bloc.

Just over 12,000 Czech refugees also spent the war in Britain, including 669 of the 10,000 Jewish children who found refuge in British homes and hostels as part of the *Kindertransport* scheme, which brought Jewish children from Germany and Austria (and later from Czechoslovakia and Poland) to Britain. One of these Czech refugees, a twenty-six-year-old clerk living in south London and travelling home at the end of 7 May, had found it difficult that afternoon 'to feel glad and happy'. While her fellow commuters discussed how they would celebrate, she was thinking of Prague, her home town, where fighting continued and 'the blood that had to flow in this last, desperate fight, of the beautiful buildings of Prague'. Later that evening the 'flat next door hoisted the Stars and Stripes and the Union Jack flag. On the other side the house had the English flag also.' Not to be outdone:

> We put out a Czech and an English flag, a coloured decoration of little flags and the picture of Mr Churchill we used to have in the sitting room which bears a Czech under-title: 'Czechoslovakia – the hour of your liberation will come!'

Two days before, at the beginning of the Prague uprising, they had 'changed the "will" to "has"'.[43] Any liberation was short-lived, however, and – like Poland by 1948 – Czechoslovakia was effectively under the control of the Soviet Union.

While refugees and displaced people were justifiably concerned with events in their home countries, other Mass Observers were preoccupied with more short-term plans. For one physiotherapist, 7 May was particularly special as it was her birthday. Both staff and patients in the hospital where she worked were 'in a mood to celebrate'. But well-laid plans for a buffet and dance at the hospital that night were interrupted when the six o'clock news failed to announce the much-anticipated peace. Feeling like a 'deflated balloon', she went to lie down, but the medical superintendent announced that, although it was too late to organise a buffet, the dance could still go ahead. Luckily a ward had fallen empty the previous week and a folding stage and piano were quickly installed, while 'the word VICTORY was hung in large red, white and blue letters from the ceiling, the walls were draped with flags [and] two magnificent lions rampant appeared behind the stage'. She went to bed later that night 'feeling that it had, after all, been another happy birthday, the war did end on the 7th May!'[44]

In Brockley, south-east London the housewife and mother who had so vividly described bombing and evacuation with her young son in 1940 was in a reflective mood that evening. She had felt 'really elated' during the day, and had listened to every news broadcast that she could with 'terrific enthusiasm'. The coming of peace gave her:

> The feeling that it was all an illusion maybe as that the years of war had been something that I had dreamed (though my bomb damaged house offered proof enough that this was not so). I could not really believe it and yet the logical 'me' knew that it was so!

After she had put her children to bed she still felt 'a restlessness that would not allow me to settle'. By ten o clock she was ironing the washing that she had done that morning, but when a neighbour came to visit, she suggested that they take a walk 'up to the hilly fields' to see whether they could spot any bonfires:

> She was game, so out we went together, leaving the children in bed asleep – a thing I have never done since the war started. It was good to know that they were safe! There was a glow in the sky which reminded me of other nights when the glow in the sky had been the aftermath of a raid. We could hear ships on the river blowing their sirens and I was filled with a desire to be

in Liverpool and to hear the ships on the Mersey letting go with theirs. I bet they made a merry row! From the hilly fields we could see many bonfires, but were surprised that so few people were about. We returned and went to bed at twenty minutes after midnight after an extra warm 'goodnight'.[45]

A member of the RAF writing for Mass Observation also had a long evening. His unit had been expecting to be deployed in Europe, but as the Allies advanced, this had been cancelled and they had had 'less and less to do ever since' in their base near Luton in Bedfordshire. That evening he was in the local village church 'with a young chap who had promised to show me the basic ideas of organ playing – a thing I have always wanted to do'. They were still there at ten o'clock when:

> A very elderly and decrepit lady enquired if she might lock the church. She said that the news had come through of complete German surrender. My friend said 'just a minute' and went back to the keyboard to play 'Praise God From Whom All Blessings Flow' then we switched off the bellow, turned off the lights and went down to the village where people were singing and dancing outside the pub while others were decorating the houses with flags and streamers.
>
> When the pub closed the people seemed to melt away. We went to a transport café and ate fish and chips... When we got back to camp we found a great deal of excitement as we were to close down from midnight until 8 a.m. Thursday. Passes were arranged for all who could possibly get home and it was arranged to run transport into Luton at 4.30 a.m. which would serve those waiting for the first trains, both for London and the north.
>
> I washed and shaved by the aid of an electric torch and then 'got down' until 4.30. We piled into the transport and raced through the semi-darkness to the town.[46]

Heading for Macclesfield in Cheshire, he was travelling in the opposite direction to so many people, who hoped to see in the victory in central London.

As the evening drew on, Mass Observation was still in Trafalgar Square, watching and recording the crowds that were drawn to the city centre that evening:

> Nine o'clock and the news is on. For a few seconds there's a strange stillness in the square as people listen to what the announcer is saying. This time the waiting crowd hear that Mr Churchill is to speak at three o'clock tomorrow, and that Wednesday is to be VE Day, with Thursday VE plus one day. Quietly and soberly the crowd disperses.[47]

This might have been the last time that evening that the crowds in central London were either quiet or sober.

Soon after ten o'clock the investigator in Trafalgar Square left for home, after describing how the crowd in the square had formed 'one large circle and arms intertwined the young people sing "Auld Lang Syne"'. At nearby Cambridge Circus, at the top of Shaftesbury Avenue, things were slightly less decorous. A large group had gathered to watch a man playing the 'hurdy gurdy' while two women danced, 'first the Lambeth Walk, then the Hokey Pokey':

> They are wearing bright colours – general effect red, white and blue, and whenever opportunity permits they pull up their skirts to show their bloomers, amid shrieks from the crowd… M45D totters about in a drunken dance and the crowd is uproariously amused… Investigator walks down to Greek Street where a large bonfire is burning. F50C to Investigator:
>
> 'Oh, you should have been here a moment ago. They had a Guy Fawkes of Hitler and they burnt him. Only thing was he didn't have a hat on. It was so silly you see, they didn't have a hat on him.

Perhaps somewhat puzzled by the lack of a hat, or by the importance attributed to this, the intrepid investigator headed towards Leicester Square, the centre of nightlife in the West End, and often of public misbehaviour, since the eighteenth century.

There she found the square and Piccadilly Circus 'filled with people'. News teams were there as well, looking for the pictures and stories that would fill the pages of newspapers the next day:

> Camera men from above Scotts [a seafood restaurant and the favoured haunt of James Bond author Ian Fleming], shouting to the crowd to 'look up.' Flashes from cameras. Flags wave and men with hooters making great noise in the streets. General noise of squawking and indistinguishable shouting. The population looks bewildered rather than elated... It is practically impossible to move across Piccadilly Circus, but when one is out of it and walking down Haymarket things are more or less normal.

Further north at Marble Arch, crowds had also gathered, but some of them at least had come together with a specific purpose:

> Groups of people singing, one particularly noticeable crowd singing hymns loudly with apparently trained voices. M55C in dark suit conducting. Other groups singing but not sufficiently loudly to make any impression against the loudness of the hymns.

While Oxford Street was 'just as Oxford Street is on any other night', Regent Street had 'more people about, and those that are for the most part rather rowdy'. Heading back towards Piccadilly, the investigator found that multiple bonfires had been lit, with a crowd dancing around a particularly large fire on Coventry Street. This fire was in fact so large that the Fire Brigade eventually arrived to extinguish it. The investigator, tiring by this point in the evening, joined a large queue for the Lyons Corner House in Coventry Street, which in its heyday served tea, cakes and light meals to around 5,000 people per day and was open around the clock. But even this large and efficient establishment was overwhelmed by the sheer numbers of would-be diners that evening:

> Sparks are rising up as huge logs of wood are hauled from a bombed building behind a wooden poster-covered wall on the south side of Coventry Street. Excited cries of 'Ooh' and 'Look' whenever the sparks are particularly spectacular. The queue, two deep, is almost indistinguishable from the thick crowd of people moving along Coventry Street past the huge circular crowd round the fire... Most people are in couples and there is quite a bit of kissing in dark corners... The queue moves forward terribly slowly...
>
> Army officer suggests burning the wooden shutter of Lyons, which is propped against the wall, and this is hauled across to the fire. F25C who can see from her position on the wall: 'Look, there's a fire engine. I wonder if it's going to put the fire out?' Cries of 'spoilsport'. Fire engine is drawn up by the side of the fire...
>
> It comes on to rain and people pass more rapidly. Young man with no trousers on walks past nonchalantly. French sailor and French tank corps roll past. Stop in front of inv[estigator]. Tank corps looks at inv., stops and kisses her. M25B (with inv.) 'Look, that's enough'. Tank corps: 'Her husband... sorry'...
> It starts to rain seriously. The bonfire crowd press back so that those people in the queue come under the shelter of the Lyons building. Police run for shelter... AFS [the Auxiliary Fire Service] with hoses gets to work on the fire and within a few

minutes it is right out. Shouts and hisses from crowd, which disperses, all except the Lyons queue. It is about two o'clock. The streets are about deserted now.

Possibly caught in that most British of situations – committed for so long to a slow-moving queue that to leave becomes unthinkable – the investigator and her husband were eventually admitted to the Lyons Corner House just before 4 a.m. There they found a clientele that was already starting to look back on the night that victory began to be celebrated:

> At 03.45 hours Inv. gets into Lyons. There is still a queue inside, but it is at least dry. When one gets allowed into the restaurant, the few empty chairs are deceptive because one is invariably told that 'they belong to someone who has gone to fetch a paper.' People come back with them. The first pictures of London celebrations.[48]

The tired investigator finally caught one of the first Underground trains home at 5.30 in the morning of VE Day.

The papers that the tired revellers in Lyons Corner House were reading were dominated by pictures and stories of London that night. The *Daily Express* told its readers of 'tens of thousands' who 'sang [and] danced around where Eros used to be. It was London's West End on its greatest night for nearly six years of war.'[49] The *Daily Mirror* carried the same story, accompanied by a photo of a young serviceman 'on top of the world' after climbing to the top of hoardings in Piccadilly 'to celebrate the lifting of the shadow from Europe'.[50] The *News Chronicle* also chose Piccadilly as the focus for its front page, describing it as 'the hub of all celebrations', where 'thousands upon thousands of people, airmen, infantrymen, flying men, sailors of all the

Allies, girls in blue and girls in khaki milled around the circus'.[51] Headlines in the *Daily Mail* explained how it had been 'all quiet until 9 p.m. – then the London crowds went mad in the West End', while readers of *The Times*, perhaps accustomed to more sober news over their breakfasts, woke to stories of 'remarkable scenes at Piccadilly', where 'civilians and service men and women thronged the road and pavement, carrying flags and wearing paper hats'.[52] Among the service women 'thronging' the streets of the West End and 'milling around Piccadilly' that night were the ATS clerk and her friends, released from their evening in barracks in Knightsbridge. After arriving in the West End, they had spent the early evening wandering between Piccadilly, Leicester Square and Trafalgar Square and soon after nine o'clock found themselves in Westminster, disappointed that neither pubs nor places of worship appeared to be open:

> Some of us want to go into Westminster Abbey for a few minutes prayer, but it is closed. So into a YMCA for a lemonade (all we can get to toast victory).[53]

Refreshed by their lemonades, they returned to the crowded streets to join in the fun that was so diligently reported on the next morning's front pages.

The nation might have had to wait until the following afternoon for Churchill's victory speech, but leaving the YMCA, she found that:

> London is really getting into the victory mood, without waiting for Mr Churchill. The Embankment is quiet but Trafalgar Square is gayer than ever, dancing and singing The Marseillaise and Knees Up Mother Brown. The Palais Glide [like the Lambeth Walk, a dance for groups of people rather than couples] in the Haymarket, and little bonfires on the

pavements, fed by newspapers. Then – Piccadilly Circus again. It is dark now, no street lights and few lighted windows. But it is one mass of yelling, laughing, singing, shrieking people; a small sports car is trying to wriggle through and its folded roof is in shreds… Most of the men are in uniform – all services and nationalities. The Canadians are noisy, the sailors are merry, the airmen are drunk (or pretend to be), the Americans have a girl apiece and are the quietest of all. Back along Piccadilly the crowds are thinning; another bus rattles by with figures clinging on all round. All the way to Knightsbridge, happy groups pass and people still hope to get buses home. This is midnight, Victory Eve – and – oh, my poor feet![54]

One destination was missing from almost all the reports for Mass Observation that evening, yet was central to much of the newspaper coverage the next morning: Buckingham Palace. The *Daily Express* described how 'a great crowd flocked to Buckingham Palace last night. Some of them danced. Some sang. At times there was a chant "We want the King!" Faces appeared at a Palace window. There was loud cheering.'[55] The *Daily Mail* explained how 'waving flags, marching in step, with linked arms or half-embraced, the people strode down the great thoroughfares – Piccadilly, Regent Street, the Mall, to the portals of Buckingham Palace'.[56] Readers of the *Daily Telegraph* were told how the same 'cosmopolitan crowd', with many representatives of the Allied nations, was a 'mile long' outside the Palace.[57] Mass Observation may not have sent an investigator to the Palace, but luckily for them an 'excited' observer was there:

> We set out with no definite aim in view, but more or less followed the crowd… The crowd carried us down the Mall to Buckingham Palace – the main focus of attention in the

whole of London that night. We were lucky. After only about a quarter of an hour's waiting – during which the crowd sang, shouted 'We want Georgie' and raised a stupendous cheer if any of the hundreds of windows opened a tiny crack – the King and Queen came out. They were greeted by a terrific roar and a forest of Union Jacks, handkerchiefs – anything that could be waved was waved – and stayed on the balcony for, I should imagine, four minutes. After having seen them we thought that we had seen the best of the sights that London could offer, and made our way back via Whitehall and St James, where the flaming torches added a touch of old London.[58]

In the absence of a speech or appearance by Churchill – a point at which the crowd could shout and cheer and embrace one another while victory was definitively announced – this impromptu appearance by the King and Queen sufficed. Buckingham Palace and its inhabitants had been chosen by the London crowds to fill the void left by the tight-lipped statement from the Ministry of Information and the official deferment of celebrations until the next day.

While not everyone joined the crowds gathering in town and city centres, with many preferring to spend the evening quietly with friends or family, almost everyone who kept a diary for Mass Observation on 7 May found time to pause and note the end of the war in Europe. For those who did participate, these celebrations were spontaneous, created by the people who were drawn to the city, town and village centres, to the pubs and bonfires and the impromptu street gatherings. The formal celebrations could wait until the next day; on the evening of 7 May the people of the people's war were going to mark the conflict's end in their own way.

PROLOGUE

8 May 1945
An End and a Beginning

The war in Europe both began and ended with a storm. The thunderstorm recorded by Mass Observers in southern England late in the evening of 7 May was still rumbling around London and the Home Counties as the clock passed midnight. Almost six years earlier a thunderstorm had hit London overnight on the 2–3 September, as Neville Chamberlain acknowledged that the policy of appeasement had failed to prevent another European conflict and prepared to declare war against Nazi Germany. The mood in Downing Street in the early hours of 8 May 1945 must have been quite different, as Churchill worked on through the night, contemplating not only victory in Europe, but the ongoing war in Asia and the complex political manoeuvres of Stalin, the leader of the Soviet Union, one of the 'Big Three' Allied nations. As the European war came to an end, the Cold War was beginning.

Stalin was as determined that Poland would come within the ambit of the Soviet Union as he had been when Molotov and Ribbentrop signed the Nazi-Soviet Pact in 1939 and divided that ill-starred country between them. Operation Barbarossa, launched on 22 June 1941, had marked the sudden and violent end of the pact and had seen Nazi troops push deep into the western Soviet Union, almost reaching Moscow by the year's end, but by early 1945 the Red Army was driving Nazi troops before it as it fought its way through Poland and towards Berlin. While Stalin had agreed to free elections in Poland at the Yalta Conference in February 1945, possession was, in practice, nine-tenths of the law, and the Polish government-in-exile, based in London, found itself effectively excluded from power. The Polish Committee of National Liberation, formed largely of Polish communist organisations and backed by Stalin's Soviet Union, expanded its authority as the Soviet army moved west.

Anthony Eden, then Foreign Secretary, was attending the San Francisco Conference that founded the United Nations and, together with America, had demanded more information about the sixteen Polish prisoners being held in Moscow's Lubyanka prison. Moscow, however, remained silent. Readers of the *Daily Mail* had been warned the previous day that not only had no reply been received, but 'it seems possible, indeed, that there will be no reply'.[1] *The Times* reported the words of Stanisław Mikołajczyk, former prime minister of the government-in-exile, who argued that 'the liberation of these democratic leaders and the honest execution of the Crimean resolutions [the Yalta Agreement] were an imperative necessity'.[2] The war in Europe was all but over, but the desire for a lasting peace – visualised in the *Daily Mirror*'s famous Zec cartoon of a wounded soldier clambering over the ruins of a European town, holding a wreath representing victory and peace in Europe and captioned 'Here you are! Don't lose it again!' – was already slipping through the world's fingers.[3]

Pockets of fighting still continued. The Silesian city of Breslau (now Wrocław in Poland), one of Hitler's 'fortress cities' to be defended at all costs, had finally surrendered to Soviet troops the previous evening. News of the end of the siege was announced in newspapers on the morning of 8 May. In the United States readers of the *New York Times* were told that 'more than 40,000 Germans and their commander General von Gnikow were captured as Breslau, capital of Lower Silesia, fell after an eighty-four-day siege – almost ten times as long as Berlin held out'.[4] *The Times* thought the siege had lasted eighty-two days and 'had been crumbling to pieces block by block, in bitter street fighting'.[5] Just 134 miles south-west of Breslau, the Prague Uprising continued even as Nazi forces across the continent were ordered to surrender. The Nazi leadership in the city had refused to recognise the German surrender announced the previous day, calling it 'enemy propaganda' and declaring their determination to fight on.[6] And fight on they did. The front pages of the *Daily Mirror* and the *Daily Express* both carried news of Prague alongside its coverage of the previous night's celebrations in London, and they made sobering reading. The *Daily Mirror* explained how:

> In a final burst of fiendishness, SS troops in Prague last night were firing the last shots of the war on helpless Czech civilians. SS men went through the streets driving people out of their homes as other SS troops waited to mow them down with machine guns.[7]

The front page of the *Daily Express* was equally alarming:

> The Germans are throwing hand grenades at houses showing national flags. German aircraft have been dropping bombs on Broadcasting House and on other public buildings in the midst of the city.[8]

A personal plea for help came from a soldier in Prague who spoke on Czech radio with a strong Scottish accent and who was 'obviously agitated and spoke without rehearsal'.[9] This was probably William Greig, a prisoner of war who had escaped from a camp on the German-Czech border and was being sheltered by a family in the Czech capital when the uprising began, and who took part in the defence of the radio station. Increasingly sporadic fighting was to continue in Prague until early in the morning of 9 May, when Soviet tanks arrived in the city centre.

Theresienstadt, the Nazi ghetto and concentration camp established by the SS in 1941 in the Czech town of Terezin, had recently seen its SS administrators flee from the advancing Red Army. The Red Cross had taken over the camp's administration on 2 May, but it was not formally liberated until 8 May, when Soviet troops overcame the remnants of the Wehrmacht nearby. Like the other camps liberated by horrified soldiers that year, Theresienstadt was suffering a typhoid epidemic, and many of those who were freed, together with those trying to care for them, would die over the coming weeks. News of Theresienstadt came too late for the VE Day newspapers, but the findings of a Soviet-led inquiry into the camps at Auschwitz-Birkenau, liberated by the Soviet Army in January 1945, had been reported on Radio Moscow and published in *Pravda* the previous day. *The Times* was among the British newspapers to summarise the report, which used the Polish name of Oświęcim (rather than Auschwitz) throughout:

> The commission finds that more than 400,000 people perished at Oswiecim between 1941 and the beginning of this year. They included citizens of the Soviet Union, Poland, France, Belgium, Holland, Czechoslovakia, Yugoslavia, Hungary, Italy and Greece… The commission, which had previously investigated conditions at Majdanek, Tremblinka [*sic*] and other

'annihilation camps' describes Oswiecim as the worst in its experience. Departments were maintained where experiments of a revolting character were conducted by German doctors named in the report... The report states that most of the deportees who arrived at the camp were killed at once in gas chambers. On an average one in six was selected for work... The Germans evacuated about 60,000 inmates when they retreated, more than 10,000 of those who remained were freed by the Russians. Seven tons of women's hair was found, ready for dispatch to Germany. Human teeth, from which gold fillings had been extracted, were piled several feet high. A vanload of used shaving brushes and nearly 100,000 children's suits of clothes, also used, were discovered in depots.[10]

Coming so soon after news of the conditions found when British troops reached the camp at Bergen-Belsen in April 1945, the emerging details of the atrocities of Auschwitz served as a reminder, if such a reminder was necessary, of the nature of the regime that had just been defeated.

While much of Europe was preparing to celebrate, portents of future conflicts, political realignment and upheaval were surfacing elsewhere, not least in Asia where the war against imperial Japan continued. Australian troops had been fighting in Papua New Guinea since 1944 and in Borneo since early 1945. Progress was slow and casualties heavy in the difficult jungle positions: in the battle for Slater's Knoll on the New Guinea Island of Bougainville just before VE Day, more than 5,600 Japanese and almost 200 Australians were killed in only a few weeks of fighting. Further north in the Philippines, US troops were battling their way north from Manila towards the Cagayan Valley, only securing Allied control there in June. The Battle of Okinawa, the bloodiest of any in the Pacific, was also grinding on. US troops had invaded the southerly Japanese island, which sits approximately halfway between Taiwan and the main islands of Japan, on 1 April; by the time fighting finished in June 1945, at least 50,000 Allied and 84,000 Japanese troops were casualties, both outnumbered by the almost 150,000 civilian dead on the small island. The heavy bombing of the Japanese mainland by the US Air Force in the Pacific, which had started with the near-destruction of Tokyo in February, was to continue until Hiroshima and Nagasaki were annihilated by atomic bombs on 6 and 9 of August. Imperial Japan would finally surrender six days later, on 15 August 1945.

Britain was, of course, also an imperial power, and its war had been fought by the Empire, led by London, but with the participation of hundreds of thousands of troops and civilians from around the world. Men from as far afield as India, Sri Lanka, Canada, Australia and New Zealand travelled to Britain to fly with the RAF; women from West Africa nursed in British hospitals; and almost 900 men from British Honduras (now Belize) volunteered to spend the war as forestry workers in Scotland. It would have been tempting for veteran imperialists like the MP Leo Amery to look back over the past five years and feel sure that the Empire was stronger than ever. To do so, however, would have been wrong. Next to reports of the German surrender and celebrations in London, several newspapers published a summary of the report of the Famine Inquiry Commission, investigating the Bengal Famine of 1943.[11] The report laid the blame for the famine, in which it estimated that one and a half million (now more widely estimated to be closer to three million) had died, at the doors of the Bengal and Indian governments, which had failed to plan for the wartime shortages and had missed opportunities to curb profiteering and corruption during the famine.[12]

Meanwhile in Delhi *The Times of India* quoted the report in its conclusion that the famine 'stands out as a great calamity, even in an age all too familiar with human suffering and death on a tragic scale'. While again apportioning most of the blame to the government of Bengal, the newspaper continued:

> The government of India… failed to recognise at a sufficiently early date the need for a system of planned movement of foodstuffs, including rice as well as wheat, from the surplus to the deficit provinces and States.[13]

Causes of the famine were multifarious and complicated: drought, the diversion of food to war workers, the disruption that the war caused to the complex networks of transport that could have supplied foodstuffs to Bengal, market failures, policy failures, corruption and profiteering. But the imperial government of India, the report argued, shared responsibility for the famine with the local government in Bengal. Presumably the military decision to employ a kind of maritime 'scorched earth' policy, by destroying both rice stocks and boats in coastal Bengal ahead of a possible Japanese invasion, also contributed to the starvation of millions there in 1943.

In a country where calls for independence had been growing for decades, the impact and legacies of the famine served to strengthen support for autonomy. More than two and a half million Indian troops had fought in the war, not only in Asia, but also in North Africa, the Middle East and Europe. In excess of 87,000 died. Their price for India's vital contribution to the war effort was to be its independence just two years later.

France was also facing increased calls for independence from some of the colonised. In Algeria this was to end in tragedy as Europe celebrated. War conditions in Algeria had provided opportunity but also hardship: while the French government needed the support of its local population, there were also high rates of unemployment among the Muslim majority, and shortages of food and other goods, which all increased support for independence, and protests were planned for VE Day. If Europe could be liberated, nationalists argued, why not Algeria? Tensions between Algerians and French settlers, which had increased during the war, exploded on the streets of the cities of Algiers and Oran, where twenty-seven settlers were killed. Thousands more – both Algerians and settlers – were to die over the next hours.

The British consul-general in Algiers recorded events in Sétif, a city in eastern Algeria, that day. In a report written for the Foreign Office, he explained how a demonstration there swiftly descended into violence:

> A scuffle then took place and a policeman drew his revolver and shot a native. More shots were fired both by the police and by French civilians who were watching the procession from balconies overlooking the street. Pandemonium then ensued. Indiscriminate firing by French and natives took place; unarmed natives seized chairs and anything on which they could lay their hands, and persons were attacked regardless of race, colour or creed.[14]

News of the violence in Sétif spread quickly, and in the surrounding countryside French settlers were attacked and around 100 killed. Retribution also came quickly: a French cruiser was sent from Algiers to bombard coastal towns in the eastern province of Constantine, while troops in armoured cars were dispatched to the province and the air force bombed towns and cities. Settlers organised themselves into militias and joined in the violence. By 10 May the uprising had been quashed, with around 15,000 Algerians dead alongside at least 100 Europeans. Brutal retaliation by the French authorities may have put an end to the independence protests and violence that marked VE Day in Algeria, but in the longer term it fanned the flames of insurrection. The Algerian independence activists who had organised the protests of 8 May learned the lessons of 1945 well: the Algerian War of Independence, initiated by the National Liberation Front (FLN) in 1954, was ultimately successful, with Algeria gaining independence from France in 1962.[15]

VE Day might have seen early shots in the war of independence fired in Algeria, but in Burma (now Myanmar), which would become independent shortly after its neighbour India in 1947, the Second World War ground on. Rangoon (now Yangon), the country's largest city and a major port, had finally fallen to the Fourteenth Army on 3 May, after troops had been held up by both determined Japanese resistance and the monsoon, which had arrived two weeks earlier than expected on 1 May. Although Japanese troops remained in pockets around the country, Operation Dracula – the codename given to the campaign to liberate Burma – was effectively over.

Unsurprisingly, any celebrations among troops based in Burma were more restrained than those at home. *The Times* summarised this in the words of a senior commander: 'The war is over. Let us get on with the war.' The article continued:

> By no means all the troops have yet heard the news. Among those who have there is deep thankfulness and rejoicing.
> The thought uppermost in the minds of the British soldier is repatriation. At last, he hopes, it will be possible to reduce the term of overseas service.[16]

Rejoicing may have been even more restrained among the Burmese population. Japanese occupation had often been brutal, but then so had the British regime that it replaced. Many had welcomed the Japanese occupation, seeing it as a form of liberation from British control, which had fundamentally altered and destabilised Burmese society in ways that still resonate today. Many Burmese and Malaysian men had fought with the Japanese, rather than with British troops, seeing them as potential liberators from colonial rule, although as it became clear that Japan was losing the war, the independence leaders had switched their allegiance to Britain. Unlike its near-neighbours India and Pakistan, Burma chose to become a fully independent republic, leaving the British Commonwealth in 1947. The wave of independence, which had begun with degrees of self-government for the Dominions in the early twentieth century, grew into a tsunami in the aftermath of the Second World War.

Trouble of a different sort was brewing in one of these Dominions. Halifax, Nova Scotia, on Canada's eastern seaboard, had been an important port for many years, home to a deep harbour and a large dockyard. The outbreak of war in 1939 meant it became a vital port at the end of the Atlantic sea lanes – a temporary home to sailors from all over the world as they waited to board the Atlantic convoys. Coming the other way, from Europe, the city welcomed refugees, diplomats, prisoners of war and, briefly, children evacuated from Britain to North America under the short-lived Children's Overseas Reception Board scheme, which ended with the sinking of the evacuee ship SS *City of Benares* in September 1940. Industry quickly grew up around the city to provide resources for the Allies in Europe: an oil refinery, a chocolate factory and a rope factory churned out their products next door to the dockyard and an air-force base. War workers, sailors, soldiers and airmen crowded into the small city, filling the speakeasies that had grown up to circumvent Halifax's strict alcohol laws and providing eager customers for the city's controlled liquor stores. The pre-war population of around 65,000 people quickly doubled, and Halifax developed a well-deserved reputation for revelry and rowdiness.

As the war in Europe came to an end, the local government of Halifax decided that the best way to prevent any disorder in the overcrowded town would be to stop tram services, to discourage troops from heading to the city centre, where, in any case, shops, restaurants and cinemas were swiftly pulling down their shutters in the hope of avoiding trouble. However, the rear-admiral in charge of the city's Canadian naval base argued that his men deserved to mark the end of the war in Europe and could go ashore to celebrate. By midnight on 7 May the city centre was a tinderbox, packed with 12,000 would-be merrymakers with nowhere to go. The result was probably inevitable: twenty-four hours of rioting, with liquor stores and shops looted, and drinking and fighting on the streets. *The Globe and Mail*, a Canadian newspaper, recorded exactly what had happened:

> The celebrations started last night, eased off this morning then broke out again with renewed violence this afternoon in an

orgy of drunken smashing and looting. Damage will run into hundreds of thousands of dollars, but no estimate is possible yet...

No buildings were flattened in the victory riot, but there is scarcely a window in the city's main business section that hasn't been smashed. Thousands of dollars' worth of goods were looted from the smashed stores, and virtually the entire liquor supply was carted out of the city's liquor stores...

As liquor flowed free in the wake of the store lootings, destruction spread rapidly through the city...

Civilian police were helpless against the hundreds of drunken looters who roamed the streets, smashing plate glass windows and entering all stores without interference... Drunken sailors reeled up to you with arms full of bottles, offering to sell it for $1 or $2 a quart, or else giving it away outright with a sudden generous impulse.

Although a curfew was imposed, by the end of VE Day at least two people were dead, many more were injured and more than 300 had been arrested. WRENS (Women's Royal Naval Service members) and airwomen, described as having gathered in groups, 'hooting and shouting as they gulped down quart after quart of beer', were confined to barracks alongside the sailors whose ill-advised leave had started the trouble. The coming of peace was anything but peaceful in Halifax, Nova Scotia.[17]

Celebrations in Southern Rhodesia (now Zimbabwe) were less eventful. Southern Rhodesia had been one of the bases of the Empire Air Training Scheme and more than 8,000 men had trained for service with the RAF there. One British man based in the capital Salisbury (now Harare) included a VE Day Diary for Mass Observation in one of his letters home, scrawling at the top 'Send this to Mass Observation when you've read it please'; and his words provide a vivid description of how service personnel based there greeted the news of the end of the war in Europe:

> On VE morning the chaps drifted into work at the usual time, 06.30, but only stood around chatting and departed in a body to hear the news at 08.00, returning at intervals to fortify themselves with nips from the invitingly open bottles.

Perhaps in an attempt to reinforce military discipline, a parade was called at lunchtime:

> Most of the paraders were somewhat tipsy, and kicked other people's topees about happily until fall in.
>
> In swaying, chattering, laughing ranks they shambled into a hollow square, in the centre of which were 'groupie' [the Group Captain], a lorry with a flight of steps, a piano, a mike, and a sheepish crew of singers.
>
> Groupie gave an informal, repetitive talk, which received much unnecessary applause throughout, while the ranks tipped topees over each other's eyes, or stuck flags in them to taste.
>
> After an unfortunate remark about fighting in the east to restore the export markets stolen by the Japs he gave way to Padre. When the 'other denominations' were dismissed, half the Station suddenly embraced the Jewish or RC religions and vamoosed.

After a brief and rather shambolic religious service, the remaining men went back to their quarters to hear Churchill's speech on the BBC. By late afternoon the camp was virtually empty, as its inhabitants had headed for Meikles Hotel, 'the rendezvous for all festive occasions'. And the evening was about to get very festive indeed.[18]

Licensing laws meant that the hotel couldn't sell alcohol until 4.30, and by then the lounge room was full, with men keenly waiting for the bar to open. The waiters were overwhelmed with orders and so:

> Foraging parties were detailed to fetch bottles from the bar, in spite of staff protests.
>
> The proportion of air force over civilians and Rhodesian troops was about 70:30, the majority of the locals lacking the low cunning of the RAF and arriving on or after 4.30 to find the place a sea of blue and beer.
>
> The heady lager beer, the only type obtainable (2/2 a Cape quart) went to the head very rapidly, and the appearance of the air force was the signal for a super sing song.
>
> All the S. African songs they played were sung with gusto by the air force, but with their own, seldom polite, words.

By early evening:

> Characters were dancing and speech-making from various tables, and the crash of breaking glass was as music in our ears.
>
> At 7.30 we had several strangers drinking our beer, and those of us who recognised that they were intruders decided to depart for 'scoff'. The narrative from this time on will be from hearsay, as the scribe, being unclasped with difficulty from an attractive pillar outside, went out like the proverbial light on the pavement.[19]

Unlike in Halifax, there seems to have been little trouble in Salisbury that evening, despite not much love being lost between the men of the RAF and 'those of Boer ancestry'. However, a description of 'natives' keeping away from the crowds because they felt unsafe, staying instead in 'their location on the town outskirts', was a forewarning of both the refusal of the white

Rhodesian government to concede majority rule (leading to its Unilateral Declaration of Independence from Britain in 1965) and, more immediately, the formal introduction of apartheid in neighbouring South Africa in 1948.

Unrest in the colonies and Dominions of the old, imperial powers, Soviet determination to impose communist rule on Poland and the continuing war in Asia and the Pacific all suggested that the defeat of Nazi Germany would neither bring a straightforward peace nor restore the pre-war world order. But as VE Day dawned, while some in Britain were – sometimes anxiously and sometimes optimistically – reflecting on the global changes that would sweep the old empires out of existence and bring in the Cold War, the majority of people were focused on what peace in Europe would mean for themselves, their families and their friends in the immediate future. And how to spend the next twenty-four hours, now that VE Day had finally been announced, was high on the list of many people's priorities.

CHAPTER SEVEN

Daytime, Tuesday 8 May
'So, This Is V Day'

Waking on the morning of 8 May 1945, one forty-year-old woman, an office worker living in Eltham, south-east London and a Mass Observation diarist since 1941, opened her diary with the laconic observation: 'so, this is V Day'.[1]

Her wartime diaries had been a mix of the public and the private, combining reflections on Roosevelt and Churchill's meeting at sea just off Newfoundland in August 1941 – a meeting that produced the Atlantic Charter, with its declared support for the rights of all people to choose their own form of government – with an amused portrayal of a 'glamour girl' on a train, whose lengthy and detailed description of her very untaxing work had united the other passengers in the belief that she should be sent forthwith to work in a munitions factory.[2] She had captured the horror and despair of the Blitz, explaining how she 'thought all was finished' as the bombs rained down on south-east London.[3] The week preceding VE Day had seen her preoccupied with international affairs, including events in San Francisco, where plans for the United Nations were being thrashed out; and with events closer to home, including a tram and trolley-bus strike that made her daily commute difficult. In her combination of occasional reflection on the 'great public events' (such as the Atlantic Charter) that have shaped the world ever since, and her detailing of the everyday life of wartime (often tedious, intermittently exciting or horrifying), she was typical of many of those who wrote for Mass Observation in the war years. These documentarians – the authors of Mass Observation's 'anthropology of our own people' – were waking to a world that was beginning to feel very different from the almost six years that had preceded it.

For some of our diarists the evening of 7 May, with all of its excitement and exhilaration, bled over into VE Day itself on 8 May. Several, including those who had ventured into London's West End and recorded their experiences there for Mass Observation, only got to bed as the next day was dawning. Others were simply too excited or caught up in events to go to sleep at their usual time. In Finchley, north London the young woman who had described toasting the peace with orangeade on the evening of 7 May explained how she and her husband had gradually become more energised and enthusiastic, hatching a plan for a late-night visit to their parents elsewhere in north London:

> This suggestion seemed to fire us with excitement once again. The thought of doing something crazy, perhaps having to walk several miles if buses were unavailable, perhaps obtaining a lift, who knows, who cares! Just an excuse to lose our inhibitions within reason for a few hours I suppose. We had excitement all right.

After visiting family and friends, they decided to head for home after midnight:

> Then came the storm but we didn't care. We were happy, we were doing something 'crazy'. We became increasingly brave and begged a lift from a heaven-sent lone lorry driving through the night.[4]

Another Mass Observer, a woman in her sixties who lived in Slough and worked in a local office, stayed up late to listen to the news and to prepare her house for VE Day:

> Midnight. The last news of the day (or is it the first) is over, and a thunderstorm is in progress. When I had finished the ironing I began to wrestle with the new cushion covers for the sitting room, and now but for sewing up the ends they are done, and the room is ready, clean and shining for VE Day.

Despite her preparations, she wrote:

> I cannot say that I was madly excited by the thought of our hardly won victory. I thought of Noel Coward's *Cavalcade* and the mothers who have lost their sons and women their husbands and lovers, and the children who have suffered and the suffering there must be now on the continent, the great bitterness and humiliation the German people have now to endure (how they will hate us) and of people like Lys who lost a very beloved brother in the RAF. Only the very young and the very insensitive can rejoice at this time freely, but no doubt I shall get drawn into the celebrations and I shall enjoy myself.
>
> It is nearly 1 a.m. I must go to bed.[5]

The feelings of these two Mass Observers on the eve of VE Day – excitement, the desire to lose oneself in a greater moment, and at the same time quiet reflection on both what was lost and an uncertain future – were shared by many of those who lived through and recorded their experiences of, and feelings about, the end of the war in Europe.

Like many others, their sleep that night was disturbed by a thunderstorm that rumbled across the southern half of the country in the early hours of the morning. A radio operator in Newport, south Wales had noticed thunder and lightning in the distance while walking home in the early hours of the morning. This was followed by a heavy storm in the morning, which led him to wonder slightly ominously, 'is this an omen of the future?' But 'when the sun shone out and drove the clouds away I hoped rather that it was'.[6] For the teacher in nearby Chepstow who had confided her worries about her family at the outbreak of war to her Mass Observation diary, the storm was an omen, but a good one: 'a victory salvo straight from heaven'; while a civil servant living in Hertfordshire felt that the storm had 'an almost biblical significance', as 'in so many of the Old Testament stories, great historical events have been accompanied by violent storms, and it seemed that this was following suit'.[7] By the morning she 'felt even more that the storm has been symbolic for it has cleared off all the heaviness and murkiness', leaving 'a perfectly glorious morning, clear and fresh and invigorating'.[8] The thunderstorm that rolled around the south of the country overnight and into the morning of 8 May seemed to some observers to be more than a meteorological phenomenon. For them it marked a break, an end to a period of disruption and uncertainty, heralding in its place a much-hoped-for new age of peace and stability.

The key moment of the day was of course Churchill's victory speech, scheduled for 3 p.m. that afternoon. Churchill, who had led the country through the war since 1940 and had become such a familiar figure to so many, was the only person who could announce victory and peace in Europe to the British people. Just as the crowds had poured into central London the previous evening, so they now started to gather in Whitehall, Trafalgar Square and other landmarks in the city centre, wanting to be close to the centres of power, and to Churchill. Others followed events in the capital over the wireless, while still others made the most of a day's holiday and found ways to celebrate close to home.

While events in London were the focus of attention, people marked VE Day in different ways across the country. In rural Devon a librarian closed her library for the day. Walking into the village that morning, she had noticed 'strings of Union flags across the lane from house windows, and one or two flags on sticks. This gave me my first feeling of jubilation. It really seemed we were celebrating.' Many villagers were waiting for the bus into Dartmouth to join in the naval town's celebrations, but she was happy in the countryside:

> Coming back, I thought how lovely the hawthorn was in the lane, against the May greenery. The smell of hawthorn was in the air. It seemed just the setting for dancing on the village green and old-fashioned English merry-making. (There is a dance in the Parish Hall tonight). Anyway, it seemed a perfect natural setting for rejoicing and festivity. Both going and coming back, the quiet of the sloping meadows seemed something precious which should fill the onlooker with rejoicing.[9]

In Reigate, Surrey, a boarding-school teacher was travelling by bus to Dorking for a special church service in the morning. It was a beautiful day and 'the country and wild flowers seemed to be all fresh and new on this first day of peace'.[10] To these observers, the English countryside appeared as it did in Frank Newbould's popular 'Your Britain, fight for it now' series of wartime propaganda posters: bucolic depictions of southern England's rolling, gentle countryside; a timeless landscape threatened by, and saved from, the destruction of war. The peace that they were welcoming was mirrored by this quiet,

*One of Frank Newbould's 'Your Britain, fight for it now'
wartime propaganda posters.*

ancient landscape where 'the air was smelling of May flower and parsley too... just like when we were children'.[11]

While the main celebrations would come later in the day, after Churchill's speech, many people set out to enjoy the morning and afternoon. Walking, hiking, camping and cycling had all become popular pastimes in the 1930s, after protests like the Kinder Scout Mass Trespass of 1932 and subsequent legislation won greater access to the countryside for many. With another war on the horizon by the end of the decade, the government was keen to ensure that the nation was as fit as possible, and the 1937 Physical Training and Recreation Act aimed to instil physical fitness in the population, supporting the growth of youth hostels and campsites across the country as a way of making the countryside more accessible. By VE Day many people planned to make use of their extra days' holiday with trips out into the countryside, weather permitting.

Across the country, diarists were packing picnics and raincoats and heading out for a day exploring the countryside. Cycling was popular, but not every encounter with the countryside was as peaceable as that of the Devon librarian. One young mother and housewife, whose husband was away, went for a bike ride while her mother put her baby son down for an afternoon sleep. She had wanted to be alone and to collect bluebells, but she lost her way and 'landed in a lane with thick mud underfoot and green caterpillars hanging from every tree'. After climbing through some barbed wire she eventually reached the bluebell wood, but she found only six, 'all the others being dead'.[12]

Sometimes, though, cycling was simply a way of getting from A to B. After a late night in Farnborough, Hampshire, one young man got up at about ten o'clock and 'cycled with my lady friend to her digs in a nearby village', while in East Yorkshire another diarist spent the morning cycling on a tandem with his wife, with their small daughter strapped on the back, to visit family in Hull.[13] Some of those who planned days in the countryside had these plans disrupted by the changeable weather of VE Day. Seven teenage friends from a local youth club in Birmingham set out on a bike ride into the countryside. As it was raining when they left the city, they called into a church that was holding a Service of Thanksgiving. Although it was a special service, 'published by the City authorities', the diarist found it uninspiring, because:

> The hymns lacked vigour, and the Service seemed to me to dwell upon the past, not laying enough emphasis on the fact that there were harder struggles ahead to repair the mental (and physical) struggles of the war.

On leaving the church, they found it was still raining, so they cycled back home for lunch. After lunch the sun came out, so they cycled to a nearby park, hoping to go boating, but the boatman had taken a holiday, so 'we moved on and took our tea in the park after doing a little light riding'. This group of young people was thoughtful about the future, and while they were keen to mark the end of the war in Europe, they were also preoccupied with questions about the coming peace. Towards the end of the afternoon they returned to a friend's house where:

> We lay on the lawn, drank tea, had our photos taken, and talked, mostly quite seriously, about our own Youth Club and about conditions. Again, everyone agreed a lot was wrong, but was not clear what we ought to do about it.[14]

Too young to have served in the war or to vote in the forthcoming General Election, they nonetheless wanted to mark the end of the war in Europe by having their photos taken, and were well aware that they would be the inheritors of the post-war world.

In Harrogate another young woman was looking forward to a day out exploring the North Yorkshire countryside with a male friend. Although it was raining, they carried on with the trip they had arranged, albeit with perhaps more stops for refreshment built in than they had originally planned:

> The rain stopped outside Harrogate and we cycled leisurely to the Black Bull at Killinghall, where we lunched. I had some cheap champagne, horrible stuff, like sweet cider. We had coffee and brandy liqueurs in the lounge. It was raining heavily now and here we stayed with a few others to listen to the radio. It was comfortable and pleasant – tho' hearing of London I

felt vaguely nostalgic. At about 4 p.m. the rain ceased and we cycled to Hampthswaite to the Farmer's Arms for our salad tea. The sun now shone and it was pleasant cycling. We made our way to Bishop Thornton – we stopped at a pub on the way for a quick drink of beer. It is delightful, undulating, well-wooded country. It was quaint how each house, however far out, had a flag or some decoration on show.[15]

They stopped at two more pubs that evening, but after the last one, where they met friends for 'a rowdy but enjoyable evening singing', she reflected ruefully that 'my friend must have been drinking rather than singing' and 'hurt himself badly' coming off his bike on the way home. Luckily, a military jeep picked him up to take him to hospital; less luckily, the jeep also crashed, meaning that 'not only did he have head injuries, but also severely hurt his leg'. They eventually got to a hospital in the small hours and he was successfully treated. The diarist finally arrived home at 4.30 a.m., too tired to sleep. The politicians of the 1930s may not have envisaged *quite* so many pub stops when they drew up their legislation in 1937, but the interwar popularity of cycling made the countryside, and country pubs, an accessible and popular leisure destination for many on VE Day.

Many other diarists spent much of the day at home or enjoying the countryside close to where they lived. One woman from North Yorkshire, however, didn't feel especially like celebrating, writing:

Indeed, I felt more like weeping on the actual VE Day. I thought of all the lads who would never return, of their families, of the crippled, of the war with Japan still to be won, and of the hopes and disappointments after the 1914–18 war. These feelings persisted all the time.

She thought though that such feelings might be generational, as 'perhaps the younger ones didn't feel sad'. Her own older children had gone youth hostelling, where they were to enjoy the sight of a large Victory bonfire on top of Ingleborough, one of the 'three peaks' of the Yorkshire Dales.[16] It rained for much of the day in North Yorkshire, but diarists in the south of England were luckier with the weather. This didn't always mean, however, that they enjoyed themselves. One young man from Middlesex described feeling 'distinctly ill and restless' during the day and, after arguing with his family who wanted to hang flags outside the house, he cycled to see his girlfriend, where 'to my irritation I found a children's party in progress outside of her house'.[17]

Rather happier was a diarist from Hertfordshire, just north of London. He was a Quaker who had kept a diary for Mass Observation throughout the war. He had missed the declaration of war on 3 September 1939 because he was attending a meeting at his nearest Friends' Meeting House. Hearing the air-raid siren that sounded in southern England as he cycled home, he found his 'family tidily collected in the dining room with shutters closed and a neighbour helping to amuse the children'. Luckily for them, it was a false alarm, because when he asked an air-raid warden whether they should have gone to the municipal air-raid shelter at the end of the street, he was told that it wasn't ready yet.[18] By the war's end he was ready to celebrate the return of peace to Europe with his family. After attending a local Anglican church service in the morning:

> We put up the tent for the children and let them have tea in it with some chocolate spread for a treat, and after tea we went

for a walk by the river. Few boats were out so we took a sort of wide canoe and paddled downstream, Laurie took a paddle for the first time and was quite helpful.[19]

Also in Hertfordshire, another diarist was hoping to spend the day with his family and planned to take his daughter camping for the first time. He wrote little of this, except for the intriguing comment that 'this is Barbara's first experience of camping, away from home, except for an isolated weekend six years ago at a nudist colony'.[20] Naturism may be more associated with Nordic and Germanic countries today, but it was a fringe element of the health-and-fitness movement of 1930s Britain, with the naturist organisation the National Sun and Air Association recording more than 2,000 members by 1937. The first naturist resort in Britain was 'Spielplatz', opened in Hertfordshire in 1927 by Dorothy and Charles Macaski, and it may well have been at 'Spielplatz' that our diarist and his family spent their 'isolated weekend' just before the war.

Picnics, walks, bike rides and camping trips may have been popular with those who could get out into the countryside and who were able to avoid the rain, but it was the cities that were the focus of attention. Unsurprisingly, the bombing raids on British towns and cities were at the forefront of many people's minds as they celebrated and reflected on the war's end. Arriving in London on the sleeper train from Glasgow that morning, Naomi Mitchison found herself struck by the differences already apparent in the city:

We left Euston about 7.30 and got to Hammersmith by underground, most of the bunks had gone already and I wondered where people were sleeping. Still the odd feeling of London being safe![21]

The government had initially attempted to stop people spending the night in Underground stations during the Blitz, fearing the consequences of a direct hit, of disease spreading in the poorly ventilated spaces and of shelterers refusing to return to the surface the next day. But pressure from Londoners – many of whom simply circumvented the rules by paying for a Tube ticket, then refusing to leave come evening – meant that the Underground stations were opened as air-raid shelters by late September 1940, just a few weeks after the London Blitz had begun. The following month, more than 124,000 people were seeking refuge on the platforms each night. By the end of the year bunk beds, toilets and first-aid posts were being installed in many stations and canteens were being opened, both in stations and on special trains that delivered refreshments, especially tea. Some stations invited shelterers to play music, others organised musical and dramatic performances and several held Christmas parties underground. Although the numbers of those regularly sleeping in the Underground dropped off after the end of the Blitz in May 1941, the stations continued to provide shelter for those who wanted it throughout the war. The last night that the Underground stations were open for shelterers was 6 May, just two days before VE Day; their disappearance must have been strange for frequent visitors to London such as Mitchison, who had no doubt become used to their presence below ground.

While the end of the threat of bombing raids was probably felt most strongly in cities like London that had been repeatedly targeted, observers in other parts of the country felt this too. In Newcastle-upon-Tyne the lord mayor made a speech as part of the civic celebrations, formally announcing Germany's surrender and inviting his audience to 'let us give thanks that our city has been saved from destruction'.[22] Battle-scarred Plymouth, where more than 1,000 people had died in air raids, celebrated with a communal party on Plymouth Hoe:

> By 10 o'clock the spirit of the day asserted itself. Flags and buntings appeared, bells were rung, guns fired and thousands paraded the streets. Celebrations were aided by brilliant sunshine, with flags and other emblems making splashes of colour on the bomb-scarred buildings. The Hoe seemed the focal point for celebrations. Thousands danced until midnight... The Lord Mayor issued the following message: 'All have borne sacrifice, hardship and loss with great understanding, fortitude and courage, and now has come the reward, a total victory.'[23]

A lonely young mother who had dressed her children in red, white and blue caught a bus into her local Norfolk town with her son after lunch. She found herself sitting opposite a woman with a three-week-old baby, who told her 'what a relief it was that she wouldn't have to take it [sic] down shelters'. This conversation cheered her up slightly:

> Thinking back on my experience of taking a small baby and a two and a half year old girl down the shelter every time the siren went, I did realise what a lot V Day means. Up to then I had rather resented the rejoicing while my husband is still overseas and my younger brother a POW in Jap hands.[24]

However, in north Cornwall a music teacher found that the air of excitement and anticipation that she had enjoyed the previous day had dissipated:

> Everybody looked very gloomy and bewildered. One said 'Seems queer don't it now it's come – can't hardly believe it.' Another: 'I was all set to celebrate last Friday and felt all

cheerful like – but it seems different now it's come – and what's all this about Russia? Are we going to fight them next?' 'God forbid', said another fervently.

Perhaps, she thought, worries about the future and a lack of excitement were more common 'in districts that have not actually suffered from the war. In those that have it is enough to know the bombs have stopped.'[25] Descriptions on the wireless that afternoon of ceremonies and festivities in London and other major cities like Plymouth could help those listening outside these centres to feel something of the spirit of relief and excitement that could be found there.

But before they could give themselves over to the celebrations, many people had another, more pressing preoccupation: whether or not the shops would be open, and what to cook and eat for lunch. Some had assiduously saved food for just such an occasion. Among them was a Sheffield accountant and his family:

> In January 1941 we purchased some tinned chicken, and as we have never been called upon to use it, we promised ourselves a treat on Peace Day, and we did open it today. As with many things, it proved something of a disappointment, for although it is genuine chicken: – bones, skin and meat – it is spoilt by aspic jelly. A tin of sausages, purchased in November 1940, proved much more acceptable for lunch.[26]

In Fleet, Hampshire an electricity sub-station worker described how his family enjoyed 'our much discussed tin of brisket of beef'. They had bought it five years earlier and 'it was reserved for use if we had no meat for a week, or for peace, whichever came first. Peace won fortunately.'[27] Many of those who kept a VE Day diary spent much of the morning queuing hopefully for something for lunch. The shop assistant from Dewsbury, West Yorkshire who had been worried about having enough food for her customers had a difficult morning, but perhaps not as difficult as that endured by Bob, her delivery man:

> Bob came with only half an ordinary day's ration. I was in despair but cheered up on learning he was only missing tomorrow. Everyone clamouring but I insisted on regular orders being fulfilled first. Bob said at Ravensthorpe [an industrial area to the west of the town] he had to lock his van between every trayful he carried into a shop because women were raiding it. By 11.30 everything was gone – bread, potatoes etc. We closed at 12.[28]

Things were fraught for shopkeeper and customer alike as people tried to secure enough food for themselves and their households to celebrate.

In a Somerset village just south of Bristol the carer and diarist was on the other side of the shop counter. She 'joined the longest fish-queue I can remember', where she eventually managed to purchase some fish and 'only just got the potatoes', as the greengrocer's was shutting by the time she arrived. Lunch that day was fried fish, boiled potatoes and mock trifle, a kind of wartime trifle-substitute that used margarine, dried egg and dried milk powder in place of custard.[29] As a full-time nurse-companion and carer, she was particularly aware of shortages and of the time needed to ensure that a household was able to eat three meals a day, and her wartime diaries are full of descriptions of shopping, queuing and cooking. Living in the country with a garden and access to hedgerows and fruit trees provided her with some foodstuffs that were harder to come across in town. In spring 1943, for example, she cooked 'bacon, fried egg, fried bread and potato, carrots, damson and custard' for lunch on 2 March, and 'fish with steamed potatoes, greens and damsons' on 3 March.[30] But while the search for food often preoccupied her, the wider war also reached her: 14 February 1945 had found her listening to news on the wireless:

> The war commentary tonight was about the plans for bombing Germany systematically. I found it rather sickening, necessary as it is if the war is to be won.[31]

That day was, of course, not only Valentine's Day, dedicated to love and thoughtfulness, but also the day after RAF Bomber Command's devastating overnight attack on the Saxony city of Dresden, which was bombed again by the US Air Force in the daytime, turning the city known as 'Florence on the Elbe' into a smoking ruin and killing at least 25,000 people, including many refugees fleeing the advancing Soviet Army.

Many Mass Observation writers were thinking of those who were not with them that day, because of their continued military service, because they were being held prisoner or because they had died during, and sometimes because of, the war. In Tayvallich in Argyll a diarist talked with her husband about 'how wonderful [it was] for Londoners to be able to go to bed with no fear of sirens or unheralded bombs'. They enjoyed a glass of burgundy each with a lunch of cold leftovers, deciding to save their long-cherished bottle of champagne for when their son returned from the war in Asia.[32] Many others shared their feelings. For those with loved ones still at war, VE Day was often something to be celebrated, or acknowledged, on a national level, not as a cause for personal celebration. One woman, living in Burnley, Lancashire was feeling melancholy that morning as her friends and neighbours were moving away from the town that day. Although she was planning a special tea with cousins, she had 'no inclination to display bunting or flags because my sons are away'. When she saw a large Union Jack later in the day it brought 'a lump in my throat and tears in my eyes', as 'the last time I saw such a flag was over the coffin of a young airman killed in a flying accident... I wonder how his mother is feeling, and whether *she* feels the war has been worthwhile.'[33]

A woman from Hatfield Peverel in Essex explained that her friend was finding the day difficult, and the celebrations on the wireless 'odious', as her son was a prisoner in Singapore; and elsewhere in Essex, in the small village of Latchingdon, the Church Committee had decided not to organise anything for teenagers and young adults as 'anyone over 14 was old enough to realise that the Jap war continues'.[34] The diary of a writer from Wallington, on the border between south London and Surrey, shows us some of the political changes that the war had wrought in the suburbs, as she was 'amused at the large and expensive hammer and sickle [flags] in front of houses where they would have been horrified a few years ago to have seen a Bolshevik sign anywhere near them'. Nevertheless, she continued:

> It was completely quiet round about us. Nobody was revelling, we were all too tired, and also we have so many sad homes near, where they have lost a son, it seemed indecent to make a fuss about V Day. For myself I felt no particular joy on that day for we had known the sure end of the E[uropean] war was coming for some time, and can't enthuse to order on a set date. Also my son had not yet returned home, so my war had not ended.[35]

Many diarists shared the uncertainty of not knowing the fate of friends and family at the end of the war in Europe. More than 170,000 British prisoners of war had been held captive in Europe, the majority captured between the retreat to Dunkirk in 1940 and the fighting in North Africa in 1942. For those who survived, the end of the war in Europe did not always mean immediate release, because although RAF Bomber Command's Operation Exodus flew many thousands of Allied prisoners to Britain in April and May 1945, others remained trapped behind Soviet lines or were too unwell to travel. While many had been able to keep in touch with those at home through the Red Cross, which delivered care packages and letters between families and prisoners, others simply disappeared from view, their fate not discovered until long after the war had ended, if then.

The nurse from Blackburn whose fiancé was a prisoner of war in Germany, and who had written at length about this the previous week, was never to hear from him again: a year later she was still wondering what had become of him. For her, the first half of VE Day felt 'flat'; in part because of her own worries and anxieties, but also because it poured with rain and she was busy, as hospital work continued and 'we had several cases for operation'.[36] In Newport, the radio operator's brother remained a prisoner of war, and he described the mixed emotions of his family, explaining:

> My brother is still a prisoner of war, last heard of in November at a place called Wolfsberg in Southern Austria. Both my parents are terribly worried about him; as my father said, they won't feel it's V Day until he comes home.

Nonetheless they marked the occasion by drinking 'a pre-war bottle of Hock', presumably saved for a special event, with their neighbours.[37] For this left-leaning diarist, his brother's safe return a few weeks later was, while a relief, also a disappointment:

> We had grown apart, even before he went. He has become a golf-playing Conservative with an unthinking contempt for all who disagree with him.[38]

Many such reunions were difficult; time apart and vastly differing wartime experiences could mean that couples, families and friends had far less in common with one another after six years of war than they had at its start.[39]

A coal miner from South Yorkshire felt as if 'a great load had been taken off', but his neighbours 'had a son, a Prisoner of War' and 'had heard nothing of him for two months'. The tight-knit community of his Yorkshire pit village shared both their wartime experiences and their politics, and the village had so many Soviet flags on display that passing hikers commented, 'Look at this place. It's bloody red.' They might have been more surprised to have seen the hammer and sickle on display in leafy Surrey, as noted by the Wallington diarist quoted above. While the flags hung there were described as large and expensive – perhaps an ostentatious display of wartime alliances and sympathies – those in the pit village were more often homemade, several of them by the miner's wife, who had cut up an old pair of red curtains for the occasion.[40] The teacher from North Yorkshire who had worried the previous week about peace being 'a flop' had cheered up and was busy 'hanging the Red Flag from the bedroom window, singing the Internationale and Red Flag to myself'. She was worried, though, that 'this was not over yet' and saw 'the struggle between Capitalism and Socialism' to be shaping the coming years.[41] Further north in the small town of Birtley, on the edge of Gateshead, one woman opened her diary with the exclamation 'VE Day – at last', but included an overheard comment about flags from her eighty-one-year-old neighbour: 'our Nellie hasn't the heart to put one out as she hasn't heard from Jackie for a fortnight'.[42] Across the country, individuals, families and communities combined excitement and relief with an awareness of their own and others' anxieties and uncertainties.

Others were living with grief, rather than uncertainty. After almost six years of war, many people were mourning losses: more than 270,000 combatants and 63,000 civilians had been confirmed dead or missing by 1951.[43] The woman who had placed flowers at the bottom of her sister's flagpole on 7 May, in memory of her nephew who had died the previous month, was 'too fagged out to go sight-seeing' when she arrived back in London that morning, and instead spent the day dusting and tidying her house, which had not been cleaned for ten weeks while she spent time in Barnt Green 'to help my sister through her sorrow'.[44] A schoolmaster from Shrewsbury had not suffered his own bereavement, but was acutely aware of those who had: his own son was in Burma, and that perhaps gave him a particular empathy with two women he knew, 'mothers of only sons killed in the war'.[45] Another teacher, living in Brentwood, Essex, found it 'hard to celebrate too much' as:

> Right opposite us there are a man and wife who have lost their only child in the RAF, and there are many others who have lost sons from the 19 houses in this road, and another with a son a prisoner in Japanese hands.[46]

While listening to wireless coverage of the crowds in London from her camp bunk-bed, a WAAF found herself feeling 'a bit sentimental and put out James' photograph (my brother-in-law who was killed at Gibraltar) – I thought of his poor mother and hoped she wasn't feeling too awful'.[47] In Bishop Auckland in the north-east of England another woman described the moving letter shown to her by a friend she had met while out shopping for food that morning:

> It was received a week ago from Boulogne-Sur-Mer from [a] Frenchman who had seen her nephew shot in the retreat of Dunkirk. He had buried him and when he, as a member of the Resistance, had to go into hiding, his friends kept flowers on the grave (in the street) all through the German occupation. When the town was freed they reburied him in the churchyard. Now they send his belongings which they had hidden and a photograph of his grave and thank the British boys for their bravery. The most moving letter I have ever read. I just wept, not for the nephew, I do not know him. I wept for all the common peoples of Britain and France and oh how I dread that this will happen again.[48]

For this observer, her sense of the losses of wartime, personalised here through the story of her friend's nephew, gave her an empathy with the bereaved and shaped her fears of yet another, devastating conflict.

During the war the bereaved had been encouraged to keep their grief and upset to themselves, for fear of its impact on public morale. Grief, they were told, could be eased by throwing yourself into the war effort, avenging the dead and helping to bring the conflict to a close. The war's end in Europe meant that some finally felt able to acknowledge their own loss, and others were keenly aware that public celebrations might inflict further upset on the bereaved. In a village in north Cornwall 'a most pugnacious Scottish woman' thought celebration was out of place entirely, asking fellow villagers out shopping that morning 'what's all this talk of celebration with all our boys lying dead and wounded and maimed for life? It's dust and ashes they should put on their silly heads.' Nevertheless, 'her house has more flags on it than anyone else's'.[49] A woman diarist in Ipswich was living with her own bereavement and had a particular reason for feeling 'no elation'. Indeed, she continued, 'emotion seemed dead in me'. Her young son, she explained, had told her 'from the next life, with whom we are able to hold communication, that VE Day would be Monday 7 May, and being put-off made it seem like an anti-climax'.[50] The links between the living and the dead, which were so real to this woman, felt very close for many as the war came to an end.

Others were preoccupied with travelling across the country, trying to reach loved ones before Churchill's speech, while some people still had to work. The airman who had described leaving his army camp north of London for an early-morning train to Manchester arrived at Piccadilly Station in the city centre, where he thought 'things seemed very odd'. He continued, 'the city was gay with bunting and people were promenading, mainly girls in their smartest frocks'. He didn't stay in the city, but instead 'hurried home' to Macclesfield.[51] Also arriving in Manchester was the barrage-balloon engineer, delivering some new equipment to a factory there. He kept a detailed diary, which he sent to his girlfriend who was stationed in Ceylon (now Sri Lanka), and faithfully copied it out for Mass Observation. Perhaps because she was based in Asia where the war continued, or perhaps because he had to work, he was disapproving of the celebrations in London the previous day, writing that the newspapers were 'full of pictures of the previous night's barbarism and mass hysteria celebrating VE Day a day too early'. He arrived in Manchester in the afternoon and found the city centre crowded as 'they were preparing to broadcast the PM's speech at 3 in Albert Square'. Like the soldier arriving in the city shortly before him, he noticed the young women celebrating in the crowds, although his disparaging portrayal of 'painted tarts emerging from dirty back entrances' was a far cry from the soldier's description of young women in their smartest clothes. With soldiers hitch-hiking into the city centre from army camps nearby to join in the celebrations, he predicted there would be 'goings on', come evening.[52]

The Glaswegian diarist who had written assiduously for Mass Observation since the late 1930s had to work on VE Day, but on her way she made sure to sit at the front of the tram, where she 'revelled in the display of flags' as she travelled into the city centre, as well as noting the large queues that were building up outside food shops.[53] All around the country, in villages, towns and cities, people started to gather in the afternoon to mark the peace and celebrate victory.

Nevertheless, for many of the observers, London was at the heart of the country's celebrations. In Brighton on England's south coast, the retired teacher, originally from London, wished keenly that she could have been in the city. She felt 'acute regret that I am not there', but found herself instead on the bus to meet friends in Eastbourne, some twenty miles away:

> People in bus very smiling and happy. Conductor said 'we can work with a better heart today.' Someone told me that Lyons waitresses who volunteer to work today were to have treble wages. Looked in vain among the flags put out for the USSR

flag. All the way by bus to Eastbourne only saw two, on the Co-op at Newhaven and Seaford, and one on a private house in Seaford... Walked on front at Eastbourne. Took chairs for service there at 3 p.m. but an official said it was to be tomorrow. So we went back to hotel for Churchill at 3 p.m.[54]

In mid-Wales a farmer's wife was feeling very fed up, wondering whether it was worth sending Mass Observation her diary, as 'we had such a dull uninteresting time' because they had no petrol to get to Builth Wells to join in any celebrations. Instead her husband worked on his accounts and she 'just did my ordinary routine', listening to details of events in London on the BBC, although 'that made us rather miserable as we longed to be there'.[55] Also wishing she was in London was the young ATS member whose diary had detailed her trip to the West End the previous night. She spent the day more quietly, at home in the Essex town of Grays with her family. Travelling home by bus that morning, she noticed that 'all through the East End the battered little streets are gay with bunting – recent V2 damage, barely tidied up, borders the bravest shows of all'. In contrast to her adventures in the West End:

> VE Day was very quiet at home. My father came home from Liverpool and we stayed in listening to the radio, and had a family party at tea time. In the centre of the table was a dish of canned pineapple, which Mother had saved through all the long years for this day... At intervals during the day, the ships and tugs in the river set up a lively chorus on their hooters and sirens – the traditional 'Cock-a-Doodle-Doo' and the 'Victory V'.

None of this, however, could compare to the excitement of the previous night and by midnight, 'wishing I were in London', she went to bed.[56]

By the afternoon many people had decided that central London was the place to be, and buses and trains heading to the city centre were crowded. The social worker who had been busy hanging the 'red flag from the window of the ladies lavatory' at work the previous day had spent the morning enjoying the sunshine in Kew Gardens, where her 'natural inclination' to 'stay here all day' lost the battle with her feeling that 'one ought to make that effort, being so near London at a time like this'. Accordingly, she and eight friends 'set off for Whitehall' on the no. 88 bus:

> Everybody on the bus seems in high spirits, exclaiming at the decorations etc. As we approach Piccadilly Circus, the streets become very congested, and in the Circus itself the traffic is held up for some time. We watch the crowds surrounding 'Eros' – and climbing to the top. We see several sailors and girls sliding down the boarded up part below the statue, and also several 'Yanks' perched on top of lamp-posts etc.[57]

Also heading into the city centre was the school owner who had taken her pupils there the day before. Today she was with her husband, her son and his friend and, after packing sandwiches, they retraced her route of the previous day:

> People – flags – favours – no real belief that FREEDOM had so crept over Europe. Chairs under tree in St James Park for picnic with raindrops pattering on leaves and on water. Sun came out. Crowds at Buckingham Palace. Greatest cheer given to old four wheeler cab. On to Piccadilly. Service in progress at bombed St James' Church. Clergyman on board placed upon bricks from debris. Offered hymn sheet. Loved singing 'Te Deum' with burr and buzz of crowds as background.[58]

Nearby, another diarist was walking down the Mall with two small children to hear Churchill's speech from outside Buckingham Palace:

> Forging our way through the crowds behind a pram. We had lunch in the park on the way, among a few thousand other picnickers, it was a perfect day for it. The crowds going towards the Palace were very gay, joining arms and singing and waving flags.

The holiday atmosphere was punctured slightly for him by a chalked sign on Hyde Park Corner saying 'Set Poland Free', a reminder of 'the unsolved problems that remain'.[59]

A diarist from Barnes in south-west London had also made the trip 'up West' with friends to savour the atmosphere that afternoon. He had kept a diary faithfully for Mass Observation throughout the war, and his descriptions of the nightly air raids of the London Blitz, and of the destruction of a house where he had lodged in Birmingham, with the death of the entire family with whom he had lived, remind us why so many people were keen to make the slow and crowded journey to the centre of the city that day.[60] He was not alone in wanting to celebrate:

> We took a bus to Hyde Park Corner and then walked up Piccadilly. Thousands of people thronged everywhere. Everyone was in a pitch of great excitement. They cheered, they sang, they laughed, they danced. They looked down from windows, they hung out of windows, they stood at the doors of houses and hotels, they stood and sat on window ledges. Every lamppost and standard had one or more onlookers perched from its summit. Cars and army vehicles made slow progress and it was hard to see what they were as they were submerged with people – on the bonnets, on the running board, on the roof, on the bumpers, you just couldn't see the vehicle itself.

They walked with arms linked, anything up to ten abreast. They marched, walked, danced and jigged in single file holding onto each other's coat tails.[61]

Having endured the conflict together, people travelled to London's West End to celebrate the end of the city's war together.

Having arrived in London that morning, Naomi Mitchison and some of her family and friends had also travelled to the West End that afternoon, where:

> I bought a small USSR flag for Val [her daughter], she was wearing a blue skirt, light blue blouse and red scarf and looked beautiful. I didn't get any myself but wore my Croix de Lorraine. She put hers in her hair. We had lunch at the Café [Royal] at 12.45… when we got out there was quite a crowd.

Mitchison's impressions of the West End crowds, however, were subtly different from those of the other diarists there that afternoon:

> Almost everyone was tired, and wanting to look, rather than do. They were sitting where possible, lots on the steps of St Martins. Most people were wearing bright coloured clothes, most of them red, white and blue in some form. (I was wearing my kilt and a blouse. Much too hot as I found). Most women had lipstick and a kind of put on smile, but all but the very young looked very tired when they stopped actually smiling.[62]

London was crowded that day, both with people who had lived in the capital throughout its war – suffering the air raids, fears and anxieties that were the common experience of the citizens of all too many cities during the conflict – and with Allied servicemen and women, volunteers from across the empire, refugees and fighters from Occupied Europe and the workers who had been so vital to the war effort 'behind the lines'. It was an international crowd, brought together by a shared desire to be at the centre of the city, and at the centre of the Empire, as peace was declared. But after the long years of war and the lively celebrations of the previous evening, many were happy, for a time at least, to be part of an audience as the afternoon built towards its central event.

The focal point of London that afternoon, and of observers around the country, was Winston Churchill's long-awaited victory speech. This was the speech that he had originally planned to deliver the previous evening – a plan that had been thwarted by Stalin's refusal to announce the end of the war in Europe to the Soviet people until the German surrender had been signed in Berlin. By early afternoon the streets around Whitehall were filling with people who wanted to mark the occasion by hearing the delayed speech as close to Downing Street as they could, and perhaps by catching a glimpse of the prime minister. Mass Observation had an investigator in place as the crowds, and the atmosphere, built up:

> Lower Whitehall, 1.45 p.m. Whitehall is jammed with people. Thousands and thousands line the pavements. From Downing Street to the Ministry of Works (Policeman estimates the crowds at 50,000). A continuous stream of people walk in the roadway and the policeman calls 'Now move along there please, keep moving'... Crowds fill the pavements and roadway. Everybody's pushing one another and laying the blame onto someone else. But it's done in good humour. The only time it does get ruffled is when some latecomer tries to wrangle a place in the front row and the crowd doesn't stand on ceremony. Latecomers soon get ticked off.

At least one fight broke out when people refused to move, resulting in the St John Ambulance having to render first aid for a split lip. As the clock ticked nearer to three o'clock, the excitement built, and some took advantage of a captive audience:

> 2.40 p.m. Service men fill the balcony of one of the houses opposite the Ministry of Works. A naval officer with lots of gold braid splashed on his sleeve imitates Hitler. He raves and gesticulates, saying 'und der Reich, und der Reich', and the crowd by way of appreciating the humour applaud loudly.[63]

He didn't have very long to entertain the crowd, because dead on three o'clock Churchill started to address not only the people who had pressed into Whitehall, but those listening across the country and around the world. After almost six years of war, those crowded into central London that afternoon were ready to listen to the man who had led them for five of those years.

Broadcasting on the BBC from 10 Downing Street, Churchill gave his much-anticipated speech, which was greeted by a hushed silence in Whitehall.

> 3 p.m. Big Ben strikes three, and silences the vast crowd assembled in Whitehall, and over the loudspeakers, specially erected for the occasion, comes the voice of the announcer, telling the people that 'the Prime Minister, the Right Honourable Winston Churchill, will speak.' And the crowd send up a mighty cheer. And then follows Mr Churchill, and for the time being the voice of the Prime Minister is the ONLY voice to be heard in Whitehall. People hang on to every word he has to say. When he tells them that as from midnight tonight hostilities will cease there's loud cheers, and again when people hear that the Channel Islands will likewise

be freed as from midnight tonight. But there's whoops of joy and waving of hats and flags when he comes to that point in his speech when he declares that 'The German war is therefore at an end.' Mention of Eisenhower's name and 'our Russian comrades' starts the crowd clapping once more. He ends his broadcast with 'Advance Britannia' and the Buglers of the Scots Guard sound the ceremonial cease fire. The band strikes up the national anthem, and soldiers standing near to Inv. smartly click their heels and stand to attention. Looking round Inv. sees the old and the young singing 'God Save Our Gracious King' with such fervour and reverence that the anthem sounds like a sacred hymn.[64]

Mass Observation's summary omitted what has probably become the most famous phrase from Churchill's speech that day – 'We may allow ourselves a brief period of rejoicing' – but many of the people listening to him through the loudspeakers set up in Whitehall, in Trafalgar Square, down the Mall, in the parks and across central London, as well as in many other cities, towns and villages, were more than ready to 'rejoice' that evening. As day turned to evening, the people of 'the people's war' got ready to celebrate peace, and victory, in Europe.

CHAPTER EIGHT

Evening, Tuesday 8 May
'This Is Your Victory'

Churchill's speech – the focal point of the day – was over soon after three o'clock, but many of the people who had crowded into London's West End to hear him speak were simply not ready to head home. The Mass Observation diarist from Barnes who had travelled to the city centre to hear Churchill thought that the speech 'was really the signal for getting celebrations going'.[1] The main question for many of those in central London was what to do next. Head for home and start to prepare for celebrations with friends, family and neighbours, or have a quiet tea before perhaps attending a church Service of Thanksgiving and listening to the King's speech at 9 p.m.? Attend one of the hourly services being held at Westminster Abbey? Picnic in one of London's parks and perhaps walk to Buckingham Palace, in the hope that the Royal Family and maybe Churchill would make an appearance on the balcony? Or simply stay in Whitehall and the West End to see what happened next?

Mass Observation's investigator in central London recorded the mood of the crowd who remained, many no doubt hoping for a replay of the spontaneous festivities of the previous evening. Like Naomi Mitchison, they thought that many people were tired, watching and waiting to see what happened rather than taking a lead in any celebrations on the city's streets:

> Westminster: 3.30. Crowds everywhere. Trams full of people both coming in and going out. Everything good humoured but somehow shapeless. People just drift about rather uncertainly. M22B had managed to get an early evening paper at Sloane Square, and they find that Churchill is to speak at 5 from the balcony of the Ministry of Health. They wander about. There are already immense queues outside the few tea shops open, and there is the general feeling that the immense crowds are going to have a thin time in the matter of eating and drinking. 'There ought to have been mobile canteens on every street corner' says F25B. 'That's where the WVS [Women's Voluntary Service] ought to have come in.'
>
> Everywhere, people are sitting on walls, or walking about with a curious aimlessness. It all seems very muddled and confused for a day of celebration. In Trafalgar Square the band is playing Gilbert and Sullivan: 'A thing of shreds and patches' drifts on the air as Inv. and friends pass down towards Whitehall. Large numbers of people are strolling away from Whitehall; evidently they don't know Churchill is expected to appear at 5. But there is still a large crowd at the end of Whitehall, waiting patiently. They join it, and soon get wedged in.[2]

In the nature of such things, the crowd waited, some aware that Churchill was due to appear, others no doubt simply drawn by the sight of a crowd and the sense that something might be happening.

Naomi Mitchison and her family were among those in the West End who were not quite sure what to do with themselves:

> Dick [her husband] wanted to book a table at the Ivy but it was shut; we tried to get ballet tickets but there were none. We

walked down to the Temple where a few people were happily resting on the benches in the gardens. It was amazing how the half blitzed trees had sprouted again... My feet were aching by this time as I was wearing comparatively tidy shoes. Dick and I went back leaving Av and Val [two of her young-adult children] to wander around. They seem to have got into a slight international incident when some people got annoyed with the Americans.[3]

Heading for home in Hammersmith, Mitchison missed one of several appearances on the Buckingham Palace balcony by the Royal Family that afternoon and evening. The diarist who had 'forged' his way through the crowds to the Palace behind a pram had heard Churchill's speech over loudspeakers there, but found the gathering to be rather subdued:

> Arrived at the Palace, and the crowd seemed to have exhausted its energies and the actual announcement was greeted comparatively unemotionally. Even the appearance of the King and Queen on the balcony did not cause riotous cheering.[4]

Churchill had driven to the House of Commons after his speech, where he gave it once again to a cheering chamber before inviting members of the House of Commons to join him for a Service of Thanksgiving at St Margaret's Church, the small church next to Westminster Abbey, known as the 'parish church of the House of Commons'. His packed schedule that day meant that he was late greeting the crowds from the Ministry of Health balcony.

By late afternoon the weather in London was hot, and the waiting crowds in Whitehall were becoming increasingly restless and uncomfortable:

Time passes. Sporadic bursts of shouting from the crowd. 'We want Winnie! We want Winnie!' There are occasional shouts of 'Here he comes' but the balcony is still empty. There is a lot of restless activity around the parapet near the balcony; men keep walking along it to further windows and back again. Now and then people look up enviously to those sitting at windows opposite or sitting down on the roofs above. A few people pipe up weakly 'He's a jolly good fellow' and there are more shouts of 'We want Winnie'. The minutes seem to pass very slowly in the intense heat. More people keep feeling ill, and the crowd makes way for them sympathetically. A stout man collapses and is helped out. Shouts of 'Hurry up Winnie old man.'

The crowd gets restive. Evidently a further disappointment after those of yesterday would be too much. Voice from the back: 'Why doan 'e come out?' Another voice, ironically "E's 'aving a drink dear!'

People fan themselves with newspapers and handkerchiefs. 'Be nice if it starts pouring.' 'Be cool anyway.' There is discontent about. Seven or eight voices start singing softly, clearly and with some hostility. 'This is a lovely way to spend an evening.' They start up several times, but it is not taken up by the crowd. By and by some male voices start shouting. 'One, two, three, four, What the hell are we waiting for?'… Somebody else adds on 'Five, six, seven, eight. Mr Churchill's always late.'[5]

Rumours started to circulate that Churchill would be appearing at 6 p.m., not 5 p.m., but at 5.40 a familiar stout figure, surrounded by a few other recognisable but slightly less familiar figures, appeared on the flag-draped balcony and put up two fingers in the unmistakable 'V for Victory' sign. Churchill had arrived.

His second speech of the day returned VE Day to the people. He began, 'God bless you all. This is your victory,

victory of the cause of freedom in every land.' The speech continued:

> My dear friends, this is your hour. This is not a victory of a party or of any class. It's a victory of the great British nation as a whole. We were the first, in this ancient island, to draw the sword against tyranny. After a while we were left all alone against the most tremendous military power that has been seen. We were all alone for a whole year.
>
> There we stood, alone. Did anyone want to give in? (The crowd shouted 'No!'). Were we down-hearted? (No!) The lights went out and the bombs came down. But every man, woman and child in the country had no thought of quitting the struggle. London can take it. So we came back after long months from the jaws of death, out of the mouth of hell, while all the world wondered. When shall the reputation and faith of this generation of English men and women fail? I say that in the long years to come not only will the people of this island but of the world, whenever the bird of freedom chirps in human hearts, look back to what we've done and they will say 'do not despair, do not yield to violence and tyranny, march straightforward and die, if need be – unconquered'.[6]

Ending with a brief reminder that the war against Japan still needed to be won, and that the task of rebuilding the nation still awaited them, this short speech was followed by Ernest Bevin, the trade unionist and Labour Party Minister for Labour and National Service in the wartime government, leading the crowd in a series of cheers for Churchill. Today the words of this speech seem to encapsulate some of the mythology that has grown up around the Second World War in Britain: the idea that Britain, the head of a large and powerful empire, fought alone, and the belief that the country was united in defiance of

Hitler, are still powerful, if not wholly accurate, views. But at 5.40 p.m. in central London on 8 May 1945 they were exactly what the crowd wanted to hear. It had been their war, and it was their victory. And it would be their celebrations – not those of the great and the good – that would mark the end of the war in Europe.

Of course most of the people that Churchill was addressing were not crowded into Whitehall, or even in London. People had tuned into their wireless sets around the country, and around the world, to listen to his earlier speech, and many stayed to listen to the BBC's coverage of the celebrations. The vast majority of the country had listened to Neville Chamberlain declare war against Germany on 3 September 1939, and they listened again as the war in Europe came to an end. The BBC had provided news, entertainment and information throughout the war. Broadcasting a reduced Home Service on just one wavelength, in a bid to prevent the enemy using its powerful transmitters to guide their aircraft, the BBC was a constant companion during the war years. It had not always been entirely popular: a Mass Observation questionnaire in May 1940 found that 'a great number [of those surveyed] were very critical of the wireless programmes'. In particular there were 'strong complaints about the amount of classical music' and 'too much talk'. There were also doubts about the accuracy of the news that people were being given, not only on the BBC, but also in the newspapers, all of which were constrained by 'Defence Notices', which were used to censor information about the war. One man remarked in 1940:

> You see, we used to get this dope put into us. Our aeroplanes flew over Berlin etc.... And they *all* returned safely. Why

shouldn't we know? That's why a lot of people at the present think the German communiques are truer than ours.[7]

But as the war went on, the BBC increased the number of comedy and entertainment programmes such as *Music While You Work* and *Workers' Playtime*. By VE Day the combination of entertainment and reporting – including vivid eyewitness accounts of battles, such as Wynford Vaughan Thomas's 1943 eyewitness report of a bombing raid on Berlin, coverage of the beach landings on D-Day in 1944 and Richard Dimbleby's famous description of the horrors of Belsen in 1945 – meant that the BBC was a largely trusted and familiar companion for the majority of its listeners, and many of them tuned in on VE Day to follow events from home.

Of course not all of those who followed events via the wireless were happy with the BBC's programming. The retired nurse living in Steyning, West Sussex had complained about the BBC in her Mass Observation diaries throughout the war. Among her many other complaints, she held the corporation at least partially responsible for the death of her sister in the United States, who had died in 1940, shortly after writing to say how much the BBC's coverage of the London Blitz had worried her:

> She comments 'It was loud enough for me' and goes on to say how she worried about my other sister (in London) and me. 'I do wonder if you are losing sleep night after night.'
>
> Within two days she was dead but we are still alive… the vicarious suffering she went through on our account helped to kill her. The radio accounts keyed her nerves to an unbearable pitch… I wonder what else the BBC will broadcast in order to give a thrill to those who sit at ease in far-off places?[8]

She wasn't much happier with the BBC on VE Day:

> To judge from the BBC no one was noticing this day of all days until the official announcement by Churchill at 3 p.m. I think the BBC and the Gov. behind it have let us down shamefully. Last evening the news lasted exactly 11 minutes. This morning at 7 and 8 a.m. it lasted 8 minutes, and one statement it made was false. It said the people in Paris were celebrating last night with singing and dancing in the street. The direct Paris radio at 7.45 p.m.... said that the French were very serious. They were remembering the million dead in the fighting forces and murdered by the Germans, and were not in a mood for rejoicing.

Nevertheless, she and some friends made sure to listen to Churchill's speech broadcast at 3 p.m. and delayed their planned walk on the South Downs to listen to 'the account of the crowds' that followed.[9]

In County Durham another diarist agreed with her judgement of the BBC programming. Turning on the wireless at lunchtime, she commented 'what rubbish for a holiday', although everyone in her household listened to Churchill's speech and stood up to join the national anthem, which the BBC played straight afterwards, even though she thought it had 'silly words, we need a new one'.[10] The sense of cohesion that led this Durham family, who were supporters of neither the Conservative Party nor the Royal Family, to stand and join in with 'God Save the King' was, in large part, a response to the shared national experience of wartime, but it was also a calculated aim of BBC broadcasting that afternoon. The corporation did its best to bring people together through the wireless, sending outside broadcast units to report from around the country, positioning well-known reporters in strategic locations and interviewing a wide range of people, not just about their feelings on VE Day, but also about their experiences of the past six years.

While much of the morning had been filled with live and pre-recorded music, the hours between Churchill's speech at 3 p.m. and the King's broadcast later that the evening at 9 p.m. were a patchwork of broadcasts, music and stories from around the nation, filled with accounts of the people's war. Interviews with passers-by, the sound of church bells (silenced since the start of the war) and reports from all over the country – from Belfast to Birmingham, Clydeside to Caernavon, Portsmouth to Puddletown – were beamed into people's homes across Britain. The BBC produced programming that wove the nation together into a shared experience of both the war and VE Day that transcended regional, class and political differences and painted a picture of a united nation, and a shared victory.

People all around the country listened to the wireless that day. For some, it was a reminder of places they knew and loved and had been unable to visit as often, if at all, during the war. A film-strip producer living in south London was 'most interested to hear the bells of Puddletown, which I have heard so often in reality. Wonder what all the folks in Weymouth and Swanage are doing today.' The end of the war in Europe, she felt, was too much to take in at once:

> It is no use trying to say how one felt. It is all much too big to realise. Feeling will come back gradually, and it will be the little things that will bring it home. The relief from bombs there has already been, and the blackout has been no serious inconvenience this winter, but the lifting of the whole pall of war over Europe, the lack of wondering how this or that other army was getting on, hope, instead of fear, for Holland, the Channel Islands etc., all this must come gradually.[11]

In Surrey the boarding-school teacher and his pupils had listened to Churchill's speech and to the broadcasts from around the country that followed. He had also enjoyed the church bells, feeling that 'they seemed to give the feeling of the whole land rejoicing in the early summer day'.[12] For those who were spending the late afternoon at home, the BBC's programming from around the country helped them to feel a part of the collective celebrations.

Others took advantage of the sunshine that southern parts of the country were experiencing. In Eastbourne the retired teacher who had counted Soviet flags as she journeyed there by bus went for a walk around the town with friends, but only found 'a few odd groups of drunken soldiers singing, and outside one pub a small group of people dancing to whistled tunes'. Things livened up later in the evening, but Eastbourne was saving its civic celebrations for the following day.[13] In Leicester one woman was musing on the end of the war, and on her hopes and fears for the future:

> Japan is still fighting, most of the wartime restrictions are still imposed on us, we are short of so many essentials and have so few luxuries. One feels the battle is but half won.

However, by late afternoon she thought that:

> Things seem to be getting a little brighter. People seem to be more lively. Windows are open and gramophones are blaring out music. Further down the road an open air communal tea has been organised. Two or three tables have been placed end to end down the centre of the road and adults as well as children are eating gaily.[14]

Public celebrations, a sense of community and sunshine could do wonders for an individual's feelings on VE Day, allowing them to enjoy the 'brief period of rejoicing' that Churchill had promised.

Many places seem to have saved the street parties, with tea and cakes made from carefully conserved and precious wartime resources such as sugar and eggs, and children's games – so central a part of the collective national memory of VE Day – until Wednesday 9 May, giving over VE Day itself to larger civic celebration. However, some places, including streets in Leicester and Coventry, held their parties on 8 May. Radford, a badly bombed industrial suburb of Coventry that had been targeted in the deadly air raid on the city in November 1940, because it was home to important munitions factories, held a party that afternoon. A diarist was there to record it:

> Tables and urns borrowed probably from some church hall, were set up on the brow of the hill on the pavement, all the children given more than they could eat, including jellies (goodness knows where from!) trifles and such like. Food was also taken to invalids and the old and anybody who didn't come out and join the throng.
>
> During the repast the Mayor and Mayoress and their two boys paid a visit and said some kind words, and moved on to another such scene…
>
> Musical games for children, boys, girls, ladies, gents, over 50s, over 70s, mixed etc. took place in succession to the music of a piano which had been hauled onto the pavement, the winners in each case getting an egg. This took a long time and was followed by dancing till dusk looked like approaching.[15]

Families, neighbours and survivors of the Coventry Blitz that had killed so many of their fellow citizens came together to celebrate both victory and the endurance of their community and their city.*

While Coventry had been a centre for the wartime munitions industry, other places had played a less immediately obvious part in the war, but had nonetheless played a role in the collective war effort. The Welsh border town of Chepstow was celebrating with a victory parade, which included the many voluntary organisations that had played a vital part in the war effort. These organisations offered those who weren't able to take a more active role in the war, through military service or work in the factories and farms, an opportunity to participate, and many of them were to become an essential element of a 'total war' that involved civilians alongside the armed services. The Chepstow teacher who had worried about her son and his new wife at the beginning of the war had helped to organise the local branch of the Girls' Training Corp (GTC), a voluntary organisation for girls and young women that trained them for potential service in the ATS by teaching drill, first aid, Morse code and other skills. She was marching that afternoon with her cadets:

> The girls did look good in their white blouses. Luckily it was very warm so they did not need coats. A full attendance showed how proud they were to be in the victory parade. Only two were absent, one ill and one on leave. As we got ready to start off I said to the Adjutant 'I am proud to be marching today.'

---

* Coventry was the first city to suffer a heavy air raid outside London, on 14 November 1940. Giving rise to the verb 'Coventrated' to describe heavy bombing, the raid killed approximately 568 people and seriously injured over 800 more. More than 4,000 homes were damaged and much of the medieval city centre, including the cathedral, was destroyed.

> The streets were thronged with people in from the surrounding villages. The girls must have had a job to keep straight faces passing the saluting base as the steps were packed with boys from the Army Technical School. 'Here's the GTC' they shouted, 'Come on let's give them a cheer' and they cheered with a will. Someone was taking photos in Bridge Street and when we got to the Dell the town clerk gave me the hymn sheets to be distributed by the cadets. We then had a place right in the front of the service, much to the disgust of the Women's Institute behind us. It was a lovely service with the parade drawn up in the hollow and the spectators around the high ground with the vicar standing under the shadow of the castle with the Chairman of the Council. The Service was short with two hymns. The Last Post was sounded from within Martyr's Tower, so-called after the regicide had executed Charles I.
>
> It had a poetic, ghostly effect, then the Reveille rang forth and the Union Jack was unfurled while we sang the national anthem. It was an uplifting moment and a memorable one.[16]

Chepstow's victory parade successfully linked the past, present and future in its combination of historical site, celebration of the town's contribution to the war effort and inclusion of young people in the event.

By the evening things in the town, at least for this teacher, had become a little more raucous and a little less reverential. She had arranged to meet a group of friends in the lounge bar of a local pub. As in many other places, beer was in short supply and the publican would only serve regular customers, who were asked not to make too much noise in case passers-by should realise there was alcohol inside. After an evening of drinking whisky, which she felt gave her 'a remarkably clear head and a ready tongue', she and her friends went to the town's victory ball at 11 p.m.:

Everyone was in a grand mood and the police had not a spot of trouble. Several of my pre-war partners were there and I had a grand time. I felt as if life was making sense again, and in the company of my own particular friends it was as if the war years had never been. I felt a sense of pride at the self-discipline of the British race when the national anthem was played and the hubbub was replaced by silence. One felt that it was the innate qualities of the British race that had made victory possible.

Such grandiose reflections did not survive into the next part of the evening. After a singalong with soldiers:

> We caught up with Arthur and Lynn and Edna outside the hall, and made a line across the road doing the Palais Glide [a popular dance]. But it was too much like hard work downhill… Arthur is a little chap, scarcely five foot, and I kept saying 'carry me Arthur, I'm tired', a rather tall order considering my bulk. Lad on the other side said 'Come on, let's take her at her word' and they crossed their hands and hoisted me up, carrying me some way before they put me down. Arthur said 'To show it's not a fluke let's do it again' and up I went and was carried in triumph down past the memorial where I had marched in dignity a few hours before… As I went along Welsh Street the floodlit castle could be seen amidst the trees. I stood on the steps and watched the twinkling lights all around the countryside and listened to the distant murmur of revellers. It was a night of pure unalloyed happiness.[17]

Chepstow had perhaps not been at the centre of the war: there were army camps in the countryside around the town and its racecourse was occasionally used as an airfield, but although some bombs had fallen in and around the town, and evacuees and Land Girls had arrived from the cities, it remained a fairly quiet backwater, spared the heavy air raids of nearby Cardiff and Bristol, and without the war factories of Hereford and Gloucester to its north. However, the war still touched the lives of the town's inhabitants: conscription, the arrival of evacuees, and rationing were just some of the ways in which the conflict shaped the life of Chepstow, and the necessity of producing more food for the country because of the dangers to shipping meant that rural areas like Monmouthshire had a crucial role in the war. Its citizens had earned the right to celebrate victory alongside the rest of the country.

Nearby Gloucester was also celebrating. Home to several munitions factories, the city had provided hostels for the war workers who were either conscripted or had volunteered for factory work. The hostels needed staffing, and among the staff were two young sisters who had kept a joint diary for Mass Observation since just before the war started, opening their first entry in August 1939 with the explanation that the diary would be 'generally muddled and badly spelled'.[18] Their wartime diaries were neither muddled nor badly spelled and provide a valuable window into the ways that the conflict shaped the lives of two young women, who started the war years working as garage assistants in Norfolk, moved to Dorset and Suffolk for war work and eventually found themselves living and working in Gloucester. Celebrations in the hostel saw the now-familiar combination of formal thanksgiving and alcohol. A married couple who lived in the hostel conducted a Service of Thanksgiving, which included a minute's silence in remembrance of the war dead:

> I ran through my mind all those I knew who had been killed and realise how lucky I am for none very near or dear to me are gone… I noticed the housekeeper was crying during the proceedings. She has lost her dearest son.

Soon afterwards the service was disrupted by some drunken heckling from attendees, and the party moved outside to enjoy the pleasant weather on the hostel lawn. After tea the sisters and their friends walked out to a country pub where they sat in the garden drinking cider and getting 'tight' before heading back to the hostel for a late-night bonfire and victory dance:

> It was a roaring blaze and seemed to have a significance in saying 'goodbye' to many wartime restrictions… We stood watching it for a long time and about quarter to 11 went in the dancehall. Here I have never seen such signs of unrestricted merrymaking. People who in the usual way never unbend were romping like healthy children in circles with joined hands. They were all young people with a larger proportion of women than men, and were simply letting themselves go in a way most joyfully and unselfconsciously to behold. Some had the necessary amount of alcohol to make them like this, but most were drunk with the spirit of victory. Everyone in the room, which was packed, had a smile on their face. The romping continued until the end of the radio music and then with exhaustion the circles were broken up. Dance records were put on and dancing began, but 'jitterbugging' and the 'conga' type of dancing was the rage, most of the crowd being at a pitch too high to concentrate on serious ballroom dancing. This went on until 12 o'clock when the ballroom was cleared. The next move was out to the bonfire. Until 3 a.m. dancing round in a circle of joined hands some of the crowd went on tirelessly.

The diarist herself was tired and went to bed, but she concluded perceptively that:

> Years of monotonous clocking-in to the war factories had brought this feeling of supreme elation to the young workers,

many of whom have turned yellow with their work. They have given vent to their suppressed feelings tonight as never before. They would not go to bed while the last ounce of energy could be summoned to carry on.[19]

Many of those young workers had given years of their youth, and sometimes their health, to the war effort. Work in the munitions factories could be dangerous: eighteen women were killed in an explosion in the Royal Ordnance Factory in Kirby, Lancashire in February 1944, and work with the toxic chemicals TNT and sulphur could not only turn a worker's skin yellow, but also cause infertility, anaemia and liver failure. Work in war industries may not have been glamorous, but these workers had more than earned their evening of abandon.

In Plymouth, where thousands had gathered on the Hoe to celebrate, things got slightly out of hand in the evening when 'during a display of high spirits about 30 deckchairs were burned on a bonfire', while in badly bombed Hull on England's east coast there was a band playing and community singing in Queen's Gardens in the city centre, but the observer who had cycled there on a tandem that morning thought that the celebrations were rather 'half hearted', with 'a large but passive crowd just milling about and wondering where to go next'.[20] They retreated to a pub, struggling to find one that wasn't either 'closed or packed to the doors', but eventually finding one a short walk from Queen's Gardens, where they had a drink before heading back out to see the coloured lights and fountains in the city centre.[21] In contrast, the normally placid town of Windsor, home to the Royal Family for most of the war, was determined to let its hair down that evening. The housemaster at Eton College who had described the water fights in the town centre the previous evening recorded a day of high spirits, starting at about eight o'clock in the morning, 'with less water throwing' than the previous evening 'but much more car stopping and mobbing of passers-by', which went on until midday, 'when the crowds were dispersed by authority'. Large bonfires were lit later in the evening and this seems to have been the signal for 'more large-scale mobs and wholesale duckings in the river'. He noted that 'I saw all [of] what is described above and joined in', concluding:

> The evening and the night all merged into one really, and it is difficult to give an account of my feelings. Having taken a full share in the festivities I was rather tired by about midnight – Lots of people went on shouting in an aimless way and breaking things, though they weren't even drunk... I for one thoroughly enjoyed letting off steam.[22]

Impromptu celebrations like these gave many a chance to 'let off steam' after almost six years of war.

Bonfires were a popular way for communities to prolong the day's festivities and bring local people together in a shared public celebration. Effigies of Hitler, made with such enthusiasm over the preceding days, replaced the traditional Guy Fawkes on the top of many bonfires. War-worn Coventry had so many bonfires that at least one person thought 'it looked almost like raid night, with bonfires in many streets lighting up [the] sky in all directions'.[23] Staid Eastbourne came to life during the evening, and the visitor from Brighton 'found a quite good bonfire and people singing and dancing' on the beach. Fittingly, the bonfire reminded her 'of the most glorious one I have ever seen, made by the Royal Engineers at Newark on November 11, 1918'.[24] In Newport the town centre was packed and lively:

People were thronging the main street, the fullest lights were on. Soldiers and girls kissed oblivious of the throng. People were dancing the 'oakee-pokee' around the policemen, who smiled and took it in good part... People let off jacky jumpers and coloured lights. The Civic Centre was flood lit and looked very lovely.[25]

The woman from Slough who had stayed up past midnight, making her home ready for VE Day, went for a bike ride with a friend as evening fell:

> As it grew darker the lights came on. Fairy lights that we hadn't seen for years decorating private doorways, arranged in V formations at windows surrounded by bunting. In the High Street some buildings with all their pre-war lights glowing, some shop windows lit, and the Town Hall deeply be-flagged, floodlit in a deep, red, rose with the clock tower at the top in lime green... Bonfires were flickering now, here, there, everywhere, in waste spaces and allotments. We had seen one or two effigies of Hitler awaiting destruction. (Will this day become another Guy Fawkes Day?) The singing in the parks had increased. It was like a dream out of a dead past.[26]

Lights – whether of bonfires, in 'V for Victory signs' made by the searchlights that had recently scanned the night sky for bombers and rockets, in the illumination of civic buildings and shop fronts, or in suburban windows and gardens – formed a celebration of the end of the dark, grey war years and in particular of the final lifting of the blackout, that ever-present reminder of the conflict, in both its threat to life and its many petty annoyances.

Simply burning Hitler's effigy wasn't enough for some communities. Radford in Coventry, which had held a street party in the afternoon, was among the many preparing to dispense with the Nazi dictator. But here they were planning a more spectacular exit for him than a simple burning. A middle-aged woman and local resident recorded the scene for Mass Observation:

> Two days previously a life-sized image of Hitler, stuffed with straw, had been suspended by the neck in the middle of the street – from bedroom window to bedroom window.
>
> As dusk came near on VE Day a self-appointed 'man and wife', both men, conducted the effigy's funeral... Some bearers brought some planks, the effigy was let down solemnly and placed on them, and the whole procession, headed by the 'Mayor' and 'Mayoress' [the 'man and wife'] forming a long crocodile of all the residents and anybody else who liked, marched singing to the common at the bottom of the road.
>
> Here had been built a huge bonfire, with all sorts of things which any other time wouldn't have been burnt.

The lighting of the bonfire, and the final destruction of Hitler's effigy at 10.30 p.m., was the signal for more dancing, the evening ending with a community rendition of the national anthem. For this woman, this marked the end 'of a day which will never be forgotten by any who were there'.[27]

Despite these widespread celebrations, not all the diarists were having a good time on the evening of VE Day. In Bury St Edmunds in Suffolk one diarist had been feeling miserable all day. This was partly because she felt unwell and had stayed in bed most of the day with bad period pains, but also because she hadn't heard from 'Martin', a German refugee and journalist to whom she had become close, for some time. The end of the war in Europe did nothing to lighten her mood; instead, she wrote, it 'makes me feel as if I am going to a funeral, and as if it is time to now bury all our dead, including the German dead'. Even the 'planes going overhead, taking food to the Netherlands and bringing prisoners home to Britain', could not improve her mood, and the victory bells pealing around the town simply annoyed her. She commented:

> I am in an exceedingly bad temper, a sort of culmination of all my hate and frustration before and during this war, and I feel like projecting it into the future after the war.

Despite describing her pity for the Germans, and explaining that 'I could not drink and make merry after committing such a slaughter and reducing them to such degradation', she allowed a friend to persuade her to go out in the evening and see what Bury St Edmunds had to offer. By late evening her mood had improved and she 'wanted to spend money and go out to eat', although she 'still did not like flags and wanted to tear them down'. After visiting the Abbey Gardens, she and her friend decided to try and find somewhere to eat, although both were adamant that they wanted to avoid Spam, the tinned pork and ham that had became ubiquitous during the war. They eventually found a rather down-at-heel restaurant and managed to sit at one of the few remaining tables:

> I thought of the dangers of infection, and the dirt one might eat in such places, but we were willing to indulge in anything. Tea tasted rather awful and served in very thick, clumsy white cups and no saucers. Food was spam and potatoes, which I ordered and Nancy refused. Then the girl returned to say no potatoes, only spam sandwiches.

Feeling hungry and miserable, she paid for their tea and headed for home, wondering whether she should leave Bury St Edmunds, her house there 'having been a refuge from bombs, but that was all'. The town and the war were linked in her mind with 'Martin', her male friend whom she was resigned to never hearing from again, as he was likely to return to Germany to try and find out what had happened to his family. Sunk in her personal misery, the end of the war meant little to her, and the future appeared to have even less to offer.[28]

The war had changed people's lives in many different ways. Relationships that had seemed solid at its beginning could break down, unable to stand the strains of separation and anxiety. Other relationships came about because of the war. For some, conscription into the military or into war work offered an escape from domesticity and an opportunity to see new places, and meet new people. The arrival of soldiers and workers from overseas could be a romantic and exciting distraction from the drudgery of wartime life. Many marriages were made in haste in the early years of the war, and were matched by a rise in the divorce rate at its end, as couples found that one or both of them had been irrevocably changed by their wartime experiences. In Leeds one woman was feeling particularly despondent about her marriage. After a slightly disappointing day, spoiled for her by unending rain, she arrived home in the late evening:

> To find husband stretched on settee, reading. No word spoken. Has not spoken to me for three weeks – don't know why, but feel that if he won't speak on V Day he'll never speak!
>
> Simply couldn't bear it. Rushed round to Mrs B. with June [her young daughter]. Had a cry and then ate a lump of her apple pie and sat and talked to her until 1 a.m.
>
> Made some tea when I went back home. No word from R! [her husband]. Sod! What a day! Wish I were back at work with my friends![29]

In December 1945 she wrote her last entry for Mass Observation, replying to a question about their writers' mental health. Although she was happy in her work as a welfare officer and industrial nurse, she was 'longing for a divorce and freedom from home ties!' Perhaps she and her husband were one of almost 30,000 couples to seek a divorce in 1946, or of more than 60,000 to part ways in 1947.[30] The end of the war may have reunited families, but not always happily.

Other diarists were having equally quiet, though usually happier, evenings. A music teacher in Leicester was babysitting for her brother and his wife, and spent the evening listening to the wireless and copying out a magazine article on music. 'How unbelievable,' she thought, 'that there was no need for black out and no fear of sirens or unexpected enemy planes.'[31] The teacher and young mother from Swansea, living with her parents and with her soldier husband home on leave, was pondering the lack of housing for married couples and the difficulty of married life in her parents' house, where she 'had a horribly "censored" feeling', particularly at bedtime when 'the look you get… is enough to make you want to make love at any time but that'.[32] The faithful Glasgow diarist, who had been at work all day, spent a contented evening at home with her mother, listening to coverage of the celebrations on the wireless. Looking out of the window in her suburb, she noticed:

> Unusually long queues at the tram stop. They suggested to me that the Glaswegians were going down town to see the flood lighting in George Square. I also saw unusually large crowds proceeding in the direction of Dowanhill Church, which was peeling its bells for a service.
>
> Walking through the city centre earlier, she had found herself singing 'the deil's awa' ('the devil's away'), explaining to

her diary that 'it was just as if a foul pestilence had gone, and the free world seemed as fair as the Garden of Eden'.[33]

The dead, the injured and the bereaved were not forgotten in the midst of the celebrations. Among many other voices heard on the BBC that evening was that of Mrs McDonald of Greenock, who reminded listeners that 'for many mothers, this evening will hold sadness as well as joy, maybe more sadness for some'. Her son Roy had been a second-year medical student when he joined up: he had been killed in Italy. Another son had lost a leg in the fighting.[34] A couple living close to Aylesbury, just north-west of London, had invited a wounded soldier, a patient at the National Spinal Injuries Centre in nearby Stoke Mandeville Hospital, to spend the day at their house. After a peaceful day they returned to the hospital to find that the patients had been given permission to stay out until midnight:

> We didn't want to go in on such a perfect evening, so we went for a walk, taking it in turns to push the chair. I don't know what we talked about, but we were very happy, and very peaceful. London's searchlights were flickering in the distance.[35]

In her Somerset village the diarist who had spent the morning shopping for food was caring for her invalid employer during the evening. Together, they listened to 'Now Thank We All Our God' on the BBC at 8 p.m., but found the Archbishop of Canterbury's address 'uninspiring'. She had gone to bed by the time 'a klaxon horn, sounded to resemble an air raid warning, gave the signal for the lighting of local bonfires', panicking horses in two nearby fields.[36] Across the country, people paused to reflect on the war in Europe's end, some celebrating in town and city centres, some grieving, or feeling quietly grateful at home while others worried about the future.

In the Surrey countryside the boarding-school teacher and his wife listened to the Archbishop of Canterbury and to the King's speech at 9 p.m. before walking out into the garden to enjoy the evening. Across the valley they could see 'the first peace time fair with blazing lights revolving merrily in the dusk'. Although he was tired, the teacher couldn't settle to anything and eventually decided to walk to the fair with some of his colleagues:

> The fair was a good mile off, up hill and down. (It is an old Ascension Day fair of great historic antiquity.) We staggered up the hill onto the Dene... Remnants of a bonfire burnt away on the grass. A few lights on the Downs three or four miles off looked cheerfully across the Valley. The fair blazed gaily and little groups of people moved about in the gathering dark. It was now about 10.30 or more. We went on to the fair and stumbled about on the grass as one always does coming up there, as you always look up at the light and never at where you're going... Plunging gaily in [I] found myself revolving on a beautiful painted horse... from there I passed with the party to the whirling motor car roundabout... we tried the skittles and the hoopla for a beautiful pearl necklace... needless to say, no success.[37]

Fairgrounds, with their bright lights, their noise and their need for fuel to power the rides, had had a difficult war. Although they were able to continue with blackout protection and dimmed lighting, they were a shadow of their peacetime selves. Music had to be muted, so that air-raid sirens could be heard, rifle ranges and coconut shies were closed, and fairground engines were conscripted to help clear debris and collapsed buildings from bombsites. The sound and noise of a historical fair, seen and heard across a rural valley, was as good a symbol as any of the coming of peace to Europe.

Things were far from peaceful in central London. A young woman living in Marylebone and working for the BBC was keen to join in the festivities after a long, but rewarding, day at work. She felt that the day's programmes were 'the climax of our work throughout the war. No one stayed away and we worked till late at night, with a feeling of a job well done.' Once they had finished work, she and her colleagues headed out to see what was happening on London's streets:

> As soon as we got into Regent Street and found everyone going mad, we went mad too. We sang, we shouted, we danced down the middle of the street, we shouted at people going by and generally behaved in a manner which I had never believed possible.

She was pleasantly surprised to see how good-natured the crowds were – something that she attributed to a lack of alcohol, as most pubs in central London were closed, out of beer or simply too crowded to fit any more revellers inside. They followed the crowd down to Piccadilly Circus and on to Buckingham Palace:

> Everyone yelled with delight at the floodlighting, and at the brilliantly lit windows of hotels etc. The crowd carried us down the Mall to Buckingham Palace – the main focus of attraction in the whole of London that night.

The King and Queen appeared on the balcony of Buckingham Palace several times that day, to the delight of the crowds below, who were eager for any kind of entertainment and anything that helped to mark the day's significance. The diarist and her friends were lucky:

> After only about a quarter of an hour's waiting – during which the crowd sang, shouted 'We want Georgie' and raised a stupendous cheer if any of the hundreds of windows opened a tiny crack – the King and Queen came out. They were greeted by a terrific roar, and a forest of Union Jacks, handkerchiefs, anything that could be waved was waved, and stayed on the balcony for, I should imagine, four minutes.[38]

'We want Georgie' – not 'God Save the King' or a reverential silence: on VE Day in central London the Royal Family, who had spent the war in Britain, visiting blitzed communities and military bases, were greeted as members of a national community who had suffered together and were now celebrating together. The Princesses Elizabeth and Margaret were allowed to leave the Palace incognito and enjoy the atmosphere on the streets below. When interviewed by the BBC in 1985, Queen Elizabeth II remembered how 'we cheered the King and Queen on the balcony and then walked miles through the streets. I remember lines of unknown people linking arms and walking down Whitehall, all of us just swept along on a tide of happiness and relief.'[39]

Naomi Mitchison and her husband had returned to the West End to meet friends and family for dinner, where they talked about 'the universe, time, Marxist psychology, the [Communist] Party line over the Poles… the BBC etc.' After dinner they wandered through the city, finding themselves, like so many others, in Piccadilly, where 'there were a lot more drunks and broken bottles than earlier, and a few people crying, or having hysterics or collapsing, and a lot of ambulances'. They decided to catch the Tube back to their London home in Hammersmith. People were dancing near the station when they arrived, and she stopped to 'dance a reel' with 'a nice drunk Glasgow Sergeant' and then 'joined in one or two "snake dances"'. They left swiftly when a 'very drunk and rather repulsive lady tried to get off with Dick' (her husband). After a short stop at a local pub where 'people were singing with the minimum of tune', they went home to their riverside house, where 'we went onto the roof and looked at the searchlights whirling beautifully around and reflected onto the river. Then we listened to the midnight news and went to bed. I just felt tired.'[40]

Back in central London, the diarist from Barnes was still enjoying the atmosphere of the West End, describing the 'torn up paper' that was 'coming down in "showers" from windows in big buildings "manned" by our American friends'. The good weather, which lasted all evening in London, allowed the crowds to enjoy the long daylight of wartime's double summer time* until after 10 p.m., and combined with the delight of the crowds to produce an experience 'which we will never forget' for this diarist.[41] Another Londoner, a young man who had served in the army since 1939, was also heading for the West End that evening. As he waited to catch a train from West Dulwich with friends, a train full of soldiers on leave stopped at the station. The soldiers, who were returning from Germany, had brought souvenirs home with them in the form of Nazi flags, which they 'were flying from the windows of the train'. The diarist had arranged to meet his friends at a pub, and after queuing outside for a while, they found a table and

---

* Double summer time – two hours ahead of GMT – was a wartime measure intended to boost productivity.

watched a South African sailor get into a drunken argument with the manager. Walking down the Charing Cross Road towards Leicester Square, they found things rather livelier than they had been in the pub:

> Outside Leicester Square Tube some youths had got a bus shelter into the middle of the road. They clambered up on top until the crowd shook it violently, when they fell off into the crowd. An old woman with a tambourine was happily dancing in the gutter. A Canadian soldier borrowed her tambourine and tried to play it. After a while she took it back and he borrowed a girl's hat and sang 'Knees Up Mother Brown' with her. The crowd stood around and grinned…

Later that night it became too dark to take notes, so he described the evening's entertainment from memory:

> In Coventry Street rockets were being fired from bottles, the Corner House was lit up, and a man was taking flashlight photographs from a window. The crush now was very tight and the best mode of progress was to link arms and form a crocodile. Alternatively, a conga chain was useful.

Arriving in Regent Street, they found that the novelty of lighted windows was attracting a crowd:

> Austin Reed's floodlighting attracts some people. A car with men in uniform on its roof races across, distributing thunderflashes and shaking a number of bystanders. It is here that we see our only organised music – a procession of medical students heading for Piccadilly Circus, with a trombone, a drum and assorted bedpans playing and singing 'Singing Ay-Ay-Ippy-Ippy-Ay'… Along the centre of Regent Street went a procession headed by an elderly man with a UJ [Union Jack] on a long pole. From this pole strings of bunting extended back

to members of the procession, two or three women and girls, and a man or two. We learn from the leader that this is all one family.[42]

Arriving home in their south-London suburb after midnight, they found bonfires burning in the street, and several houses with 'elaborate lighting arrangements' outside their windows. Opening a long-cherished magnum of champagne, the diarist and his friends sat around having 'a very philosophical discussion'. He already found that he missed some elements of the war:

> I had enjoyed the war because I felt that I was fighting for something worthwhile – or rather *against* something. I had felt important up to now... I was afraid that I should wake up in the morning and find myself back in 1939, with all the pleasure of my wartime experiences and the friends I had gained proving to be nothing but a long dream.[43]

For some, the war had brought new opportunities and new friendships. A sense of 'living through history' and of being a part of something important, with shared aims and values, was something that this diarist, and others, were worried they would miss in the post-war years. He had found a sense of belonging in the military; others found this in their workplace or in their local communities. But by December 1945 his fears were proving unfounded: he was looking forward to leaving the army and training as a teacher, facing 'the future with eagerness', even though, he joked, 'I think we have at least a year before we are atomised; let's all make the most of it.'[44]

Others, however, were looking back on the war years with mixed emotions. The noise, light, bonfires and fireworks that marked the end of the European war in so many towns and cities inevitably put some people in mind of the Blitz. A diarist from badly bombed Eltham in south-east London – an area that had been under the path of the V-1 'flying bombs' and V-2 rockets of the last years of the war, as well as the night-time air raids – went to the large Woolwich barracks late in the evening, where a concert was followed by a fireworks display. She thought this was:

> Reminiscent of the blitz, with hand-grenades and Very Lights [military flares] going off, and various other noisy fireworks adding to the din. Several children round here were frightened, thinking no doubt that it was a raid, but the men no doubt loved it.[45]

In Burnley in Lancashire, a diarist dismissed the searchlights of the evening as 'nothing to compare with the scores of searchlights seen at one time round here when the blitz was on', while in Swansea the light of bonfires reminded the diarist teacher of 'the nights when the houses were burning during the blitz'.[46] The secretary in Southend, who had been woken by the thunderstorm the previous night and had thought, in her confusion, that it was an air raid, was surprised that 'people, generally, weren't sick of fire, explosions and sudden noise'.[47] Germany's surrender may have meant that the attacks on British towns and cities were over, but their impact on the landscape, on individual lives and on memory, would have a long afterlife.

In the genteel Glaswegian suburb of Bearsden the young social worker living with her parents and their Polish lodgers, while her husband was fighting in Burma, found herself reminded of the devastating air raids on nearby industrial Clydebank in 1941. She had been unwell and was confined to bed, something that she found frustrating as she longed to be out, witnessing what was happening. Late in the evening her mother and the son of their Polish lodger set out on a bike ride to 'see what was happening in the way of celebrations'. They reported back on numerous bonfires, fireworks and 'beautifully decorated houses among the new bungalows between here and Glasgow – fairy lights round the windows and flood lighting here and there'. This wasn't enough to drive the darkest days of the war from her mind. As she looked out of her bedroom window she:

> Could see nothing… but a little twinkle through the trees and a faint red glow in the sky – very different from that bright red glow on that cold March night when all Clydebank was ablaze, and the smoky flames of the oil tanks leapt up in the moonlight. Thank God we'll never see that again and all the desolation that followed it.[48]

Clydebank was one of the most heavily bombed places in Britain: more than 1,200 people were killed and almost all the houses in the small town were damaged, with many thousands made homeless. Communities like this would take a long time to recover from the ravages of war.

Heswall on the Wirral had been much luckier. Close to the industrial centres and docklands of Liverpool and Birkenhead, where nearly 4,000 people were killed during the Merseyside Blitz, suburban Heswall survived relatively unscathed, with just seven civilian deaths recorded on the town's war memorial on Dee View Road. Among those named are three members of one family: Dorothy, George and Lilian Shone. Names on a war memorial today are generally simply that: names, a reminder of the dreadful cost of war, but the individuals being commemorated there often long forgotten. But on VE Day the Shone family's tragedy was not forgotten. The young clerk who had recorded her excitement at the end of the European war had spent the evening with friends in two of Heswall's pubs, arguing over politics and the potential for a revolution in Britain. On their way home they stopped to look at a bonfire 'built up in the rubble of a blitzed house'. She remembered how:

> On May 30th 1941 an HE [high-explosive] bomb, followed by an oil bomb had fallen where this bonfire now blazed. The house had been smashed then set on fire. Five children had been able to escape, but NFS [National Fire Service] and ARP men had been unable to reach either Mr and Mrs Shone, who must have been killed instantly, nor Dorothy, who had been burnt to death. Dorothy was a small, laughing young girl of 19, engaged to a soldier, great fun at a party or in a dance. People had stood away from the blazing ruins, helplessly, as she screamed in agony, trapped.

Going to bed that night, she thought about the meaning of VE Day, and of the symbolism of a celebratory bonfire in the ruins of a family home. If the fire was built from the ashes of lives lost, honouring them with a lasting peace, then 'that is good'. If, however, it was a false dawn, with more conflict and more losses to come, then 'this country deserves all the desolation and damnation that will result from the stupidity and short-sightedness of its people'.[49]

As VE Day came to an end, some diarists were still celebrating, determined to wring every scrap of excitement and pleasure out of this day, keen to make sure that 'they were there' – whether in the crowds of central London, around the bonfires or in the pubs of regional cities, towns, villages and suburbs. The long war in Europe was over; the war in Asia, for those without loved ones there, felt both a long way away and certain of eventual victory. For others, though, the day was simply a pause: a time to celebrate or to reflect on the past six years of conflict, comradeship and suffering. Some diarists lived in the moment, others looked back over the past years, while others looked forward – some with hope and others with anxiety.

What would come next was unclear. Hitler had been defeated, but the wartime coalition with the Soviet Union was breaking down. Indian calls for independence had only grown stronger during the war and were the augury of an era of decolonisation. Domestic politics too were unclear, as the country prepared for a summer election and began the long job of reconstruction. Britain had survived the war, but not unscathed; the human and economic cost was enormous. Like the rest of Europe, it stood on the edge of an uncertain future.

Afterword

'It Is All Very Difficult to Imagine We Have Peace'

Many of those who so diligently recorded their wartime feelings and experiences for Mass Observation between 1939 and 1945 agreed with the sixty-three-year-old teacher from Great Missenden in Essex whose wartime diary concluded with the announcement of victory in Europe on the evening of 7 May 1945: 'This war diary – thank goodness – can now be laid aside forever.'[1] For many observers the extraordinary circumstances of war – the sense that they were living through remarkable times – was the catalyst for writing. Over the past six years Mass Observation had repeatedly asked them to reflect on how they were feeling (January 1940: 'How do you feel about holidays this year?'; October 1943: 'What do you feel about the recent bombing of Germany?'), and by the war's end they were seasoned self-observers, able to consider their own feelings about and responses to events as well as recording the actions and sentiments of those around them. Such continued self-reflection was demanding and perhaps, as the war came to an end, the immediacy of recording everyday events and feelings seemed less urgent, less a means of contributing to history, of saying, 'I was there too.'

But many other diarists had picked up the habit of regular writing and felt they had a personal relationship with Mass Observation, developed over years of regular reporting, posting often-intimate details of their lives to the organisation and receiving regular letters, requests and reports in return. By the last months of the war this connection felt familiar and personal to some of the writers. One woman, a company secretary living in Croydon, had sent Mass Observation a lengthy description of her feelings on VE Day, including an apology:

> Sorry I sound gloomy. I'm not, dear old MO. I am sure you must have a grand picture of this war-worn land stored up by now, in peace or war I just have to do all a full-time city job and a house and family and garden require as if I were two people.[2]

She, and many other writers, had built up a rapport with the organisation, which was intensified by the extraordinary circumstances of war, meaning that the diaries and responses to questions that they so diligently wrote are unlike the material collected by other social-survey or polling organisations at the time. For many, it was as if they were writing to an old friend.

This wasn't to last. Mass Observation gradually became a more straightforward market-research organisation in the years after the war, as government funding for surveys of public feeling and reports on morale dried up, and advertising agencies and producers became keen to gauge the mood and desires of the new consumer society. In the immediate aftermath of the war, however, Mass Observation continued to ask its 'National Panel' to record their thoughts on a wide and eclectic range of topics, from thoughts on Christian names (May 1946: 'What do you personally *feel* about your Christian name?'); the supernatural (September 1946: 'What are your thoughts and feelings about a) spiritualism, b) astrology, c) telepathy, d) fortune telling?'); reading (November 1946: 'What are your feelings towards paper covered books in general?'); and the atom bomb (February 1947: 'What are your feelings about the atom bomb?'). Almost two years on from VE Day, in April 1947, they asked their remaining writers for their 'six main grumbles', noting that 'This is a question that we asked regularly through the war, but have not yet asked in peacetime. Will observers who answered this question during the war years do their best to answer it now.'[3]

And they did. Rationing, and shortages of food and fuel, had only got worse since the end of the war as Britain struggled to rebuild and reconstruct. Although the basic petrol ration had been restored in 1945, bacon allowances were cut in the same year and allowances of butter, sugar and tea all remained at their lowest wartime level. Bread rationing had been introduced for the first time in 1946 and potatoes were rationed in 1947, after an especially long, cold winter had destroyed much of the crop in storage. Top of the list of grumbles were housing, shortages, strikes and queues. Some of the unity that was felt in wartime was clearly dissipating two years later. A Watford teacher was disgruntled about the continuation of some of the irritations of wartime life, especially for women. She argued that 'Needlessly long waits in queues make women fed up, resentful of young men who do not seem to realise what wartime was like for women.'[4] Naomi Mitchison in Kintyre was also feeling thoroughly grumpy about the continued shortages of supplies and labour, and the perceived slowness of reconstruction:

> Being so tired and everything being so difficult to do. Lack of domestic help which stops me from doing my own jobs which I am good at. Difficulty of getting spare parts, tractor tyres etc. Having to think about food so much of the time. Not being able to get on with public work, houses, roads, etc., most of which I promised, thinking they could be given to people. Most people being so stupid.[5]

However another respondent – an ex-teacher, wife and mother living in Accrington, Lancashire – complained about other people complaining, which she saw as motivated by a dislike of the Labour government:

> So many people spend so much time finding fault instead of trying to improve things. E.g. THE HOUSEWIVES LEAGUE. This is a disgusting society, simply out to sabotage the government.

She went on to criticise 'people who talk as if war were inevitable' and 'people who refuse to be economical with fuel and other scarce commodities'.[6] The Chepstow teacher who had spent VE Day parading and partying was also cross with those she believed wanted the government to fail, and who resented the social and economic changes that were shaping post-war Britain:

> I have a grumble against the grumblers. They are either people who are out to sabotage the government, people who had too much before the war, or people who had not enough who try to improve their caste by pretending that they had.[7]

While she was optimistic about the future, she believed that others were failing to build on the achievements of wartime. The joy and unity that she and others had felt on VE Day had clearly faded two years on.

And the months and years since VE Day had been eventful ones. While Wednesday 9 May (VE Day plus one, and a second public holiday) had been quiet, largely given over to nursing hangovers, seeing family and children's street parties, it was a brief pause in a turbulent few months. The young mother living with her parents in Swansea had waved goodbye to her husband as he returned from leave that morning. In the afternoon she went for a walk around her neighbourhood, stopping first to look at a street party being organised:

> There are plates of sausage rolls, cakes and bread and butter – four huge trifles… they are covered with hundreds and thousands and cream (?). Two big girls are running from house to house collecting the children… further along the police sergeant who lives in the road is helping the boys to build a bonfire… as we go along the road boys and a few girls pass us dragging bushes of gorse behind and between them to their various bonfires.[8]

Meanwhile in Leeds another observer had decided to carry on celebrating, visiting local pubs and enjoying 'free dancing in the parks under the "big tops"' organised by the local council.[9] But many people spent the day more quietly. Near Rochdale the woman who had written so evocatively of 'the little bunches of people clustered around the paper sellers' on the eve of VE Day had stayed home all day, feeling 'afraid of having to see the world drift away from the energy and vision that peace demands'.[10] In Leicester 'everything was quiet', while a woman in Great Missenden spent the day taking down 'the last of the black-out curtains' and depositing 'a jar of anti-mustard gas ointment' in the dustbin.[11] Clearly, many aspects of the war years would not be missed.

In July 1945 Britain held its first General Election since November 1935, when Stanley Baldwin's Conservative-led National Government had been returned with more than 50 per cent of the votes cast. During the war the major parties agreed not to stand against one another in by-elections, guaranteeing a stable parliament for the vast majority of the war years. The Labour Party left this wartime coalition government just two weeks after VE Day and was elected in the July election with a landslide swing of almost 10 per cent. Churchill, the great war leader, lost power, handing the premiership to the unassuming figure of Clement Attlee, Labour Party leader and deputy prime minister in Churchill's Cabinet for much of the war. There was no great enthusiasm for the election, and the overall mood in the country leaned towards scepticism about any government's ability to deliver on its promises, and even apathy. Why, then, did voters reject Churchill so soon after he led the country to victory in Europe, and just two months after crowds had cheered him loudly on the balcony of the Ministry of Health? The answer lies in large part in the middle of the war years, and in the aims and desires of the 'people's war'.

Attlee's Labour Party promised voters it would deliver the 'New Jerusalem' of a welfare state, and was more widely trusted than Churchill's Conservative Party to deliver on this promise. Out of power for the 1930s – Auden's 'low, dishonest decade' – it was easier for Labour to promise the reforms to social and economic policy that so many people desired.[12] The 1945 Labour Party election manifesto, *Let Us Face the Future*, promised to 'harness the spirit of Dunkirk and the Blitz' to provide the 'food, work and homes' that people needed. It promised to embrace the recommendations of William Beveridge's popular wartime 'Social Insurance and

Allied Services Report', with its commitment to tackling the 'five giants' of 'want, disease, ignorance, squalor and idleness', creating a welfare state that rewarded people for their wartime sacrifice with a 'safety net' from cradle to grave. Labour, not the Conservatives, was widely seen as the party to deliver this.

If Beveridge and the 'spirit' of the 'people's war' were key to Labour's appeal in the 1945 election, then Churchill was believed to be the Conservative's not-so-secret weapon. This weapon, however, was tired and struggled to connect with his audience on the campaign trail. Midway between VE Day and the General Election, Mass Observation asked its writers to record their feelings about the forthcoming election and their hopes for the post-war years. A full 50 per cent of them were 'unimpressed' with Churchill's infamous 'Gestapo' speech, when in a party political broadcast on the BBC he warned listeners that Attlee's Labour Party would, if elected, 'fall back on some form of Gestapo'.[13] This speech has been widely seen as a misstep by the Conservative Party leader. Churchill's rhetoric may have been designed to warn the British people, who – as we have seen – had anxieties about the intentions of Stalin's Soviet Union in the aftermath of war in Europe, against the potential for a homespun totalitarianism. Its result was disastrous for a Conservative Party already trailing in the polls and over-reliant on the wartime popularity of its leader. Looking at the mild-mannered Clement Attlee, a close colleague of Churchill during the war, the electorate was more likely to agree with wartime Home Secretary Herbert Morrison that this was 'Churchill's crazy broadcast', rather than with Churchill's warning that Attlee was a dictator-in-waiting.[14]

Election Day itself, Thursday 5 July, dawned bright and dry for most of the country. In Penzance the war-disabled diarist was amused to find himself picked up and taken to the polling station by a 'Labour car', even though he intended to vote for the Liberal candidate.[15] In Fleet, Hampshire, the diarist who had enjoyed a long-saved tin of brisket of beef with his family on VE Day proudly recorded that both he and his wife had voted for Tom Wintringham, the Common Wealth candidate, whose party had seen some success in the war years by offering voters a left-of-centre alternative in the otherwise uncontested by-elections.[16] The end of the wartime coalition, however, also marked the end for Common Wealth, which only retained one seat, in Chelmsford in Essex, which was itself lost when the sitting MP joined the Labour Party the following year.

The *Daily Mirror* had reminded its readership of what they had been fighting for, reproducing Philip Zec's famous cartoon, first published on VE Day, showing an exhausted British soldier clambering over the rubble of a continental town, holding a wreath labelled 'Victory and Peace in Europe' and accompanied by the words: 'Here you are! Don't lose it again.' 'Vote for Them,' *Daily Mirror* readers were told:

> Vote on behalf of the men who won the victory for you. You failed to do so in 1918. The result is known to all. The 'land fit for heroes' did not come into existence. The dole did. Short-lived prosperity gave way to long, tragic years of poverty and unemployment. Make sure that history does not repeat itself. Your vote gives you the power. Use it. Let no one turn your gaze to the past. March forward to new and happier times. The call of the men who have gone comes to you. Pay heed to it. Vote for THEM.[17]

The results were delayed for several weeks as the votes of servicemen and women overseas were returned and counted.

When they were finally tallied, on 26 July, the scale of the Labour landslide was a surprise to many: 393 elected Labour MPs, giving the party a huge 146-seat majority.

Among the new MPs was Naomi Mitchison's husband, Dick, who beat the young Conservative politician John Profumo to take the seat of Kettering in Northampton. As the candidate's wife, the campaign was hectic for Mitchison, with days spent 'driving all out at 60mph with Labour ladies in the back chatting about bottling jam'.[18] Travelling back to Scotland the next day, she was unable to get a bunk on the sleeper train to Glasgow, or even a seat, and spent the journey dozing in the train's corridor before returning to her home on Kintyre. There she continued to be busy, harvesting hay, collecting fruit, hosting endless visitors and dealing with an unexpected delivery of furniture from their home in Hammersmith. Returning from Scotland to Kettering for the election result, she again failed to get a sleeper carriage, but did get a third-class seat 'by dint of looking sad and unprotected'. The results were exciting: although 'Dick was fairly confident', the margin at first seemed to be narrow. He eventually won the seat by a majority of 6,444 and Mitchison celebrated his victory, and that of the Labour Party overall, in the pub, where 'there was a bowl of gaillardias… and I stuck two in my hair.'[19]

Profumo returned to politics in 1950 and went on to rise through the ranks of government until the notorious 'Profumo affair' of 1963 when, while serving as Secretary of State for War, he admitted to an affair with Christine Keeler, who was also in a relationship with a senior naval attaché at the Soviet Embassy. Profumo was young in 1945, but other, more established figures also lost their seats, including the National Labour MP Harold Nicolson, husband of Vita Sackville-West, and the Conservative Leo Amery, who was famous for urging the Labour MP Arthur Greenwood to 'speak for England' in a 1939 debate on the German invasion of Poland.*

Although she was a socialist who believed in the need to redistribute wealth and build a fairer society, Naomi Mitchison was both wealthy and very well connected. Perhaps a more typical experience of the 1945 election was that of Nella Last in Barrow-in-Furness, a seat gained for Labour by Walter Monslow, who beat the sitting Conservative MP by more than 12,000 votes. As the results became known, Nella had gone into the town centre to buy some groceries and have her hair done. She found that everyone she met 'was eager to speak of the election' and was surprised that 'beyond real grief at the "dirty trick" played on Churchill, there was no real lament from my Tory friends'. She thought this stemmed from the war, which had unified people and left an optimistic belief that 'it might turn out all right', from voters of all loyalties and none. One woman, pleasantly surprised by the amount of food available in Barrow's shops that day, joked, 'By God, Labour is beginning to show what it will do for us all. They have soon seen we have plenty of fish and potatoes!'[20]

The optimism that Last detected on a sunny summer's day in Cumbria was both strengthened and challenged just a

---

* National Labour was formed of that small section of the Parliamentary Labour Party that supported, and served with, the Conservative-led National Governments of the 1930s. Nicolson was elected in 1935, representing Leicester West. Leo Amery was a prominent Conservative politician, ally of Churchill and opponent of appeasement. Like Churchill, he was an ardent imperialist. His oldest son, John Amery, was executed for treason in 1945 after making propaganda broadcasts for Nazi Germany and encouraging British prisoners of war in Germany to join the so-called British Free Corps, a unit of the Waffen SS.

month later, when the war came to an abrupt and shocking end: strengthened because the war in Asia and the Pacific ended in victory over Japan before the planned, and dreaded, ground invasion of the Japanese home islands; challenged by the form of Japan's defeat and its legacies for the world, based as it was on the United States's decision to use the atomic bomb against the cities of Hiroshima and Nagasaki. Mass Observers would have learned of this powerful new weapon over their breakfasts on 7 August 1945, the day after the first bomb was detonated above the Japanese city of Hiroshima. 'The bomb that has changed the world,' bellowed the front page of the *Daily Express*, while two days later readers of the *Daily Mirror* discovered that 'practically all living things – human and animal – were literally seared to death by the tremendous heat and pressure'.[21] As the war came to its end, Mass Observation asked its panel of writers two key questions:

> Describe in detail your own feelings and views about the atom bomb, and those of the people you meet.
>
> How do you feel about the peace now?[22]

The replies show us how some of the people whose descriptions of VE Day have filled the pages of this book were feeling about the emerging post-war world just three months later.

In response to the first question, Mass Observation writers were divided about this new, devastating weapon. Many, though, were also pragmatic. The Allies were planning for the invasion of the home islands of Japan, known as Operation Downfall and scheduled to begin in the autumn of 1945. Although the operation was to be led by the United States, some 55,000 British, Australian, Canadian and New Zealand troops were earmarked for the invasion, which was expected to be both difficult and bloody, with high casualties predicted among both combatants and civilians. Japan's surrender on 15 August meant that the eventual Allied occupation of Japan was a peaceful one, and that Malaya and Singapore returned, temporarily at least, to the British Empire without further fighting. A housekeeper from Durham explained that:

> It frightened me, for I have read bits about splitting the atom. But both Tom [her husband] and I were mad at those priests etc. against its use. We said save our own men at the expense of *all*.

But her irritation with those who opposed the weapon's use was tempered by her strong sense that the destructive power of the atom, once used, could not be forgotten. Worrying that it would only be a matter of time before other countries developed their own weapons, she concluded, 'God help the world.'[23] The film-strip producer from London, who had listened to the BBC recording of church bells on VE Day with such pleasure, thought that for 'aggressor nations' like Japan 'the swift death of even these large numbers seems no more to be deplored than slow deaths from torture, or starvation, indeed rather less'. Women whom she overheard while out shopping, and dismissed rather disparagingly as 'unintelligent and on the callous side', thought that 'they asked for it and now they got it' and 'expect they'll blow the whole world up now and we shan't know nothing about it, like a judgment'.[24] The Eton schoolmaster who had had such fun on VE Day was writing from his home in Shropshire during the school holidays and was even more unyielding. He wrote:

> My first reaction to the news of the destruction caused by the atomic bomb was amazement, but it was unmixed with any feelings of pity for the Japanese. I was irritated by the stupidity of the people who persisted in writing to the papers, or saying it was un-Christian and brutal, and like German methods. Total war has shown us that civilians are as much military targets as front line soldiers, and since the Japanese at home are compelled to make munitions etc., they are not to be exempted from our attacks.[25]

Six long years of war, with destruction rained upon civilians of European and Asian nations, had clearly left some not only war-weary, but hardened to its cost.

When asked to reflect on their feelings about the new atomic weapons, most Mass Observers looked to the long term, rather than the end of the war against Japan. Overwhelmingly they felt that it would bring about significant changes in world history. Some were optimistic about what these changes would mean, their thoughts and hopes reading like a forerunner of the doctrine of Mutually Assured Destruction that prevailed throughout much of the Cold War. A draughtsman from Surrey, who had spent VE Day pottering on his allotment, thought that over time the enormous power of these new weapons would mean that current military tactics would become obsolete, as 'a country the size of the Isle of Man… could wipe out half of Europe'. He argued that 'nations must sink their political differences in the international spheres, and endeavour to really get together to make warfare impossible on a major scale'.[26] Likewise the miner from South Yorkshire, whose wife had made red flags for their friends and neighbours out of a pair of curtains on VE Day, found reason to be optimistic:

> The day has gone when thousands of young men could be shipped to the war, and politicians could sit back and await results. Kings, emperors, butlers, dustmen, housewives, children. We are now *all* in the front line. All the more reason to expect a bigger, better effort to nip war in the bud.[27]

A retired contributor from Tring in Hertfordshire thought that 'it may be the turning point in human moral history', while a young sergeant in the air force, who heard the news of Hiroshima in a Bournemouth hotel 'full of deaf old ladies and retired Indian Army Colonels', hoped that:

> It will certainly end all war as we know it. War can never be declared again, as obviously whoever gets the other with the first atomic bomb will win. Perhaps we will really be able to have a working League of Nations [the interwar forerunner of the United Nations] now, backed by the atomic bomb.[28]

As one war ended, and leaders of forty nations met in San Francisco to try and create just such an organisation – the United Nations – that would have the power to prevent future such catastrophic conflicts, it's noticeable how few Mass Observers felt that two world wars had taught nations and political leaders the value of peace.

Others, though, were even more pessimistic, often overwhelmed by the horror of a weapon that could kill some 20,000 people in a moment and reduce a city to ruins. A soldier agreed with the retired writer from Tring that the atom bomb *could* be a turning point in world history, but thought that 'it won't be, and... sooner or later we shall wipe ourselves out'.[29] The retired nurse in West Sussex, who had spent so much of the war complaining about the BBC's coverage of the conflict, found herself 'terrified at the spirits we have called up from the "vasty deep"'. She did not share the optimism of some other writers about the power of the new weapon to ensure world peace. Indeed, she continued, 'I cannot see any such wisdom in the settlement to date of world affairs that would let me think there is wisdom enough among leading men to be allowed such terrible powers.' 'Anyway,' she thought, 'it is another reason for not regretting that my life is nearly over.'[30] The young secretary from the Wirral who had described her feelings on VE Day in such detail was reminded of reading a novel by H. G. Wells in 1940:

> In which he described an atom-bomb raid on Paris. The description was vivid – how the earth was churned to black liquid, how the devastated city glowed red with flames. I shuddered with horror to think that the Luftwaffe raids experienced at the time could ever be so horrible. Then I was comforted, thinking to myself that such bombs would never be invented in *my* lifetime. When the news of the first atom bomb raid on Japan was announced my first thoughts were again of the gory description in that book by H. G. Wells. I was again shaken with horror. Such bombs *had* been invented in my lifetime![31]

Some Mass Observers ignored the request to record their feelings, and instead chose to set out their thoughts and predictions for the future. The young man from Middlesex who had been irritated by a children's party outside his girlfriend's house on VE Day was similarly pessimistic. Describing himself as a pacifist, he wondered whether 'present civilisation as we know it will destroy itself with bigger and more devastating atom bombs'.[32] A farm worker from Worcestershire agreed. He thought the use of atomic weapons meant that:

We are in for the Age of Fear, the age of atavisms, of return to the primitive needs of physical life, and to the hoary myths of history, famine and nationalism. People may even come to look on the atomic bomb as a kind of drug; for it can't hurt very much to be vaporised.[33]

The thoughts of a new mother were more personal. For her, the potential of this new weapon to destroy life was real rather than abstract and was expressed through a description of her feelings, just as Mass Observation had requested:

My feelings about the atom bomb? Hard to describe – a sort of primal shudder and at once the thought 'if this can happen then what is the good of anything?'… I feel my children cannot escape annihilation, and understand for the first time the mothers who poisoned their children in the face of the enemy advance… I can't talk about it, so have no friends' views to add. I am afraid. I AM AFRAID. And where will it get me? We are impotent.[34]

Relief at the end of one war was replaced for this observer by profound, almost paralysing anxiety about what the 'post-war' world might look like and, in the shadow of the bomb, how long it would last.

This knitting-together of public events and private, domestic life was common to much of the writing that Mass Observation collected during the war years. By the end of the war many of their writers were highly skilled at describing their feelings and relating them to the events of the war. The thoughtful and prolific Nella Last – with her interest in the world and her assured descriptions of her more private feelings, thoughts and experiences – was disappointed to discover that other people were not always as preoccupied with the wider world as she was. She had gone for a day out in the Lancashire resort town of Morecambe with her husband and some friends on 11 August, two days after the second atom bomb was dropped on Nagasaki, and was keen to record what people were saying about the news:

> We sat on the slope of the Head to watch the circus, and I saw a group sitting near in very earnest conversation, with their heads together. I'd have loved to go and butt in. I love being in an argument and thought 'perhaps they are talking about the atomic bomb, or the result of the election.' I've got very good hearing, and when I'd got used to the different sounds around I could hear what they *were* discussing – the new cold perm! Every woman I know is interested in it – another revolution, when curly hair can be assured by a method so simple that it can be done at home.[35]

Of course we don't know what this group of friends talked about when Nella wasn't listening or whether some were keeping their fears, or their hopes, to themselves, maybe unwilling to risk spoiling a day out with an argument about politics or the future of humankind. But their emphasis on the personal, on a new hair technology rather than the atom bomb, the election or the new world that was taking shape, should not be so surprising after almost six years of being asked to put the national good above individual desires.

Given the celebrations of VE Day, repeated in a far more muted fashion on 'Victory over Japan' (VJ) Day on 15 August, we might expect the dominant mood in the first weeks of peace to be happy, or optimistic. The war was over and Britain had been on the winning side. Not only that, but it had recently elected a reforming government that was promising to put the key proposals of Beveridge's popular wartime report into practice and build a new welfare state that should ensure security and stability for all. But the answers to Mass Observation's second question in August 1945, 'How do you feel about the peace now?', show a much more mixed picture. According to a report published by the organisation that year, three out of five of their writers felt pessimistic, and 'the election of a Labour government has done "unexpectedly" little to change the prevailing mood'. This, they thought, was less to do with world events, and more to do with the sense that people's lives were changing too slowly. For the individual, 'the impact of today's events overwhelms any major feeling of satisfaction about the nationalisation of the Bank of England'.[36]

The feelings of Mass Observers about the world they were emerging into were, predictably, mixed. For some, their pleasure at the victory of the new Labour government, and all that this promised, outweighed any anxiety or fear about what the future might hold. The retired nurse from Steyning was a Labour Party supporter and described how, after her long years of apprehension during the war, 'how wonderful to go to bed, or to leave the house, and know that it will be all right'; and the Yorkshire coal miner was 'glad to have lived to see July 26th, 1945'.[37] The music teacher from Leicester who had spent VE Day babysitting for her brother's family was similarly:

> Very optimistic. With a socialist government in power I feel we are moving in the right direction at last. There is still a lot of hard work and sacrifice ahead but I feel that most people realise this and though they will grumble (as the English always do) they will get on with it and make the best of a bad job.[38]

Mass Observers writing in August 1945 were not especially prone to grumbling, but they did sometimes feel rather flat, after the heightened emotions of wartime. Peace might demand 'a lot of hard work and sacrifice', but it perhaps didn't feel as important and immediate as the demands of war.

Much of this disquiet stemmed from the sense that although the war was over, in some ways it didn't *feel* over: victory had been anticipated long before it was achieved, and although the bombing and fighting had stopped, rationing, shortages and many wartime restrictions remained. The teacher from Watford thought that 'the peace is so much like war time after the war's gradual ending that it is difficult to know what to say'. And the young man from Middlesex found that 'apart from blackout bombs and sirens, for me life is just the same'.[39] In Sheffield another Mass Observer, a young married woman who was still employed in her wartime job of welding instructor, agreed:

> Personally, I still feel rather 'numb' – unable to appreciate that it is really over – but I recognise that it is only a reaction after the strain and will wear off in time. I think that everyone is bound to feel a certain flatness after the excitement of the last months of war news – it is difficult to adapt oneself when one is still living a more or less wartime life.[40]

The 'wartime life' that continued immediately after the war was largely made up of the tiring, tedious elements of the war years: endless bureaucracy, interminable queues, shortages of fuel, food, housing and clothing, continued rationing and ceaseless exhortations to continue saving, recycling and reusing. The accompanying sense of unity, cooperation and common purpose that so many had found in wartime was less apparent. Post-war austerity, while it may have been an unavoidable after-effect of the costs of war and of building the peace, was nonetheless a largely unwelcome one.

The Eton schoolmaster, who described himself as 'Tory by inclination', was highly sceptical about the new government's ability to build a 'brave new world' and thought that 'everyone who believed that peace will bring immediate relief from war conditions will be, and are already being, sadly disillusioned'. Instead, he believed, 'we must be resigned to the fact that things must get worse before they get better'.[41] None of those who were still writing for Mass Observation seemed to be under the impression that peace would bring 'immediate relief' from the demands and controls of wartime. Rather, they were concerned that the loss of a 'wartime spirit' would make the personal sacrifice and acceptance of shared hardships that would be necessary to build the peace much harder to achieve.

The film-strip producer from south London was quite resigned to the difficulties inherent in motivating people for a collective effort in peacetime. There was, she thought, certain to be a 'sense of slackness' as people gradually unwound from the heightened tensions of wartime:

> After individual and national efforts have been keyed up, and directed towards a single definite objective, there is bound to be a period of readjustment when that objective has been achieved. So I am not really pessimistic about the irritations and misunderstandings of this early post-war period.

She hoped that 'some new, simple, or simplified, objective may soon be devised to pull efforts together into a common direction once more'.[42] Others agreed: the common cause of wartime needed a peacetime equivalent, if the desired post-war world was to be built on both the national and the international stage. The teacher from Thornaby-on-Tees in Yorkshire was 'dreadfully impatient to start building the new world' and relieved 'not to live in imminent danger of death from the sky'. Nevertheless, she worried that 'we have already begun to lose the peace' and found herself longing 'for a "mission" – something new and *positive* to work for'.[43] Another diarist agreed that the spirit of wartime endeavour was going to be essential to 'build the peace', because 'without the consenting goodwill of the people even the best schemes will fail'; and a housewife in Bishop Auckland, County Durham was missing the sense of purpose that she had found in the war:

> Now and again I suddenly realise that peace is *here*, not something to wait for like the bombs falling. Then I feel so mad that I am of no help. I'm just a housewife with no outlet for constructive work. Things will be very little altered for me, I have no one to return from the war, it is all very difficult to imagine we have peace. Then I sometimes realise how very hopeful I should be – at least the fighting is over and others are getting their broken lives patched up slowly. Then I smile to myself when I think 'well, after all, we have got a Labour government to lead us along in peace' – so surely it must be a better peace than I had ever hoped. But I still cannot see the wood for the trees.[44]

Wartime might have been difficult, sometimes frightening and often boring, but in these immediate post-war days – as people started to adjust to a life *without* the rhythms of wartime, but *with* many of its annoyances and irritations – a nostalgia for the unity and aims of the war years was already starting to emerge.

The reflections of the woman from Leeds whose husband wasn't speaking to her on VE Day, and who was longing for a divorce by the end of the year, show how, for some, the war felt like something out of the ordinary: a period of liberation, bringing opportunities, new friendships and a sense of fulfilment that weren't part of their usual peacetime life. She wrote:

> To me, it has been similar to having a conversation broken by someone barging in, and when that person has gone, one simply carries on from where one left off. I'm glad we had a war for one reason – it has shaken me out of a state of single-mindedness. Now I see things and people 'face to face' as it were, and I wouldn't have missed it for anything.
>
> Whether I was sheltering for six hours in the basement of the 'Spotted Cow' from the bombs above, or sleeping with my torch in my hand, or running like hell to the other end of the hospital train on which I worked for the milk for my afternoon cup of tea (¼ mile away), or whether we'd had a siren free night and I'd slept like a log for once – whether or not I was doing any of those things, I *lived* every minute of the war.[45]

For her, the war was a period 'out of time', taking her away from her everyday life, showing her exactly what she was capable of and offering experiences and sensations that wouldn't exist in peacetime. The return to peace, with families and couples reunited after many years apart, continued hardships and the expectation that most people would return to their pre-war lives, would be hard for many to navigate.

The post-war world was to be shaped by the war, and the individuals who wrote for Mass Observation, who described their feelings and experiences on VE Day in such detail, were to understand this post-war world through their wartime experiences. For some, peace was welcome: a relief after long years of hardship, loss and anxiety. For others, the thrill and excitement of wartime would dominate their lives for the next decades. Life had been lived at an intensity during those years that would be difficult to recapture. The war might have been over, but it would cast a long shadow on the world, and on the individual lives of those who took time out of their war to record their thoughts and feelings for Mass Observation, and whose words are recounted here.

Acknowledgements

I wish to thank and acknowledge the Trustees of the Mass Observation Archive, University of Sussex, for permission to quote from the Archive. I also want to thank the current Mass Observation staff – Fiona Courage, Kirsty Patrick, Suzanne Rose, Jessica Scantlebury, Lottie Robinson and Ellie Turner-Kilburn – for their help, support and collective dedication to the Archive.

Dorothy Sheridan, Mass Observation Archivist from 1990 to 2008, has shaped this book in ways that are too numerous to mention. Dorothy was the archivist when I was a doctoral researcher at the University of Sussex in the 1990s, feeling intrigued and overwhelmed in equal measure by the material in Mass Observation, and her kindness and sense have shaped my work ever since. She is an excellent role model and I hope that she enjoys this book. Most important of all are all those anonymous writers who made the time not only to reflect on their lives, experiences, hopes and fears, but also to write them down and post them off to Mass Observation. Without them, and without their dedication and the tenacity of those who ran Mass Observation through the difficult wartime years, there would be no book.

My colleagues in the School of Philosophical, Historical and Interdisciplinary Studies at the University of Essex have been excellent sounding boards and collaborators through difficult times in British higher education. I especially want to thank Alix Green, Nadine Rossol, Andrew Priest, Diana Presciutti and Michael Roper, and all of my students on the final-year module 'Britain's Second World War: Mass Observation, Myth and Memory'. Gordon Wise at Curtis Brown has been a constant source of wise guidance, and James Nightingale and Harry O'Sullivan at Atlantic have been encouraging and enthusiastic editors. Away from Essex, Martin Evans continues to listen to me talk about my work with the patience needed of a partner, while Claire Langhamer in Brighton and Susan Grayzel in Utah are unfailingly generous with time and wise advice.

For a long time I have wanted to write a book that my parents, aunts and uncles might read. All were born during or just before the war years, and lived through the war in south London and Coventry, so this is their book. I hope they enjoy it.

Lucy Noakes
Brighton, UK

Notes

Prologue: 'An Anthropology of Our Own People'

1. *New Statesman*, 2 January 1937.
2. The National Archives (TNA), Ministry of Information (MoI), INF1/264, Summaries of Daily Reports, 8 June 1940.
3. Mass Observation Archive (MOA), Diarist no. 5414, 3 & 10 September 1940.
4. MOA, File Report (FR)0640, 'Hull', April 1941.
5. MOA, FR601, 'Bristol', March 1941.
6. MOA, Directive Respondent no. D1165, March 1943; Respondent no. 1165, March 1943; Respondent no. 1420, November 1939.

1. The Second World War in British Myth and Memory: 'I Had a Pretty Quiet War Really'

1. *Beyond the Fringe*, 1960.
2. *Evening Standard*, 12 March 1960, p.4.
3. *Daily Mail*, 20 May 1961, p.3.
4. *Daily Mail*, 1 August 1968, p.3.
5. Winston Churchill, House of Commons Debate, 4 June 1940.
6. The government's statistical analysis of the war gives the number of civilian dead through air raids as 60,595. Peter Howlett, *Fighting With Figures: A Statistical Digest of the Second World War* (London: HMSO, 1995), p.ix.

7. *Daily Telegraph*, 6 July 1982.
8. *Daily Star*, 17 October 1990.
9. *Daily Telegraph*, 15 March 2020.
10. HM Queen Elizabeth II, BBC, 5 April 2020.
11. *Daily Mirror*, 24 June 1996.

2. Mass Observation and the Second World War: 'They Speak for Themselves'

1. Jeremy Gould, *Plymouth: Vision of a Modern City* (Swindon: English Heritage, 2010).
2. 'The War in the West – A Child's Perspective', BBC, *WW2 People's War* archive, Article ID A3253475, www.bbc.co.uk/history/ww2peopleswar/stories/75/a3253475.shtml
3. Mass Observation Archive (MOA), Directive Respondent no. 3684, May 1945.
4. Astrid Lindgren, *A World Gone Mad: The Diaries of Astrid Lindgren 1939–45*, translated from the Swedish by Sarah Death (London: Pushkin Press, 2016), p.207; Anonymous, *A Woman in Berlin*, translated from the German by Philip Boehm (London: Virago, 2011 [first published in English 1954]).
5. Virginia Woolf, ed. Anne Oliver Bell, *The Diaries of Virginia Woolf: Vol. V, 1936–1941* (London: Penguin Books, 1984), p.39.
6. *Daily Express*, 7 December 1936, p.2.
7. *Daily Mirror*, 7 December 1936, p.12.
8. Tom Harrisson, Charles Madge and Humphrey Jennings, Letter, 'Anthropology at Home', *New Statesman and Nation*, 30 January 1937, p.155.
9. 'Anthropology at Home', 30 January 1937, p.155.
10. Quoted in James Hinton, *The Mass Observers, A History 1937–1949* (Oxford: Oxford University Press, 2013), p.7.
11. Hinton, *The Mass Observers*, p.8.
12. MOA, File Report (FR) A26, *They Speak for Themselves*, June 1939.
13. MOA, FRA26, *They Speak for Themselves*, June 1939.
14. Hinton, *The Mass Observers*, p.30.

15. MOA, FRA4, 'Directives', January 1937.
16. MOA, FRA4, 'Directives', January 1937.
17. Humphrey Jennings and Charles Madge, *May the Twelfth: Mass Observation Day Surveys* (London: Faber & Faber, 1937), p.92.
18. Jennings and Madge, *May the Twelfth*, p.184.
19. Jennings and Madge, *May the Twelfth*, pp.218–19.
20. MOA, Day Diarists, Diarist no. A001, 12 June 1937.
21. MOA, FRA4, 'Directives', January 1937.
22. Cited in Joe Moran, 'The Science of Ourselves', *New Statesman*, 29 January 2007.
23. MOA, Topic Collection (TC), Box 27, *Armistice Day, Coronation Day, Wakes, Valentine's Day, Xmas* (November 1938).
24. Quoted in Charles Madge and Tom Harrisson, *Britain by Mass Observation* (Harmondsworth: Penguin, 1939), p.41.
25. MOA, Day Survey, Respondent no. 833, 25 September 1938.
26. MOA, Day Survey, Respondent no. 1035, 28 September 1938.
27. MOA, Day Survey, Respondent no. 1033, 28 September 1938.
28. MOA, Respondent no. 1006, January 1939.
29. MOA, Directive Questionnaire, March 1939.
30. MOA, Respondent no. 1016, March 1939.
31. MOA, Respondent no. 1017, March 1939.
32. MOA, Respondent nos 1028 & 1035, March 1939.
33. Cited in Tom Picton, 'A Very Public Espionage', *Camerawork*, September 1978, p.3.
34. *Daily Mirror*, 6 December 1938, cited in David Mellor, 'Mass Observation: The Intellectual Climate', *Camerawork*, no. 11, September 1978, pp.4–5.
35. Tom Harrisson and Charles Madge, *War Begins at Home* (London: Chatto & Windus, 1940), p.29.
36. Harrisson and Madge, *War Begins at Home*, p.33.
37. MOA, Diarist no. 5353, 31 August 1939.
38. MOA, Diarist nos 5205 & 5230, 3 September 1939.
39. MOA, Directive Questionnaire, November 1939.

40. James Hinton, 'The "Class" Complex': Mass Observation and Cultural Distinction in Pre-War Britain', *Past and Present*, no. 199 (May 2008), p.211.
41. Sadly, nobody from Northern Ireland seems to have contributed to the material on VE Day.
42. This map can be found on the Mass Observation Online website, Adam Matthew Digital, *Mass Observation Online*, resources-amdigital-co-uk. uniessexlib.idm.oclc.org/mo/map/
43. Harrisson and Madge, *War Begins at Home*, p.20.

3. Mass Observers at War: 'War Begins at Home'

1. Astrid Lindgren, *A World Gone Mad: The Diaries of Astrid Lindgren, 1939–45*, translated from the Swedish by Sarah Death (London: Pushkin Press, 2016), pp.15–16.
2. Cited in Nicholas Stargardt, *The German War: A Nation Under Arms, 1939–45* (London: Vintage, 2015), p.30.
3. Renia Spiegel, Diary entry for 6 September 1939, reproduced in *The Smithsonian Magazine*, www.smithsonianmag.com/history/hear-o-israel-save-us-renia-spiegel-diary-english-translation-holocaust-poland-180970536/
4. Mass Observation Archive (MOA), Respondent no. 1006, August 1939.
5. MOA, Respondent nos 1018 & 1029, August 1939.
6. MOA, Diarist no. 5156, 29 August 1939.
7. MOA, Diarist no. 5426, 1 September 1939.
8. MOA, Diarist no. 5161, 29 August 1939.
9. MOA, Diarist no. 5397, 31 August 1939.
10. MOA, Diarist no. 5010, 1 September 1939.
11. Tanya Evans & Patricia Thane, *Sinners? Scroungers? Saints? Unmarried Motherhood in Twentieth-Century England* (Oxford: Oxford University Press, 2019), p.55.
12. MOA, Diarist no. 5141, 29 August 1939; Diarist no. 5458, 31 August 1939.
13. MOA, Diarist no. 5353, 31 August 1939.

14. MOA, Diarist no. 5397, 2 & 3 September 1939.
15. MOA, Diarist no. 5378, 3 September 1939.
16. MOA, Diarist no. 5141, 3 September 1939.
17. MOA, Diarist no. 5340, 3 September 1939.
18. MOA, Diarist no. 5010, 3 September 1939.
19. MOA, Diarist nos 5458 & 5080, 3 September 1939.
20. MOA, Diarist no. 5366, 3 September 1939.
21. MOA, Diarist no. 5282, 3 September 1939.
22. MOA, Diarist no. 5390, 2 October 1939.
23. Humphrey Jennings and Harry Watt, *London Can Take It* (Ministry of Information, 1940).
24. Tom Harrisson and Charles Madge, *War Begins at Home* (London: Chatto & Windus, 1940), pp.64–5.
25. Harrisson and Madge, *War Begins at Home*, p.69.
26. Harrisson and Madge, *War Begins at Home*, p.80.
27. Harrisson and Madge, *War Begins at Home*, p.97.
28. Winston Churchill, Hansard, House of Commons, vol. 360, col. 1502, 13 May 1940.
29. *Daily Mail*, 14 May 1940; *Daily Express*, 14 May 1940.
30. MOA, Diarist nos 5175 & 5297, 14 May 1940.
31. MOA, Diarist no. 5353, 11 May 1940.
32. Winston Churchill, Hansard, House of Commons, vol. 361, col. 796, 4 June 1940; vol. 362, col. 61, 18 June 1940.
33. J. B. Priestley, *Postscripts*, 5 June 1940 (London: William Heinemann, 1940), pp.1–4. This was Priestley's first broadcast, on a Wednesday evening. All others were on Sundays, straight after the nine o'clock news.
34. MOA, File Report (FR)0173, *Morale Today*, 6 June 1940.
35. National Records of Scotland, ED31/528, 17 March 1941.
36. Public Records Office of Northern Ireland, MPS2/3/99, *Deaths Due to War Operations: Lists of Dead Identified at St George's Market*.
37. 'The Blitz', Swansea Museum, www.swansea museum.co.uk/swansea-a-brief-history/world-war-two/the-blitz
38. MOA, Diarist no. 5285, 9 September 1940.

39. MOA, Diarist no. 5285, 15 November 1940.
40. MOA, Diarist no. 5443, 7 September 1941.
41. MOA, Diarist no. 5277, 13 October 1940.
42. MOA, Diarist no. 5277, 14 October 1940.
43. MOA, Diarist no. 5277, 31 October 1940.
44. MOA, Diarist no. 5277, 14 November 1940.
45. MOA, Diarist no. 5024, 7 October 1940.
46. MOA, FR2121, *A Survey on the Pilotless Planes*, May 1945.
47. Priestley, *Postscripts* (1940), pp.36–7.
48. George Orwell, *The Lion and the Unicorn: Socialism and the English Genius* (London: Secker & Warburg, 1941).
49. *The Times*, 1 July 1940.
50. W. H. Auden, 'September 1st, 1939', first published in *The New Republic*, 18 October 1939.
51. MOA, FR913, *Notes on Some Reconstruction Problems*, October 1941.
52. Hansard, House of Commons, vol. 388, col. 496, *Beveridge Report (Sales)*, 6 April 1943.
53. MOA, FR1538, *First Reactions to the Beveridge Report*, December 1943.
54. William Beveridge, *Social Insurance and Allied Services* (London: HMSO, 1942).
55. MOA, Diarist no. 5311, 2 December 1942.
56. MOA, Diarist no. 5176, 1 December 1942.
57. MOA, Diarist no. 3321, 1 December 1941; MOA, Respondent no. 340, December 1942.
58. MOA, FR1565, *Public Reactions to the Beveridge Report*, January 1943.
59. *Daily Mail*, 10 August 1946.
60. Julie Anderson, 'Homes Away From Home and Happy Prisoners: Disabled Veterans, Space and Masculinity in Britain, 1944–1950', *Social History*, vol. 53, no. 3, 2020, pp.698–715.
61. MOA, Respondent no. 1015, August 1944.
62. MOA, Respondent no. 1065, August 1944.
63. MOA, FR2257, *Youth and the Election*, June 1945.
64. MOA, Diarist no. 5340, 4 September 1939.
65. Lucy Noakes, *Dying for the Nation: Death, Grief and Bereavement in Second World War Britain* (Manchester: Manchester University Press, 2020), p.251.

66. MOA, FR2270A, *A Report on the General Election, June–July 1945*, October 1945.

4. 1–6 May 1945: 'A Week of Confusion and Fluctuating Emotions'

1. Mass Observation Archive (MOA), Diarist no. 5004, 11 December 1841.
2. MOA, Diarist no. 5045, 7 December 1941; Diarist no. 5341, 14 December 1941.
3. The quote comes from Churchill's own six-volume *History of the Second World War*, cited in International Churchill Society, 'Pearl Harbor!', winstonchurchill.org/publications/churchill-bulletin/bullertin-162-dec-2021/pearl-harbor/
4. Cited in Peter Gatrell, *The Unsettling of Europe: The Great Migration, 1945 to the Present* (London: Allen Lane, 2019), pp.20–21.
5. Anonymous, *A Woman in Berlin* (London: Virago: 2011), pp.22–3.
6. Christabel Bielenberg, *The Road Ahead* (London: Corgi, 1992).
7. 'Flight over Kattegat', BBC, *WW2 People's War*, Article ID A4174931, www.bbc.co.uk/history/ww2peopleswar/stories/31/a4174931.shtml
8. BBC World Service, *My Century: The Story of the Twentieth Century – Told by Those Who Made It*, Josef Chalupsky, www.bbc.co.uk/worldservice/people/features/mycentury/ww2.shtml
9. MOA, Diarist nos 5378 & 5443, 2 May 1945.
10. MOA, Diarist no. 5239, 2 May 1945.
11. MOA, Diarist no. 5443, 1 May 1945.
12. MOA, Diarist no. 5372, entries for the week of 1–7 May 1945.
13. MOA, Diarist no. 5455, 20 April 1945 and 2 May 1945.
14. MOA, File Report (FR)2263, *Report on Victory in Europe*, June 1945.
15. *Daily Express*, headlines for 1–7 May 1945.
16. MOA, Diarist no. 5443, 2 May 1945.
17. MOA, Diarist no. 5030, 29 April 1945.
18. MOA, Diarist no. 5098, 2 May 1945.

19. MOA, FR2263, *Report on Victory in Europe*, June 1945.
20. MOA, Diarist no. 5205, 17 September 1939, 3 May 1945.
21. MOA, Diarist nos 5372 & 5310, 2 May 1945.
22. MOA, Diarist no. 5318, 3 May 1945.
23. MOA, FR2263, *Report on Victory in Europe*, June 1945.
24. MOA, Diarist no. 5030, 7 May 1945.
25. MOA, Diarist no. 5353, 4 May 1945.
26. BBC Archive, '1945: Richard Dimbleby Describes Belsen', originally broadcast 19 April 1945, www.bbc.co.uk/archive/richard-dimbleby-describes-belsen/zvw7cqt
27. MOA, Diarist no. 5205, 3 May 1945.
28. MOA, FR2248, *German Atrocities*, May 1945.
29. MOA, Diarist no. 5098, 5 May 1945.
30. MOA, Diarist no. 5098, 3 May 1945.
31. MOA, FR2248, *German Atrocities*, May 1945.
32. MOA, FR2248, *German Atrocities*, May 1945.
33. MOA, FR2248, *German Atrocities*, May 1945.
34. MOA, FR2248, *German Atrocities*, May 1945.
35. MOA, FR2263, *Report on Victory in Europe*, June 1945.
36. MOA, Diarist no. 5318, 4 May 1945.
37. MOA, Diarist no. 5318, 6 May 1945.
38. MOA, Diarist no. 5205, 3 May 1945.
39. MOA, Diarist no. 5402, 6 May 1945.
40. MOA, Diarist no. 5239, 1 May 1945.
41. MOA, Diarist no. 5314, 3 May 1945.
42. MOA, Diarist no. 5378, 4 May 1945.
43. MOA, Diarist no. 5344, 2 May 1945.
44. MOA, Diarist no. 5344, 6 May 1945.
45. MOA, Diarist no. 5344, 7 May 1945.
46. MOA, Diarist no. 5344, 25 May 1945.
47. MOA, Diarist no. 5344, 8 May 1946.
48. MOA, FR2263, *Report on Victory in Europe*, June 1945.
49. MOA, Diarist no. 5401, 1 May 1945.
50. MOA, Diarist no. 5239, 2 & 5 May 1945.
51. MOA, Diarist no. 1046, 7 May 1945.

52. MOA, Diarist no. 5310, 5 May 1945.
53. MOA, Diarist no. 5337, 5 May 1945.
54. MOA, FR2263, *Report on Victory in Europe*, June 1945.
55. MOA, FR2263, *Report on Victory in Europe*, June 1945.
56. MOA, FR2263, *Report on Victory in Europe*, June 1945.
57. MOA, Diarist no. 5443, 6 May 1945.
58. MOA, Diarist no. 5358, 6 May 1945.
59. MOA, Diarist no. 5338, 6 May 1945.
60. MOA, Diarist no. 5376, 6 May 1945.
61. MOA, Diarist no. 5275, 5 May 1945.

Prologue: 7 May 1945: The Funeral of Germany

1. *News Chronicle*, 5 May 1954, p.1.
2. *Daily Express*, 7 May 1945, p.3,
3. *Daily Express*, 7 May 1945, p.1.
4. *Daily Telegraph*, 7 May 1945, p.1; *The Times*, 7 May 1945, p.5.
5. *The Manchester Guardian*, 7 May 1945, p.6.
6. Carl Christian Givskov, 'The Danish Purge Laws', *Journal of Criminal Law and Criminology*, vol. 39, no. 4, 1949, p.448.
7. *Daily Mail*, 7 May 1945, p.3.
8. Roly Evans, 'Lessons from the Past: The Rapid Clearance of Denmark's Minefields in 1945', *The Journal of Conventional Weapons Destruction*, vol. 22, issue 1 (2018).
9. *The Age*, 9 May 1945, p.1.
10. Letter of 20 May 1945, quoted in Ruth Winstone (ed.), *Tony Benn, Years of Hope: Diaries, Letters and Papers 1940–1962* (London: Hutchinson, 1994), p.90.
11. *The Times*, 7 May 1945, p.3.
12. *The Times*, 7 May 1945, p.5.

5. Daytime, Monday 7 May: 'The Most Unsettling Day of All'

1. Mass Observation Archive (MOA), Diarist no. 5307, 7 May 1945.
2. MOA, Diarist no. 5307, 7 May 1945.
3. MOA, Diarist no. 5076, 7 May 1945.
4. The National Archives (TNA), Records of the Prime Minister's Office (PREM), 4 41/3, *'Minutes of War Cabinet, Monday 7 May 1945'*.
5. *New York Times*, 8 May 1945, p.3.
6. MOA, Diarist no. 5358, 7 May 1945.
7. MOA, Respondent no. 3642, May 1945.
8. MOA, Respondent no. 2486, May 1945.
9. MOA, Diarist no. 5376, 7 May 1945.
10. MOA, Diarist no. 1046, 7 May 1945.
11. MOA, Respondent no. 1563, May 1945.
12. MOA, Respondent no. 1651, May 1945.
13. MOA, Respondent no. 1213, May 1945.
14. MOA, Respondent no. 1682, May 1945.
15. MOA, Diarist no. 5378, 7 May 1945.
16. MOA, File Report (FR)2263, *Report on Victory in Europe*, June 1945.
17. MOA, FR2263, *Report on Victory in Europe*, June 1945.
18. MOA, FR2263, *Report on Victory in Europe*, June 1945.
19. MOA, Respondent no. 1015, May 1945.
20. MOA, Diarist no. 5307, 7 May 1945.
21. MOA, Diarist no. 5271, 7 May 1945.
22. MOA, Respondent no. 3642, May 1945.
23. MOA, Respondent no. 1668, May 1945.
24. MOA, Diarist no. 5408, 7 May 1945.
25. MOA, Respondent no. 3666, May 1945.
26. MOA, Respondent no. 1213, May 1945.
27. MOA, Respondent no. 1345, May 1945.
28. MOA, Respondent no. 1490, May 1945.
29. Kathleen E. Gales & P. H. Marks, 'Twentieth Century Trends in the Employment of Women in England and Wales', *Journal of the Royal Statistical Society*, vol. 137, no. 1, 1974, pp.60–74.

30. MOA, FR1522, *Morale in November 1942*, December 1942.
31. *News Chronicle*, 2 May 1945, p.4.
32. MOA, Respondent no. 1668, May 1945.
33. MOA, Diarist no. 5283, 7 May 1945.
34. MOA, Diarist no. 5098, 7 May 1945.
35. MOA, Respondent no. 1980, May 1945.
36. MOA, Diarist no. 5310, 7 May 1945.
37. MOA, Diarist no. 5390, 5 May 1945; Diarist no. 5331, 7 May 1945.
38. MOA, Diarist no. 5331, 7 May 1945.
39. MOA, Respondent nos 2811 & 2794, May 1945.
40. MOA, Respondent no. 2711, May 1945.
41. MOA, Respondent no. 3009, May 1945.
42. MOA, FR2263, *Report on Victory in Europe*, June 1945.
43. MOA, FR2263, *Report on Victory in Europe*, June 1945.
44. MOA, FR2263, *Report on Victory in Europe*, June 1945.
45. MOA, FR2263, *Report on Victory in Europe*, June 1945.

6. Evening, Monday 7 May: 'I Still Rejoiced with All My Heart'

1. *Daily Telegraph*, 8 May 1945, p.1.
2. *Daily Mail*, 7 December 1945, p.2.
3. The National Archives (TNA), Records of the Metropolitan Police Office (MEPO) 2/6476, *V.E. Day: Preparations for Celebrations by the Public*.
4. TNA, MEPO 2/6476, *V.E. Day: Preparations for Celebrations by the Public*.
5. Mass Observation Archive (MOA), Diarist no. 5307, 7 May 1945.
6. MOA, Diarist no. 5221, 7 May 1945.
7. MOA, Diarist no. 5331, 7 May 1945.
8. MOA, Respondent no. 3426, May 1945.
9. MOA, Respondent no. 2575, May 1945.
10. MOA, Respondent no. 3642, May 1945.
11. MOA, Respondent no. 3642, May 1945.
12. MOA, Respondent no. 2043, May 1945.
13. MOA, Respondent no. 2811, May 1945.

14. MOA, Diarist nos 5303 & 5240, 7 May 1945.
15. MOA, Respondent no. 2463, May 1945.
16. MOA, Respondent no. 2486, May 1945.
17. MOA, Diarist no. 5088, 7 May 1945.
18. MOA, Diarist no. 5088, 7 May 1945.
19. MOA, Diarist no. 5375, 7 May 1945.
20. MOA, Respondent no. 1682, May 1945.
21. MOA, Diarist no. 5378, 7 May 1945.
22. MOA, File Report (FR)2263, *Report on Victory in Europe*, June 1945.
23. MOA, Diarist no. 5358, 7 May 1945.
24. MOA, Diarist no. 5132, 7 May 1945.
25. MOA, Respondent no. 3527, May 1945.
26. MOA, Respondent no. 1680, May 1945.
27. Charles Madge & Tom Harrisson, *Mass Observation* (Frederick Muller: London, 1937), p.30.
28. MOA, Respondent no. 3230, May 1945.
29. MOA, Diarist no. 5205, 7 May 1945.
30. MOA, Respondent no. 3659, May 1945.
31. MOA, Respondent no. 1563, May 1945.
32. MOA Topic Collection (TC) 23, Box 8, *23-8-D Birmingham*.
33. MOA, Diarist no. 5307, 7 May 1945.
34. *Birmingham Gazette*, 8 May 1945, p.1.
35. MOA, Respondent no. 3650, May 1945.
36. *Leicester Evening Mail*, 7 May 1945, p.4.
37. MOA, Respondent no. 3683, May 1945.
38. MOA, Respondent no. 3613, May 1945.
39. MOA, Diarist no. 5310, 7 May 1945.
40. MOA, Respondent no. 3533, May 1945.
41. MOA, Respondent no. 3388, May 1945.
42. MOA, Respondent no. 3545, May 1945.
43. MOA, Respondent no. 3555, May 1945.
44. MOA, Respondent no. 3621, May 1945.
45. MOA, Respondent no. 2465, May 1945.
46. MOA, Respondent no. 2512, May 1945.
47. MOA, FR2263, *Report on Victory in Europe*, May 1945.

48. MOA, FR2263, *Report on Victory in Europe*, June 1945.
49. *Daily Express*, 8 May 1945, p.1.
50. *Daily Mirror*, 8 May 1945, p.1.
51. *News Chronicle*, 8 May 1945, p.1.
52. *Daily Mail*, 8 May 1945, p.1; *The Times*, 8 May 1945, p.5.
53. MOA, Diarist no. 5358, 7 May 1945.
54. MOA, Diarist no. 5358, 7 May 1945.
55. *Daily Express*, 8 May 1945, p.2.
56. *Daily Mail*, 8 May 1945, p.1.
57. *Daily Telegraph*, 8 May 1945, p.1.
58. MOA, Respondent no.3119, May 1945.

Prologue: 8 May 1945: An End and a Beginning

1. *Daily Mail*, 7 May 1945, p.1; 8 May 1945, p.1.
2. *The Times*, 8 May 1945, p.1.
3. *Daily Mirror*, 8 May 1945, p.2.
4. *New York Times*, 8 May 1945, p.11.
5. *The Times*, 8 May 1945, p.8.
6. *Daily Mail*, 8 May 1945, p.8.
7. *Daily Mirror*, 8 May 1945, p.1.
8. *Daily Express*, 8 May 1945, p.1.
9. *Daily Express*, 8 May 1945, p.1.
10. *The Times*, 8 May, p.5.
11. On the Bengal Famine, see Janam Mukerjee, *Hungry Bengal: War, Famine and the End of Empire* (London: Hurst, 2023); Yasmin Khan, *The Raj at War: A People's History of India's Second World War* (London: Penguin, 2015).
12. *The Guardian*, 8 May 1945, p.6.
13. *The Times of India*, 8 May 1945, p.7.
14. The National Archives (TNA), Foreign Office (FO)171/49275, *Political Situation in North Africa*.
15. See Martin Evans, *Algeria: France's Undeclared War* (Oxford: Oxford University Press, 2012).
16. *The Times*, 9 May 1945, p.3.
17. *The Globe and Mail*, 9 May 1945. The extracts can be found on the website of the Canadian War Museum, www.warmuseum.ca/

18. Mass Observation Archive (MOA), Respondent no. 2799, May 1945.
19. MOA, Respondent no. 2799, May 1945.

7. Daytime, Tuesday 8 May: 'So, This Is V Day'

1. Mass Observation Archive (MOA), Diarist no. 5443, 8 May 1945.
2. MOA, Diarist no. 5443, 14 & 18 August 1941.
3. MOA, Diarist no. 5443, 7 September 1941.
4. MOA, Respondent no. 3692, May 1945.
5. MOA, Respondent no. 3320, May 1945.
6. MOA, Diarist no. 5233, 8 May 1945.
7. MOA, Diarist nos 5282 & 5338, 8 May 1945.
8. MOA, Diarist no. 5338, 8 May 1945.
9. MOA, Respondent no. 1642, May 1945.
10. MOA, Respondent no. 3441, May 1945.
11. MOA, Respondent no. 3441, May 1945.
12. MOA, Respondent no. 1653, May 1945.
13. MOA, Respondent nos 3434 & 3351, May 1945.
14. MOA, Diarist no. 5221, 8 May 1945.
15. MOA, Respondent 3533, May 1945.
16. MOA, Respondent no. 3035, May 1945.
17. MOA, Respondent no. 2575, May 1945.
18. MOA, Diarist no. 5216, 3 September 1939.
19. MOA, Diarist no. 5216, 8 May 1945.
20. MOA, Respondent no. 3359, May 1945.
21. MOA, Diarist no. 5378, 8 May 1945.
22. MOA, Respondent no. 2457, May 1945.
23. MOA, Respondent no. 3684, May 1945.
24. MOA, Respondent no. 3537, May 1945.
25. MOA, Respondent no. 2895, May 1945.
26. MOA, Diarist no. 5076, 8 May 1945.
27. MOA, Diarist no. 5201, 8 May 1945.
28. MOA, Diarist no. 5331, 8 May 1945.
29. MOA, Diarist no. 5283, 8 May 1945.
30. MOA, Diarist no. 5283, 2 & 3 March 1943.
31. MOA, Diarist no. 5283, 14 February 1945.
32. MOA, Diarist no. 5313, 8 May 1945.

33. MOA, Respondent no. 1032, May 1945.
34. MOA, Respondent nos 1070, 2977, May 1945.
35. MOA, Respondent no. 2885, May 1945.
36. MOA, Diarist no. 5344, 8 May 1945.
37. MOA, Diarist no. 5233, 8 May 1945.
38. MOA, Diarist no. 5233, 8 June 1945.
39. See Alan Allport, *Demobbed. Coming Home After the Second World War* (Yale: Yale University Press, 2009).
40. MOA, Respondent no. 1226, May 1945.
41. MOA, Respondent no. 1974, May 1945.
42. MOA, Respondent no. 1016, May 1945.
43. Central Statistical Office, *Fighting With Figures: A Statistical Digest of the Second World War* (London: HMSO, 1995), p.vi.
44. MOA, Respondent no. 1015, May 1945.
45. MOA, Respondent no. 1622, May 1945.
46. MOA, Diarist no. 5310, 8 May 1945.
47. MOA, Respondent no. 1651, May 1945.
48. MOA, Respondent no. 1974, May 1945.
49. MOA, Respondent no. 2895, May 1945.
50. MOA, Respondent no. 3385, May 1945.
51. MOA, Respondent no. 5212, May 1945.
52. MOA, Respondent no. 1213, May 1945.
53. MOA, Diarist no. 5390 8 May 1945.
54. MOA, Diarist no. 5408, 8 May 1945.
55. MOA, Respondent no. 4365, May 1945.
56. MOA, Diarist no. 5358, 8 May 1945.
57. MOA, Respondent no. 1563, May 1945.
58. MOA, Respondent no. 1046, May 1845.
59. MOA, Respondent no. 3427, May 1945.
60. MOA, Diarist no. 5132, 6 November 1940.
61. MOA, Diarist no. 5132, 8 May 1945.
62. MOA, Diarist no. 5378, 8 May 1945.
63. MOA, File Report (FR)2263, *Report on Victory in Europe*, May/June 1945.
64. MOA, FR2263, *Report on Victory in Europe*, May/June 1945.

8. Evening, Tuesday 8 May: 'This Is Your Victory'

1. Mass Observation Archive (MOA), Diarist no. 5132, 8 May 1945.
2. MOA, File Report (FR)2263, *Report on Victory in Europe*, June 1945.
3. MOA, Diarist no. 5378, 8 May 1945.
4. MOA, Respondent no. 3427, May 1945.
5. MOA, FR2263, *Report on Victory in Europe*, June 1945.
6. Winston Churchill, Speech from Ministry of Health, London, 8 May 1945, International Churchill Society, https://winstonchurchill.org/resources/speeches/1941-1945-war-leader/to-v-e-crowds/
7. MOA, Topic Collection (TC) 74, *Radio Listening*, 74-1-C Programme Surveys, May 1940.
8. MOA, Diarist no. 5399, 8 October 1940.
9. MOA, Respondent no. 1980, May 1945. This woman was one of several who both kept a diary and responded to Mass Observation Directives during the war. The organisation allocated separate identification numbers for each activity.
10. MOA, Respondent no. 1016, May 1945.
11. MOA, Respondent no. 1075, May 1945.
12. MOA, Respondent no. 3441, May 1945.
13. MOA, Diarist no. 5408, 8 May 1945.
14. MOA, Respondent no. 3650, May 1945.
15. MOA, Respondent no. 1644, May 1945.
16. MOA, Diarist no. 5282, 8 May 1945.
17. MOA, Diarist no. 5282, 8 May 1945.
18. MOA, Diarist no. 5324, 24 August 1939.
19. MOA, Diarist no. 5324, 8 May 1945.
20. MOA, Respondent nos 3684 & 3351, May 1945.
21. Respondent no. 3351, May 1945.
22. MOA, Respondent no. 3683, May 1945.
23. MOA, Diarist no. 5318, 8 May 1945.
24. MOA, Diarist no. 5408, 8 May 1945.
25. MOA, Respondent no. 1688, May 1945.
26. MOA, Respondent no. 3320, May 1945.
27. MOA, Respondent no. 1644, May 1945.

28. MOA, Diarist no. 5271, 8 May 1945.
29. MOA, Respondent no. 3368, May 1945.
30. Office for National Statistics, *Victory in Europe Day: How World War II Changed the UK*, 2015, www.ons.gov.uk/people populationandcommunity/ birthsdeathsandmarriages/ articles/victoryineuropeday howworldwariichangedthe uk/2015-05-08
31. MOA, Respondent no. 3022, May 1945.
32. MOA, Respondent no. 1668, May 1945.
33. MOA, Diarist no. 5390, 8 May 1945.
34. You can listen to this broadcast on the *History of the BBC* webpage: www.bbc.com/historyofthebbc/100-voices/ww2/ve-day/. There are further details of the BBC's wartime programming in David Hendy, *The BBC: A People's History* (London: Profile Books, 2022).
35. MOA, Diarist no. 5239, 8 May 1945.
36. MOA, Diarist no. 5283, 8 May 1945.
37. MOA, Respondent no. 3441, May 1945.
38. MOA, Respondent no. 3119, May 1945.
39. This comes from a BBC interview with HM Queen Elizabeth II in 1985, quoted in Emily Burack, 'Did Queen Elizabeth and Princess Margaret Really Leave the Palace on V-E Day?', *Town and Country*, 22 December 2023, www.townandcountrymag.com/society/tradition/a46068670/queen-elizabeth-princess-margaret-ve-day-ritz-true-story/
40. MOA, Diarist no. 5378, 8 May 1945.
41. MOA, Diarist no. 5132, 8 May 1945.
42. MOA, Respondent no. 1680, May 1945.
43. MOA, Respondent no. 1680, May 1945.
44. MOA, Respondent no. 1680, December 1945.
45. MOA, Diarist no. 5443, 8 May 1945.
46. MOA, Respondent nos 1032 & 1668, May 1945.
47. MOA, Respondent no. 3613, May 1945.
48. MOA, Respondent no. 3545, May 1945.
49. MOA, Respondent no. 3642, May 1945.

Afterword: 'It Is All Very Difficult to Imagine We Have Peace'

1. MOA, Diarist no. 5402, 7 May 1945.
2. MOA, Respondent no. 3474, May 1945.
3. MOA, Directive Questionnaire, April 1947.
4. MOA, Respondent no. 1048, April 1947.
5. MOA, Respondent no. 1534, April 1947.
6. MOA, Respondent no. 3035, April 1947. The British Housewives' League was formed in 1945 to campaign against continued rationing, queuing and shortages. It has been described by the historian Peter Hennessy as 'a thorn in Ministerial flesh'. Peter Hennessy, *Never Again: Britain 1945–51* (London: Penguin, 1992), p.276.
7. MOA, Respondent no. 1079, April 1947.
8. MOA, Respondent no. 1668, May 1945.
9. MOA, Respondent no. 3660, May 1945.
10. MOA, Respondent no. 3666, May 1945.
11. MOA, Respondent nos 3650 & 1056, May 1945.
12. The phrase comes from W. H. Auden's poem 'September 1, 1939', written just after the German invasion of Poland.
13. This was broadcast on the BBC on 4 June 1945.
14. Cited in Richard Toye, 'Winston Churchill's "Crazy Broadcast": Party, Nation and the 1945 Gestapo Speech', *Journal of British Studies*, 49 (July 2010) pp.655–80; here p.656.
15. MOA Diarist no. 5030, 5 July 1945.
16. MOA Diarist no. 5201, 5 July 1945.
17. *Daily Mirror*, 5 July 1945, p.1.
18. MOA, Diarist no. 5378, 28 June 1945.
19. MOA, Diarist no. 5378, 25–8 July 1945.
20. MOA, Diarist no. 5353, 28 July 1945.
21. *Daily Express*, 7 August 1945, p.1; *Daily Mirror*, 9 August 1945, p.1.
22. MOA, Directive Questionnaire, August 1945.
23. MOA, Respondent no. 1016, August 1945.
24. MOA, Respondent no. 1075, August 1945.
25. MOA, Respondent no. 3683, August 1945.

26. MOA, Respondent no. 1108, August 1945.
27. MOA, Respondent no. 1226, August 1945.
28. MOA, Respondent nos 1099 & 1651, August 1945.
29. MOA, Respondent no. 1645, August 1945.
30. MOA, Respondent no. 1980, August 1945.
31. MOA, Respondent no. 3642, August 1945. The H.G. Wells novel was probably *The World Set Free: A Story of Mankind*, first published in 1914.
32. MOA, Respondent no. 2575, August 1945.
33. MOA, Respondent no. 1093, August 1945.
34. MOA, Respondent no. 1022, August 1945.
35. MOA, Diarist no. 5353, 11 August 1945.
36. Mass Observation, *Peace and the People* (London: Longmans, Green & Co., 1947), pp.12–13. The Bank of England was nationalised in 1946.
37. MOA, Respondent nos 1980 & 1226, August 1945.
38. MOA, Respondent no. 3022, August 1945.
39. MOA, Respondents nos 1048 & 2575, August 1945.
40. MOA, Respondent no. 1490, August 1945.
41. MOA, Respondent no. 3683, August 1945.
42. MOA, Respondent no. 1075, August 1945.
43. MOA, Respondent no. 2975, August 1945.
44. MOA, Respondent nos 3666 & 1974, August 1945.
45. MOA, Respondent no. 3368, August 1945.

Index

abdication crisis (1936), 1, 34, 36–7, 42
'Aftermyth of War, The' (comedy sketch), 8–9, 11
air raids, 2–4, 144
 ARP (Air Raid Precautions), 59
 see also Blitz
Algeria, 32, 204–5
 French settlers, 204–5
 War of Independence (1954–62), 204–5
Allen, Fred, 177
Amery, John, 286*n*
Amery, Leo, 202, 286
Anderson shelters, 17
apartheid, 211
Armistice Day *see* World War I
Army Film and Photographic Unit, 110
Asia, 171, 180, 197, 201, 211, 277–6, 287
Astor, Nancy, 28, *29*
Atlantic Charter, 213
atomic weapons, 202, 287, 289–93
Attlee, Clement, 90, 91, 282–3
Auden, W. H., 83, 282

Auschwitz-Birkenau concentration camp, 200–201
austerity, post-war, 90, 295
Australia, 201, 288
Austria, 104, 186

Bader, Douglas, 7–8
Baedeker Raids (1942), 80
Baldwin, Stanley, 282
Bank of England, 294
Banks, Arron, 20
Bath, Somerset, 80
Battle for Slater's Knoll (1945), 201
Battle of Berlin (1945), 95–9
Battle of Britain (1940), 7, 23, 73, 75–6
Battle of Kursk (1943), 94
Battle of Okinawa 1945), 201–2
Battle of Stalingrad (1942–3), 94
Battle of the River Plate, The (film), 13
BBC (British Broadcasting Corporation), 11, 59, 104,

135, 138–40, 156, 158, 163, 241
  Home Service, 248
  VE Day broadcasts, 248–52, 266
Belfast, Northern Ireland, 76
Belgium, 72
Bengal, 202–3
  Bengal Famine (1943), 169, 202
Benn, Anthony Wedgwood 'Tony', 131–2
Bennett, Alan, 7–11
Bergen-Belsen concentration camp, 109–11, 249
Berlin, Germany, 61, 126, 137
  fall of, 95–9, 116
Bernays, Edward, 40
Beveridge, William, 85–6, 282–3, 293–4
Beveridge Report, 85–8, 90
Bevin, Ernest, 247
Beyond the Fringe (revue show), 8–10
Bielenberg, Christabel, 97
Birmingham, England, 179–80
Birmingham Gazette, 179
Black, Peter, 12
blackout, 4, 30–31, 57, 59
Blitz (1940–41), 2–4, 17–18, 22, 23, 51, 73, 75–80, 213, 224, 238, 273
  'Blitz spirit', 4, 24, 30, 79, 81
  'Little Blitz' (1944), 80
Blitzkrieg, 72
Bloom, Godfrey, 21
Board of Trade, 153
Bogarde, Dirk, 13

Bolton, Lancashire, 1, 40, 52–3
Braun, Eva, 96
Breslau (now Wrocław), Poland, 199
Brexit, 16, 20–21
Briggs, Asa, 5
Bristol, England, 4, 80
British Commonwealth, 206
British Empire, 202, 206
British Free Corps, 286*n*
British Legion, 89
British Mandate for Palestine, 132
British Union of Fascists, 17, 36, 40
Buchenwald concentration camp, 111
Buckingham Palace, London, 194–5, 238, 245
Burma (now Myanmar), 100, 151, 170, 205–6
Bury St Edmonds, Suffolk, 263–4

Canada, 206–8, 288
Cardiff, Wales, 80
Cardington, Bedfordshire, 144
census (1951), 153
Chalupsky, Josef, 99
Chamberlain, Neville, 24, 49, 60, 64–6, 68–70, 73–4, 197, 248
Channel Islands, 32, 99–100
Chaplin, Charlie, 105
Chepstow, Wales, 254–7
Children's Overseas Reception Board scheme, 207
China, 169

Churchill, Winston, 15–16, 20, 73–5, 91, 94, 133, 137–8, 157, 163, 173, 193, 197, 213, 282–3, 286
  'Gestapo' speech, 283
  VE Day speech, 216–17, 238, 240–42, 243–8
City of Benares, SS, 207
Clydebank air raids, Scotland (1941), 76, 273–4
Coal Face (film), 37–8
Cold War, 101, 197, 289
Communist Party of Great Britain, 88–9
concentration camps, 185, 200
  see also names of individual camps
conscription, 60, 76
Conservative Party, 282–3
Cook, Peter, 9
Copenhagen, Denmark, 129–30
Covid-19, 21–3
Coward, Noël, 25
Crazy Gang, The, 105
Critchley, Julian, 19
Crown Film Unit, 51
Czechoslovakia, 32, 48, 59, 98, 185–6, 200

D-Day landings (1944), 17, 81, 94, 249
Dad's Army (TV sitcom), 11–12
Daily Chronicle, 106
Daily Express, 33, 73, 104, 111, 127, 128–9, 192, 194, 199, 287
Daily Mail, 9, 12, 73, 88–9 130, 163, 193–4, 198
Daily Mirror, 24, 33–4, 51, 192, 198–9, 284, 287
Daily Star, 20
Daily Telegraph, 19, 33, 86, 129, 194
Dam Busters, The (film), 13
Darkest Hour (film), 15–16
'death marches', 109, 117
'Defence Notices', 248–9
Denmark, 72, 129–30
  Danish Resistance, 129
Diary for Timothy, A (film), 38
Dimbleby, Richard, 109–10, 249
Dixon of Dock Green (TV series), 158
Doctor in the House (film series), 13
'doodlebugs' *see* V-1 flying bombs
Dresden, Germany, 228
Dunkirk evacuation, 2, 16, 23, 72–6, 230
Dunkirk (film), 14, 20

Ealing Film Studios, 10
Eden, Anthony, 198
Edward VIII, King of the United Kingdom, 32–4
Eisenhower, Dwight D., 123, 136
Eksteins, Modris, 95
Elizabeth II, Queen of the United Kingdom, 22–3, 269

Elizabeth, the Queen Mother, 195, 268–9
Empire Air Training Scheme, 208
English Journey (Priestley), 39
Entertainment National Services Association (ENSA), 70
Eton, England, 180–81
Europe, victory in, *see* VE Day
European Championships (1996), 24
evacuation, 59–60, 76
Exeter, England, 80

Falklands War (1982), 19–20
Famine Inquiry Commission, 202–3
Farage, Nigel, 20
Fifth Chair, The (film), 177
Fifth Column, 2
film (World War II in), 12–15, 37–8, 105
Fires Were Started (film), 38
Firth of Forth, Scotland, 126
Fisher, Geoffrey, Archbishop of Canterbury, 266
Flanagan and Allen, 71
Formby, George, 105
Foyle's War (TV drama), 14
France, 59, 204–5
  fall of (1940), 2, 23, 72–3
  liberation of, 94
  VE Day, 129
Francois, Mark, 20
Frank, Anne, 110
Frank, Margot, 110
Freud, Sigmund, 40

Galtieri, Leopoldo, 19
Garrison Theatre (variety show), 158
'Gas Mask Sunday' (1938), 45
Gasbags (film), 105
General Election (1945), 90–92, 243, 268–9, 282–5
George VI, King of the United Kingdom, 195
  coronation (1937), 1, 41
  VE Day broadcast, 251
Germany, 36, 94–5, 98, 109, 138, 151, 185–6, 197, 200, 248–9
  Armed Forces High Command, 125
  civilians, 169
  Condor Legion, 67
  German Instrument of Surrender, 125
  surrender, 98–100, 125–9, 141, 148, 156, 167
  Third Reich, 61
  troops, 126, 137, 169
  see also Nazi regime
Gestapo, 'HIPO Corps', 129–30
Girls' Training Corp, 254–5
Globe and Mail, The, 207
Gloucester, England, 257–9
Gnikow, General von, 199
Goebbels, Joseph, 96
Goebbels, Magda, 96
GPO Film Unit, 37–8, 51
Grays, Essex, 3
Great Dictator, The (film), 105
'great Sunday squat' (1946), 88–9

Greenwood, Arthur, 286
Greig, William, 200
Grierson, John, 37
Gulf War (1991), 19–20

Halifax, Nova Scotia, 206–8
Hancock, Matt, 22
Hardy, Tom, 15
Harrisson, Tom, 1, 5, 34, 38–40, 49, 51, 151
Heswall on the Wirral, Merseyside, 274–5
Hewins, Ralph, 130
Himmler, Heinrich, 102
Hiroshima, Japan, 202, 287–9
Hitler, Adolf, 2, 30, 48–9, 93–7, 105–6, 124, 248, 276
   death of, 96–8, 104–8
   effigies of, 172, 260–62
   in film, 105
Hitler Youth, 96
Holocaust, 109–13, 124, 169
Home Fires (TV series), 14
House of Commons, 73, 245
Hull, East Yorkshire, 4, 80, 259
hunger marches, 36, 83
Hussein, Saddam, 19

In Which We Serve (TV series), 25
India, 169, 202–3, 276
infant mortality rates, 83
Interdepartmental Conference (1944), 164–5
Irgun (paramilitary group), 132
'Iron Curtain', 133
Ismay, Hastings 'Pug', 136
Israel, 132

It's That Man Again (ITMA) (radio comedy), 85
Italy, 36, 93
   surrender of, 94, 98, 100
ITV, 14

Jankowski, Jan Stanisław, 133
Japan, 17, 31, 88, 169, 201–2, 205–6, 247
   atomic bombs, 202, 287, 289–93
   defeat of, 202, 287–9
   Pearl Harbor, 93–4
   VJ Day, 293
Jarrow hunger march, 36
Jennings, Humphrey, 34, 37–8, 51, 70
Jews/Judaism, 80, 96, 111, 132
   children, 185–6
   see also Holocaust
Jodl, Alfred, 125, 126, 137
Johnson, Boris, 21

Keeler, Christine, 285
'Keep Calm and Carry On', 71
Kinder Scout Mass Trespass (1932), 218
Kindertransport scheme, 185–6
Kitchen, Michael, 14
Korda, Alexander, 66
Korean War (1950–53), 88
Krosigk, Schwerin von, 138

Labour Party, 90, 92, 247, 282–5, 294
Land Girls (TV series), 14
Last, Nella, 53, 64, 74, 89–90, 109, 286, 292–3

Le Mesurier, John, 11–12
Lean, David, 25
Led By Donkeys, 21
Leicester, England, 180
Leicester Evening Mail, 180
Lend-Lease Scheme, 94
Let George Do It! (film), 105
Let Us Face the Future (Labour manifesto), 282
Lindgren, Astrid, 31, 60–1
Listen to Britain (documentary), 51
'Little Blitz' (1944), 80
London, 76–8, 80, 118–19, 142–3, 146, 158–62, 173–7, 189–95, 237–8, 268–72
 air raids, 3–4
 bombings (7 July 2005), 24
 London Underground, 224
 see also Blitz
London Can Take It! (documentary film), 38, 51, 70
London School of Economics, 85
Lowe, Arthur, 11–12
Lubyanka prison, Moscow, 198
Luxembourg, 72
Lynn, Vera, 22–3

Macaski, Charles and Dorothy, 223
Macmillan, Harold, 9
Madge, Charles, 1, 26, 34–7, 39, 40, 49, 51
Malaya, 288
Manchester Guardian, 129

Margaret, Princess, Countess of Snowdon, 269
Marriage Bar, 153
Martin, Kingsley, 34
Mason, Herbert, 13, 17
Mass Observation, 1–5
 'Crisis Diary', 46
 Day Diaries, 41–5
 Directives, 2, 47–8, 54–5, 61–2
 finances, 51–2
 origins, 34–5
 post war, 278–81, 287
 volunteer writers, 55–6
 wartime diaries, 49–51
May the Twelfth (Mass Observation publication), 41
Means Test, 83
Meikles Hotel, 209–10
Merkel, Angela, 20
MI5, 17
Mikołajczyk, Stanisław, 198
Miller, Jonathan, 9
Ministry of Food, 154
Ministry of Health, 245
Ministry of Information, 2, 38, 49, 51, 57, 71, 139, 158, 163, 171
Mitchison, Dick, 66, 244–5, 270, 285
Mitchison, Naomi, 100, 116, 145, 173, 223–4, 239, 243, 244–5, 269–70, 279–80, 285–6
Mitford, Diana, 17
Molotov, Vyacheslav, 197

Monslow, Walter, 286
Montgomery, Bernard Law, 98
Moore, Dudley, 9
Moore, Tom, 22
Moorehead, Alan, 128–9
More, Kenneth, 7
Morrison, Herbert, 283
Moscow, Russia, 133, 197–8
Mosley, Oswald, 17, 36
Munich Crisis (1938), 1, 43, 59
Music While You Work (radio programme), 249
Mutually Assured Destruction doctrine, 289

Nagasaki, Japan, 202, 287–9, 293
Nakba (ethnic cleansing of Palestinian Arabs), 132
Naomi, Mitchison, 65–6
National Health Service (NHS), 1, 22
National Insurance, 86
National Labour, 285, 286*n*
National Liberation Front (FLN), 205
'National Panel', 40, 44, 47, 50, 89, 151, 278
National Service, 60, 88
National Sun and Air Association, 223
naturism, 223
Nazi regime, Germany, 31, 36, 59, 60, 61, 94, 109, 110, 185, 197–9
collapse of, 93
Nazi-Soviet Pact (1939), 197

Netherlands, 72
New Statesman and Nation, 1, 34, 44
New York Times, 199
New Zealand, 202, 288
Newbould, Frank, 217–18, *218*
Newcastle-upon-Tyne, England, 224
News Chronicle, 126–7, 154, 192
NHS (National Health Service), 86
Nicolson, Harold, 285, 286*n*
Night Mail (film), 38
Nolan, Christopher, 14, 20
Non-Aggression Pact, 60
Nordhausen concentration camp, 111
North Africa, 94, 230
North Sea (film), 38
Now Thank We All Our God (hymn), 266
NS-Frauenschaft (Nazi women's organisation), 61

Okulicki, Leopold, 133
Oldman, Gary, 15
Olivier, Laurence, 62
Operation Barbarossa, 93, 197
Operation Downfall, 31, 287
Operation Dracula, 205
Operation Exodus, 230
Operation Pied Piper, 49–50
Orgel, Kurt, 61
Orwell, George, 39, 82–3
Oswiecim *see* Auschwitz-Birkenau

outbreak of World War II, 59–70

Pacific theatre of war, 151, 201–2, 211, 287
Palestine, 131–2
Passport to Pimlico (film), 10–11
Patton, George, 125
Pearl Harbor, 93–4
People, The, 64
'people's war', 14, 19, 58, 90, 251, 282
photography (in World War II), 13
Physical Training and Recreation Act (1937), 218
Plymouth, Devon, 27–30, 225, 259
Poland, 59, 60–61, 133, 184–5, 197
  Polish Home Army, 133
  Polish Underground State, 132–3
  Polish Committee of National Liberation, 198
post-war reconstruction, 83–5
Postscripts (radio programme), 74–5, 82
Prague, Czechoslovakia, 32, 99
  Prague Uprising (1945), 122–3, 125, 186, 199–200
Pravda, 200
Priestley, J. B., 39, 74–5, 82
prisoners of war, 91, 230–31
  camps, 169
Profumo, John, 285
propaganda, 49

posters, 217–18, *218*
Purper, Liselotte, 61
Pyke, Geoffrey, 34

queuing, 4
Radford, Coventry, 253–4, 261–2
Radio Moscow, 200
RAF (Royal Air Force), 202, 208
  Balloon Command, 144
  Bomber Command, 228, 230
  see also Battle of Britain
Raine, Kathleen, 35
Rangoon (now Yangon), Burma, 205
rationing, 4, 88, 153–5, 279, 295
Reach for the Sky, (film), 7, 13
Red Cross, 200, 230
Rendell, Joan, 66
Rhodesian Unilateral Declaration of Independence (1965), 211
Ribbentrop, Joachim von, 197
Road to Wigan Pier, The (Orwell), 39
Roosevelt, Franklin D., 137, 213
Royal Family, 245, 269
Royal Ordnance Factory explosion, Kirby, Lancashire (1944), 259
Russia *see* Soviet Union
Rylance, Mark, 15

Sackville-West, Vita, 285
San Francisco, United States, 101, 132, 183, 198, 213, 290
'scorched earth' policy, 203
Sétif, Algeria, 204
Shape of Things to Come, The (Wells), 66
Shone, Dorothy, 274
Shone, George, 274
Shone, Lilian, 274
Shute, Nevil, 67
Simpson, Wallis, 32–4
Sinden, Donald, 13
Singapore, 288
Singh Pujji, Mohinder, 16–17
Social Insurance and Allied Services Report, 282–3
Social Insurance Committee, 85
social security, 86
Socialist Medical Association, 178
Southampton, Hampshire, 67
Southern Rhodesia (now Zimbabwe), 208–11
Soviet Union, 36, 60, 94–5, 97–8, 117, 122–3, 126–8, 132–4, 137, 151, 169, 185–6, 197–9, 276, 283
  Red Army, 123, 198
Spanish Civil War (1936–9), 36, 67
Spare Time (film), 38
Spiegel, Renia, 61
'Spielplatz', Hertfordshire (naturist resort), 223
'Spitfire Summer', 23

SS (Schutzstaffel), 96, 109, 123, 199–200
  Waffen SS, 286*n*
St Andrew's Church, Plymouth, 28
St Margaret's Church, London, 245
St Paul's Cathedral, London, 13, 17
Stalag Luft VIII-B prison camp, 117
Stalin, Joseph, 123, 126, 133, 137–8, 185, 197, 240, 283
Stauffenberg plot, 97
Sudetenland, 59
Swansea, Wales, 76
Sweden, 60–61
Swedish Red Cross, 101

Tass (Soviet news agency), 133
Theatre Royal, Brighton, 7
Theresienstadt, Czechoslovakia, 200
They Speak for Themselves (radio programme), 37, 38–9
Things to Come (film), 66
Thomas, Wynford Vaughan, 249
Thousand-Year Reich, 95, 97, 124
Times of India, The, 202
Times, The, 33, 83, 129, 133, 193, 198–200, 205
Torrin, HMS, 25
Toynbee Hall, London, 85
Trinder, Tommy, 71, 85
Trinity College, Dublin, 130–31

Truman, Harry S., 137–8

United Kingdom
  Independence Party
  (UKIP), 21
United Nations, 101, 198, 289
United Nations Conference on
  International Organization,
  San Francisco, 101, 132,
  183, 198, 290
United States, 93–4, 134, 137,
  151, 202, 287–8
  Air Force, 202, 228
  Third Army, 125, 127

V-1 flying bombs
  ('doodlebugs'), 80, 101, 273
V-2 rockets, 101, 144, 273
VE Day (8 May 1945), 5,
  28–31, 57–8, 149–51
  announcement of, 163–74
  anticipation of, 119–22,
    135–62
  celebrations, 91–2, 207–11,
    249–76
  eve of, 173–83, 189–95,
    213–42
  food, 154–6, 226–7, 253
  protests, 204–5
Versailles Treaty, 36
VJ Day (15 August 1945), 293
Volkssturm (militia), 96

Wannsee Conference (1942),
  111
War Begins at Home (Mass
  Observation publication),
  52, 71

Warner, Jack, 158
Warsaw, Poland, 62–3
  Warsaw Uprising (1944),
    123, 185
Watt, Harry, 70
We Have Ways Fest, 13–14
Weeks, Honeysuckle, 14
welfare state, 90, 282–3, 294
Wellard, James, 127
Wells, H. G., 66, 291
What Happened to the Corbetts
  (Shute), 67
Whisky Galore! (film), 10–11
Willcock, H. A. 'Bob', 52
Windsor, Berkshire, 180–81,
  259
Wintringham, Tom, 284
Woman in Berlin, A (book), 32,
  96–7
women (in World War II), 60,
  102–3, 152–3, 279–80
Women's Institute (WI), 14, 18
Women's Voluntary Service
  (WVS), 18, 244
Woolf, Virginia, 32–3
Workers' Playtime (radio
  programme), 249
Worktown project (Bolton),
  40, 52–3
World War I (1914–18), 36,
  76
  Armistice Day (11 November
    1918), 45, 149
WRENS (Women's Royal
  Naval Service), 208
Wright, Joe, 15
Wuthering Heights (film), 62

Yalta Conference (1945), 185, 198
York, England, 80

Zec, Philip, 198, 284
Zhukov, Georgy, 99, 126